Some Survived

Some Survived

by Manny Lawton

with an introduction by John Toland

Algonquin Books of Chapel Hill
Chapel Hill, North Carolina
1984

Algonquin Books of Chapel Hill
P.O. Box 2225
Chapel Hill, N.C. 27515-2225

LIBRARY OF CONGRESS CATALOGING IN PUBLICATION DATA

Lawton, Manny, 1918–
    Some survived.   *030941*

    16.95

    1. World war, 1939–1945—Prisoners and prisons,
Japanese. 2. Lawton, Manny, 1918–   . 3. World War,
1939–1945—Personal narratives, American. 4. World War,
1939–1945—Concentration camps—Philippines. 5. Prisoners
of war—United States—Biography. 6. Prisoners of war—
Philippines—Biography. I. Title.
D805.P6L38 1984 940.54′72′52 84-16940
ISBN 0-912697-13-X

The photographs of the Death March and other scenes of Japanese captivity are furnished through the courtesy of NBC-TV and by Mr. Stan Sommers, Marshfield, Wisconsin.

The sketch of American POWs is furnished through the courtesy of Mr. Ben Steele, Billings, Montana.

THIRD PRINTING

To Peggy, my beloved, who captured me within the year of my liberation from three and one-half years as a prisoner of war and became my wife. Over the ensuing years she has made each place we lived a Garden of Eden. She helped me salvage what might have been a wasted life and brought me a love and companionship which enabled me to forget the bitter and dreadful years that went before.

Contents

List of Illustrations

List of Maps

Preface

In August of 1985 the survivors of Bataan and Corregidor will mark the fortieth anniversary of their liberation from the hell of prisoner of war camps in the Philippines and Japan. In those four decades the world has seen more dramatic scientific progress and greater political realignment than in any previous span of history. The high speed jet airliner has become commonplace. The computer, developed in the last few years, affects every phase of our lives. Man has flown to and walked upon the moon. The Soviet Union, our wartime ally, has become our chief political competitor. Since taking over central Europe after World War II, she has moved into Cuba and Afghanistan and has gained strong footholds in Africa and Central America. Her communist philosophy now rules a great portion of Southeast Asia. The Soviets have made great progress toward their avowed aim of taking over the world. Japan, our wartime enemy, is now closely allied with America in trade and national defense.

When we came home after three and one-half years of slavery under the Japanese, we were so happy to be free that few of us wasted time hating our former enemies. While not many of our number admitted to hatred of them, very few spoke of love and forgiveness. Such feelings should be easily understood if the observer is informed as to the physical and mental abuses to which we were subjected. In these pages the reader will be taken into the very camps and prison ships in which so many lives were lost from disease and starvation. He will be pleased to see that some never lost the capacity to help and to care for their fellow man, and he will be saddened to learn that in some cases when the thin veneer of civilization is rubbed off, man can deteriorate to little more than an animal.

The loss of life was extremely high in Japanese prison camps. The exact number or percentage will probably never be recorded. From what I have read and heard from others who have put considerable thought to the subject, it would appear that over fifty percent of those captured did not survive. In their documentary, "Bataan: The Forgotten Hell," the National Broadcasting Company said fifty-seven percent died. That is probably close to the right figure. We do know that close to 5,000 were lost at sea when their unmarked prison ships were bombed or torpedoed by our own Navy. Those ships were: *Shinyo Maru*, torpedoed off Sindangan Point, Mindanao, P.I., December 7, 1944, with a loss of 688 prisoners, 83 reached shore; *Arisan Maru*, torpedoed October 24, 1944, in South China Sea, 1,792 lost, 8 survived; *Oryoku Maru*, December 15, 1944, off Bataan coast near Subic Bay. Survivors from the latter were put on the *Enoura Maru* and the *Brazil Maru*. After a forty-seven-day journey they reached Japan with 375 survivors, 1,243 having been lost in two bombings. Dr. Julien M. Goodman is quoted as having said that another ship, name unknown, was torpedoed on October 18, 1944, with a loss of 1,100 prisoners. There were at least a half-dozen other ships which transported prisoners from Manila to Japan. Due to the heat and thirst and crowded conditions, at least three hundred died on those ships.

On land, in camps that I have heard of, the losses totaled 5,950. They were: on the Death March, approximately 1,000; camps, O'Donnell, 2,200; Cabanatuan, 2,600; Palawan, 150. Throughout the Philippines, Japan, Formosa, Korea and Manchuria there were at least fifty other camps with prison populations ranging from 150 to 500. All had deaths. The lowest figure was in Jinsen, Korea, where only one died, while another camp in Japan had over one hundred deaths. A reasonable guess would be an average of ten per camp which would add up to another five hundred. When we add all of the above losses together the figure comes to 11,573. That is no doubt a very conservative number. In the years following the war the mortality rate of the survivors has been much higher than in the population as a whole. Before they reached the average age of sixty, it was estimated that only about 5,000 of the approximately 24,000 who were captured in the Philippines were still alive. Many of the present-day survivors are in very poor health as a result of the stress and strain they were forced to withstand.

In recent years I have seen approximately one thousand of the survivors and have grown to love them more and more. To a man and woman, they are some of the finest Americans I have ever known. Their loyalty to their country and to each other radiates a quality of human love which would melt the hearts of even the most cynical. It is their story that is being told in these pages. I am sure that the survivors join me in paying tribute to our courageous comrades who lost their lives in service to our country.

Acknowledgments

I should like to thank the gallant men mentioned in these pages both for being my friends and for giving me subjects to write about. Being closely associated with most of them during the trying times of our prisoner of war ordeal helped me to endure. In recent years brave men such as Victor Mapes, Calvin Graef and Philip Brodsky told me their remarkable stories of survival, which I have recorded as accurately as I could. Their courage, stamina and determination were an inspiration, and had a great influence on my decision to write this book. Since the war I have come to know many other survivors, with whom I have developed a bond of friendship stronger than I ever imagined possible among a group of men and their wives. I am grateful to each of them for their love and camaraderie.

In addition to those who are a part of the story, there are others who were a great help to me in this undertaking, and not to mention them would be impolite and certainly ungrateful.

Sky Beaven, that lovely lady of letters, not only encouraged me to undertake this project but also did a detailed job of editing the first draft as to dates, places and historical facts. William Emerson, author, former editor of the *Saturday Evening Post*, and professor of journalism at the University of South Carolina, taught me some of the skills of writing and convinced me that I should get going with the book. Dr. Robert H. Walker, author and professor of American Studies at George Washington

University, made some very valuable suggestions and also found me a publisher. Dr. Louis D. Rubin, Jr., did a masterful job of editing. John Toland, Pulitzer Prize—winning author and good friend, had some kind introductory words to say about the book. Duane Schultz, author of *Hero of Bataan*, gave his encouragement and warm friendship. Finally, I should like to thank the many friends who, having read some of my stories in local newspapers, insisted that I should write a book.

MANNY LAWTON

Introduction

Among America's greatest unsung heroes of World War II are those prisoners of war in the Pacific whose captivity for more than three years was marked by far more deprivations and suffering than any American prisoner had experienced since Andersonville.

The experiences of Manny Lawton, while incredible to those ignorant of the facts, were shared by many comrades and that is what makes this book significant. Their ordeal was so horrendous that even today few Americans know what their countrymen went through and some readers may perhaps find it difficult to believe that anyone could have survived. My research over the past twenty-five years confirms that what you are about to read is not an exaggeration but the grim truth.

The case of Lawton is of special interest for he is a sensitive, objective man with a remarkable sense of recall, and these qualities make his memoirs a testament of man's ability to rise above his travails rather than a litany of horrors. He tells in detail of the last catastrophic days of fighting on Bataan, the Death March, and the months of deprivations and beatings at their first camp. "It was at O'Donnell," said one of Lawton's comrades, Robert W. Levering, "we learned that Hell is not a place but a condition. . . . The living lived because we were able to adjust ourselves to the gradually worsening conditions." At their next camp, Cabanatuan, they were faced not only with more beatings but starvation. The men were reduced to trapping rats, dogs and such to augment their meager rations. Lawton was wakened one night by two comrades arguing over the division of a snake. One claimed the larger portion because he had seen it first.

"You crippled thief," yelled the other man, "the damn snake was getting away when I came along. You never would have caught him."

"It's my snake. I found it. Consider yourself lucky if you get any at all."

"I'm having half or a chunk of your hide."

Such are the scenes from Hell related by Lawton to which he gives illumination by his reactions. "As I listened," he observed, "I laughed at first. Then it saddened me to realize that the two men were willing to tear each other apart over an item of food which neither would have considered edible in better times. The incident demonstrated two sad truths: 1) We had sunk to a terrible low and 2) friendship was a fragile thing which has little elasticity when survival is threatened."

Once MacArthur finally retook Leyte in late 1944 it seemed as if liberation were near, but this great victory ironically brought death to many prisoners who were hurriedly shipped to Japan as hostages. Lawton was one of the 1,619 men embarked from Manila on the so-called Hell Ships. His chronicle of this voyage of the damned is appalling. Only one in four made it and those who did had to endure eight more months of oppression.

"The amazing thing," one prisoner told me, "is how anyone survived the years of captivity. The damned Army gave us only one instruction on being captured: reveal name, rank and serial number. They didn't tell us the important things about organizing camps democratically and sanely. We weren't taught how to handle hunger or cold or heat or pain or boredom. And for that I blame the Army."

Captivity, as illustrated by this book, brought out the best and worst. Some men remained indifferent to the fate of others; some gave their lives for friends; some stole; some gave up food, and fought for the rights of others. Many of those who survived did so because of their selfishness. Others, like Manny Lawton, survived because of faith in God, country and their fellow men. I have met many of this latter group at the reunions of the Survivors of Bataan and Corregidor. These men served their country and their comrades well in prison and, after freedom, finally lost their hatred of the Japanese. It is time we honored these unsung heroes who got no promotions or medals and who endured without losing their humanity.

JOHN TOLAND

Some Survived

1. The Fall of Bataan

The rapid rings of my field telephone startled me as I sat talking to Lieutenant Sese. It was ten o'clock in the morning of April 8, 1942.

"This is Colonel Erwin," the serious but calm voice snapped. "The line has broken in the Mount Samat area to our left. Large numbers of enemy troops are pouring in. General Bluemel has given orders to withdraw. Move your battalion approximately two kilometers back and assemble on the Provincial Road. Wait there for further orders."

"Is this the end, sir? What do we do next?"

"Just wait and pray. General King is trying to negotiate a surrender. In the interest of saving lives there should be no further resistance."

"Yes, sir. Good luck, Colonel. God be with you."

Those solemn words ended my last official conversation with my commanding officer. The last gallant stand of American and Filipino defenders of Bataan had come to a bitter halt.

Lieutenant Sese, reading the troubled expression on my face, anxiously asked, "What is it, Captain?"

"The end has come. Inform Major Ibanez to withdraw."

Lieutenant Alfredo (Fred) Sese, forty, was among the brightest and most well-informed Filipino officers I had come to know. Of mixed Spanish, Chinese and Filipino blood, the father of six children, he was handsome and much larger than the average man of his country. Standing five feet eight inches and carrying

170 pounds made him appear half again the size of most men in our unit. An eager student of American literature and history, he made easy conversation on things American. He and I had become close personal friends and through him I had learned much about Filipino customs and mores.

Major Ibanez, a short, neat, crew-cut forty-five-year-old career Filipino officer, was battalion commander. With twenty years' service divided between the Philippine constabulary and army, he had a reputation for courage, leadership and devotion to duty. He knew combat, and had the experience and judgment to cope with emergencies. Now he would be confronted with something new and undescribed in military handbooks—surrender.

At twenty-three years of age, a graduate of Clemson University and its Reserve Officer Training program and a crash course at the Army Infantry School, I served as battalion military advisor. Though the only American with the 500-man unit (1st Battalion, 31st Infantry, Philippine Army), I had become a part of it and felt perfectly at ease with its officers and men, in spite of differences in language and customs.

As sergeants barked orders and men began pulling back from the line in preparation for an orderly withdrawal, my thoughts switched to Colonel John (Jack) Erwin. At this very moment he was seeing his last command, the 31st Infantry Regiment, Philippine Army, fold up in defeat. A professional officer of the United States Army, he had enjoyed an outstanding career of thirty years' service dating back before World War I. Now his career was falling apart in something far short of glory and pride. A large man, Erwin was six feet two and weighed 250 pounds. He walked with a quick step, always wore a cigar in his mouth, seldom lit, and always carried two or more of everything he thought he might need—wristwatches, fountain pens, knives, compasses and pistols. His appearance was tough, but his heart was kind and his words seldom gruff. He was easy to approach and talk to, but he demanded efficiency and results. Whether virtues or quirks of character, his traits were of little importance now as he and I and all the rest faced the most dreaded of all military experiences—bowing down to the enemy, defenseless, in humiliation and defeat.

It had been exactly four months since the Japanese struck their crippling blow on December 8, 1941. On that very first day our planes, caught on the ground at high noon, had been wiped out. Within the week the Navy Yard at Cavite on Manila Bay had been destroyed and most of its fighting ships had fled south to the Dutch East Indies. Enemy control of the skies and sea foreclosed any prospect of reinforcements coming in.

For two weeks following the first air attacks, we had deployed our forces and nervously awaited enemy landings. My battalion was assigned a beach defense position, including the town of Iba, on the China Sea coast in Zambales Province, and extending one mile south. Iba Air Base and all of its P-40 fighter planes had been destroyed on that first fateful day.

Rumors of enemy landings began shortly after the initial bombings. Rumors became reality with small landings at Aparri and Vigan on December 10th and at Davao on the island of Mindinao on December 20. The big blow fell on December 22 when Lieutenant General Masaharu Homma landed 43,000 troops from eighty-five transports at several points along Lingayen Gulf in the north of Luzon.

To oppose the invading force General Jonathan M. Wainwright had the unseasoned Eleventh and Twenty-first Divisions and the Ninety-first Infantry combat team. These troops, only recently inducted, were hardly more than recruits. However, in reserve was the well-trained and disciplined Twenty-sixth Cavalry of 699 men and 28 officers, the last unit of horse cavalry in the United States Army. Its officers were American and the enlisted men were proud Philippine Scouts with long years of service.

The untrained Philippine Army troops could not stop the enemy at the beaches. The Twenty-sixth Cavalry had to be committed on the very first day. Though they sustained heavy losses themselves, they inflicted greater casualties on the enemy. After the initial rout, the Eleventh, Twenty-first and Ninety-first regrouped and were able to help with the delaying action which cost the Japanese dearly at key river crossings as Wainwright fought a delaying action back toward Bataan.

The bulk of the Luzon forces completed the withdrawal into Bataan on New Year's Day, 1942. All that remained engaging the enemy were 5,000 men of the Forty-first and Fifty-first Infantry Regiments, Philippine Army, and the proud, disciplined Fifty-seventh Infantry Regiment, Philippine Scouts. They organized a defensive position known as the Abucay Line, stretching from Abucay on Manila Bay westward to Mt. Natib. There the Japanese suffered more than 2,000 casualties before breaking through. In addition to the loss of manpower, Japanese General Homma had to answer to his superiors for another three weeks' delay in getting his conquest rolling again. He had been under constant pressure from Tokyo to complete the Philippine campaign. The Japanese General Staff had predicted a short operation: thirty days at most. Now two months had passed and victory still eluded him.

Just before January ended, the Fil-American defenders were forced to abandon the Abucay Line. General James Weaver's Provisional Tank Group, with 75 mm self-propelled artillery, covered the withdrawal. Those guns, raining down shrapnel, thwarted several opportunities for the enemy to exploit his victory. Without the cover of those merciless explosives, most of the weary, battered fighters would have been surrounded and destroyed. On January 28 the last of the unwashed, unshaven, bleeding infantrymen wearily plodded down the East Coast Road to temporary rest and security behind the new Pilar-Bagac Line.

General Homma, having let the defenders elude his grasp at Abucay, meant to crush MacArthur's forces in short order. The new line stretched fourteen miles across the middle of the Bataan peninsula from Manila Bay on the east to the China Sea on the west.

A determined thrust on January 27, down Trail 2 just east of Mt. Samat, failed. Again and again Homma's troops tried for the next three nights. The stubborn defenders refused to yield.

An amphibious flanking attack against the rugged cliffs of the west coast met with disaster. Of the 900-man landing party, a mere handful survived. Those spurts of intensive effort were followed by a stalemate throughout the balance of February and March. Homma, having been stopped, much to his embarrassment, had to petition for reinforcements.

General MacArthur, on March 11, acting on orders from President Roosevelt, turned his command over to General Jonathan Wainwright and departed for Australia. Day by day the plight of the defenders grew more desperate. Of the less than 80,000 troops in Bataan, only 27,000 were listed as combat forces. Of those, three-fourths were suffering from malaria; all were hungry and faced with starvation. Wainwright notified Washington that the meager food supplies would be completely exhausted by April 15.

On Good Friday, April 3, reinforced with fresh infantry, more artillery and bombers, General Homma unleashed the most savage artillery barrage of the entire campaign. It commenced at 10 A.M. and continued without hesitation for two hours. High explosive shells from more than one hundred 155 mm cannon seemed to explode one on top of the other. No square yard seemed to be missed. A two and one-half mile sector directly forward of Mt. Samat was pulverized. The shelling was followed by wave after wave of bombers dropping high explosives over the same area. The first wave dropped incendiaries, which ignited the matted jungle into a terrifying inferno.

In their foxholes, the defenders felt some degree of security from the shelling, but now a decision had to be made. Staying in the foxholes required withstanding the intense heat plus the possibility of being burned alive; getting out to move to the rear posed the threat of being cut to pieces by shrapnel. As the wild flames closed in, each man made an attempt to dash to safer ground, only to be greeted by artillery reaching beyond the burning zone. By 5 P.M., when the Japanese infantry attack was launched, two Philippine Army regiments were in a shambles. The door was open for Lieutenant General Akira Nara's Sixty-fifth Brigade to smash through.

April 4 brought another fierce artillery and air bombardment. By evening, enemy troops had swarmed up and over Mt. Samat and descended its south slope.

On April 5, Easter Sunday, the defenders made a brave attempt to mount a counterattack. It was to no avail. With two miles of the front line laid open and two divisions wiped out, there was no possibility of stopping the onslaught.

General Clifford Bluemel, Commander of the Thirty-first Division, Philippine Army, tried doggedly on April 6 and April 7 to regroup elements of any units he could find. He was powerless in his attempt to inspire beaten men. The weak, hungry, demoralized troops had no fight left in them. Major General Edward P. King, Commander Bataan forces, realized that further resistance could only mean slaughter for his men, and on April 8 made his anguished decision to surrender. Calling his staff together, he tersely announced that the end had come and that he was going forward under a flag of truce requesting surrender terms from General Homma.

As he was being driven forward in his jeep on the morning of April 9 to meet Homma, he recalled that General Robert E. Lee had surrendered at Appomattox on the same date. He even recalled what Lee had said: "Then there is nothing to do but to go and see General Grant, and I would rather die a thousand deaths."

Now it had ended. The high command had feared from the outset what the ultimate fate of Bataan would be. In the ranks, to the bitter end, there was hope. There had been rumors of actual sightings of huge convoys of reinforcements gunning their way in. No doubt such hope ignited, time after time, the will to resist against overpowering odds. We were forced back at Lingayen, Aparri and Abucay. Each time, our troops regrouped and fought back with a fury which took many Japanese lives and at times forced the enemy to yield ground which he had already claimed as his own.

For three months and twenty-two days, an army of 100,000 plus reinforcements had tried and failed to subdue less than 80,000 ill-supplied defenders on Luzon. In early April, the last and crucial week, a fresh enemy army and a battered, bleeding defense force met for the final death struggle. On the Fil-American side, there were no replacements for the dead and wounded. Neither was there medicine for the constantly increasing malaria, nor food for hungry bellies. General King's decision to surrender was correct. He had no options. Final defeat was neither a surprise nor a disgrace for those involved. The mystery is: how did they resist so long?

By noon of April 8 we were moving toward the road on a jungle trail. On either side of us were thick, matted vines, mango trees and huge mahogany trees. Some of the giant hardwoods were six feet in diameter and their tall branches overlapped the trail, forming an umbrella against the sun. In contrast to the front line which overlooked a large rice field, where there were no trees and the glare was hard on the eyes, this looked like semidarkness. I felt as if I were being swallowed up by the jungle.

Except for the thump, thump of marching feet, there was silence among us. A few birds fluttered from the trees ahead. Occasionally, a startled monkey squealed as he raced up the trunk of a large tree, dashed out to the end of a high limb and jumped to another. Very little wildlife was left in the Bataan jungle. Our hungry men had slaughtered and eaten every type of living creature, including lizards, monkeys and fowl.

Major Ibanez, Lieutenant Sese, Corporal Bautista and I marched together. Bautista, tall and wiry, with a prominent jaw and searching brown eyes, had joined the outfit six months earlier as part of a training cadre. An excellent soldier in every way, he had learned his military skills in six years of service with the Forty-fifth Infantry, Philippine Scouts. Naturally alert and well adapted to jungle warfare, he had saved my life one day in January. We were scouting an area to the west flank of the Abucay Line. Walking ahead of me in tall cogon grass, he suddenly stopped, spread out his left arm knocking me to the ground and covering me with his body. As quickly as a western gunman, he drew his 45 pistol and fired rapidly into a large tree thirty yards ahead. A man slid to the ground.

"Japanese," he remarked calmly.

We waited for a while. Seeing and hearing nothing more, we cautiously approached the spot. Splotches of blood marked a trail leading toward the river.

I was thinking of that incident and others in which Bautista had performed so exceedingly well. It was always he who was called on for special missions which required great skill and natural ability. Now, as we marched toward our uncertain fate, his penetrating eyes were searching every bush and tree, his keen ears picking up every sound.

"What do you think they will do to us, sir?"

"It may not be too bad, Bautista. There are rules of international law with regards to treatment of prisoners of war, you know."

"What do they care about rules?" Sese commented. "Those Japanese are uncivilized. What about the way they abused the people at Singapore and China?"

"Yes, we have heard of atrocities, but we don't know for sure. Maybe since we gave them a good fight they will have more respect for us."

Trying to seem confident and hopeful, I plodded along. Though my doubts and fears were just as strong as any of the men, I knew that panic would lead to greater disaster. To myself I reasoned that there was nothing else to do but go in the direction we were headed. With the enemy behind us along what had been the front line, and to the right where they had swarmed over Mt. Samat, as well as to our left with full possession of the main highway, there could be only one area of temporary security. It would be better to assemble there unarmed and let them come to us, than to run head-on in the jungle into ruthless enemy troops still filled with the excitement of battle and the smell of victory. Escape was impossible and further resistance would be suicide.

Silently, fearfully, we moved along, each minute bringing us nearer to that dreaded act of surrender. Humiliation and shame, added to our built-up burdens of hunger and disease, made each weary step hesitant and heavy. Heaped on top of these very real and certain afflictions was the gnawing dread of the unknown.

There was no doubt in anyone's mind that the Japanese would be tough and unsympathetic. The unspoken question in my mind was just how brutal and merciless they might be. I had visions of individual enemy soldiers, or groups of them, bayoneting or clubbing to death any of our group whom they might come across, or of Japanese officers ordering their men to set up machine guns to slaughter us by the hundreds. There was nowhere to go, and no way to avoid whatever might lie ahead. In such a helpless situation, I am convinced that the dread of the unknown is much more unnerving than the terror of battle itself.

We reached our designated area in late afternoon. No Japanese were there. Exhausted, we fell out in the shade of large trees in a cleared area beside the dusty highway. After a brief rest I got to my feet and walked among the men, thinking to offer some encouragement. However, I soon realized there was nothing much to be said. I could make no promises . . . for there was no prospect of fulfillment. I wished them good luck—it was all I could muster. Having done that, I rejoined the staff at our temporary command post.

During the previous night, chills and fever of malaria had hit me for the first time since my arrival in the Philippines six months earlier. Now, in late afternoon, I could feel them coming on again. As we sat around and waited in the dread certainty of becoming prisoners of war, we explored various possibilities of coping with what lay ahead. Escape for me seemed out of the question. For a blonde Caucasian to melt into the Oriental populace and be unnoticed, I reasoned, would be impossible. Hiding in the jungle and gradually working my way north to the uninhabited mountain area held some promise, I thought, but even to start on such a course would require a supply of medicines—especially quinine with which to combat malaria. None was available. My final decision for my own self was to stay put and await whatever might lie ahead in the hands of the Japanese. I suggested that anyone who wished to was free to try an escape. None chose to do so.

It was now late afternoon. With nothing further to do but

wait, we decided to try to get some sleep. Being restless and anxious, Lieutenant Sese came over to where I lay, to chat further. Seeing that my face was flushed and my shirt wet from perspiration, he reached over and felt my forehead. "Captain, you have a high fever. Shouldn't you go to the hospital?"

"If I were already there it would be good. To walk eight or ten kilometers tonight, not even knowing where the hospital is, would do more harm than good. I will do better to sweat it out here and try to go there tomorrow morning."

"Maybe that would be best," he answered with some doubt in his voice. For the next hour or more, Sese busied himself with bathing my face and head with wet cloths. After finally satisfying himself that the fever was reduced, he fell asleep.

The following morning I was awakened at dawn by the noise of passing trucks; some headed north and some south. They were American. No Japanese were yet on the scene.

Feeling somewhat rested and a little less feverish, I prepared to leave for the hospital. As I was saying farewell to the staff, I noticed Alberto, my servant and cook, staring at me with tear-filled big brown eyes and a bewildered expression on his face. Alberto was only sixteen; too young to be a soldier. The oldest of eight children in a peasant farm family, he had come to our training camp at San Marcelino, Zambales, in September looking for work. Lieutenant Red Williams had hired him as house boy. After I moved in with Red in October, he continued in the job and proved to be efficient as a housekeeper and devoted to both of us.

At the outbreak of war on December 8, 1941, we advised him to go home to his family.

"No, sir, I will go with you."

"But there is a war to be fought, Alberto. You are not a soldier. It will be safer for you at home."

"I will be safe with you. I will cook for you."

Reluctantly we consented, being apprehensive both about his safety and the liability a young boy might be. Once in the field, however, he proved to be an imaginative cook and adaptable to operating in the wild.

First Lieutenant "Red" Williams had joined the unit two months before I came in October. Williams was a cool-headed, courageous young officer from Oregon. He stood five feet ten inches tall and had red hair and a neatly trimmed moustache. Though rather quiet, he had an air of self-confidence about him which quickly established him as a leader. Williams was one of the few men I have known who had no fear of death. He and I quickly became good friends.

Our unit was moved up to an assembly area behind the Abucay Line on January 17. That same afternoon I went forward and consulted with the battalion commander of the unit we were to replace. Early the following morning, just as we finished breakfast, the quiet and stillness of the jungle around us erupted with the sounds of battle. It seemed that automatic fire was coming in from all directions. We jumped into foxholes and tried to assess the situation. At first it sounded to me like machine guns. Then after listening for a minute or so I decided that the enemy was somehow projecting packages of firecrackers from a distance. Just when I had myself convinced that the Japs were practicing psychological warfare by shooting firecrackers among us and that there was no danger, I suddenly heard several live bullets ricochet from trees and rocks around me. I sent out a patrol to find the source of the disturbance.

Before the search squad had gotten out of sight, Red Williams calmly strolled by with a rifle in his hand. I asked him what he was up to. He said, "I'm going out to find the Japs who are playing games with us."

With those last words, Williams quickly moved out of sight among the tall trees. I never saw him alive again. A few hours later his body was recovered. A Japanese sniper, perched in a tree, had shot him through the temple. It was January 18, 1942.

After Williams was killed at Abucay, I became Alberto's sole responsibility. He learned to drive the panel truck containing my supplies, prepared my meals, and with his machete could cut bamboo poles and quickly throw up a shelter. He even kept what money I had brought along. Looking at the frightened lad now and thinking of the comfort he had been to me, I felt remorse for not having made him go home.

"Shall I go with you now?" he asked with a choking voice.

"No, Alberto. That would not be best for you. Do you think you can find your way home?" (Home for him was across the Zambales Mountains more than fifty miles away.)

"I think so, sir, if the Japanese will let me."

"Well, first of all you must get out of that uniform and put on your civilian clothes. If you mix with the civilians you may get by as one of them. Take what canned food you can carry from my panel truck. Don't hang around. Get going before the Japs come in."

Hesitating for a moment, he reached into his pocket and pulled out some folded bills and handed them to me.

"Your money, sir."

Counting out half of it, I handed him twenty pesos with my left hand and grasped his right in a farewell handshake.

With tears running down both cheeks, he blurted out "Thank you, sir. I hope you will be safe." With that emotionally restrained farewell, he quickly turned and walked away. Realizing at that late moment that he had looked on me as a father and protector, my throat choked up and my heart pounded. It was one of those cruel points in life when a burst of tears would have relieved my tension, but at the same time could have undone the last semblance of strength which Alberto had looked up to. My tears would have to flow in private.

Bidding farewell to grown men and fellow officers was a different matter. Under normal conditions speeches would be called for. Here and now, no words would fit. What could I say to the daring and imaginative Lieutenant Alejo Santos, who had confiscated the panel truck and helped me fill it with food supplies from abandoned stores? What words from me could convince the courageous Major Ibanez that all would be well? I could only shake their hands and wish them well.

There was much I wanted to say to Lieutenant Fred Sese, but words were difficult. I looked him in the eyes and haltingly said,

"Fred, you have been a good officer and a dear friend. I hope things will be all right."

"Thank you, Manny. You have caused me to understand and love America more. May God be with you."

As I headed south on the crowded, dusty road, I noticed a brown skinned Filipino boy, wearing a large straw hat and blue denim shirt and shorts, slip into the jungle. On his back he carried a small sack of supplies. I prayed that my plan for Alberto would be successful.

Trudging slowly down the East Coast Road, I saw Filipino and American soldiers coming and going aimlessly as if lost. All wore dazed looks. Some still carried rifles, which seemed unwise to me, but I made no suggestions. My days of giving orders had come to an end. The sun seemed hotter than usual; no doubt my fever made it seem worse. Passing trucks churned up clouds of dust. There was no breeze to blow it away. My uniform was soon soaked with sweat, which made the dust cling to me like mud.

At five in the afternoon I reached Cabcabin. Hospital #2 was filled to overflowing. Patients with more serious ailments than mine were lying around under shade trees. I found a very busy medical corpsman and asked to see a doctor.

"I'm sorry, captain," he said in a sympathetic tone. "The doctors are trying as best they can to take care of the many wounded. They can't possibly see you now."

"I have high fever. I need quinine."

"There is no medicine," he answered. Handing me a blanket from the supply tent, he said, "Here, take this and bed down under a tree. A night's rest and some hard praying might help."

I picked a spot in the bushes near the road, wrapped my body in the blanket and flopped down. Shortly I was in a deep sleep. Being exhausted, neither the nearby rumble of trucks nor the distant explosions of munitions dumps disturbed me. It was the night of April 8, 1942. Not only did the setting sun signal the end of another day, it also drew the final curtain on four months of heroic struggle by the army of Bataan.

2. The Death March

Dawn of April 9, 1942, was surprisingly still and calm at Cabcabin. Gone were the shouts of distressed voices, the rumble of heavy trucks and the thunderous explosions of yesterday and the days before. It was a ghostly, unreal change. I had the feeling that someone had turned off the time machine and brought all activity to an eerie halt.

Sitting up and looking around, I noticed that three other Americans, a sergeant among them, were sleeping nearby. They, too, had been issued blankets by the medics. Their ailment was malaria also. I passed around a pack of cigarettes. Each took one.

"What do you think they will do to us?" asked one of them in a soft Southern voice.

"Be prepared to be lined up and shot," suggested his companion, a man of above average size and reddish hair and good looks. He wore the insignia of the Thirty-first U.S. Infantry.

"You can expect the worst," the sergeant informed us. "I have talked with some of the Marines who were in China last year. They told me the Japs were really brutal to the Chinese there." His dark brunette complexion and Brooklyn accent identified him as a second generation Italian. Also, he spoke with authority, as did most men from Brooklyn whom I had known.

"Well, there is no use in working up a lather over what might happen. We will just have to try to take what comes," I advised.

Remembering that I had some canned food in my bag, I invited them to have breakfast with me. Among the four of us, we divided one can of corned beef and one of salmon. They were the last of my supplies and the last meat any of us would taste for many weeks.

Just as we finished eating, the sergeant commented under his breath, "We are about to find out what kind of bastards they are. Here they come."

It was 6:30 A.M. Three Japanese soldiers with bayonets on their rifles approached at a brisk walk. They were short, stocky and extremely young looking. With jabbering and motioning of the arms, they indicated that we were to line up. None of us could understand the language, but all could interpret the nudging of a bayonet. It meant move quickly and don't hesitate or resist.

Once we were lined up and standing at attention they began shaking us down for valuables. One indicated that we were to empty our pockets. The first one who got to me took my last twenty pesos. I wished I had given them to Alberto. The second ripped off my wristwatch. None seemed to want my class ring. It was the military type, and probably didn't look gold enough to suit them. Each of us lost everything of value in our possession. Satisfied that we had nothing more, the Japanese soldiers gaily walked away laughing and jabbering among themselves.

Having no new cuts and bruises and not having been physically abused, we felt relieved. One of our men commented with some optimism in his tone, "Though they are thieves, at least they weren't rough. Maybe the Japs aren't so bad after all."

"Don't make hasty judgments. We've seen only three of them. There are 100,000 more on the way," warned the sergeant.

As we stood beside the road nervously anticipating what would happen next, a truck pulled up and stopped. Ten Japanese soldiers climbed out. Their leader, probably a corporal, motioned for us to come forward. Evidently our response was not quick enough, for he gave a gruff order to his men. Immediately they charged forward and began kicking and slapping us

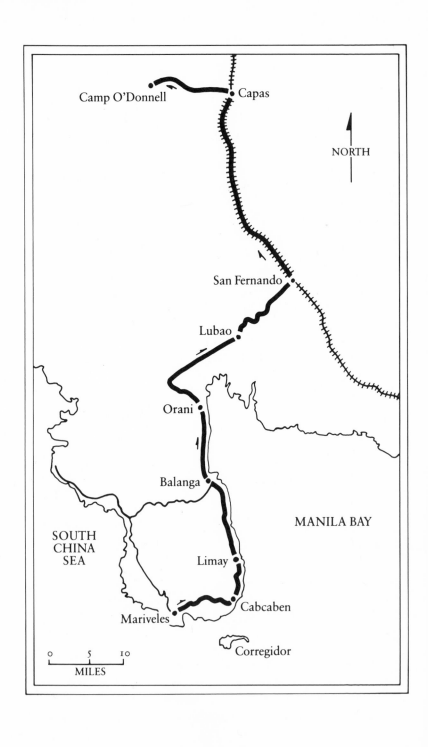

Camp O'Donnell

Capas

NORTH

San Fernando

Lubao

Orani

Balanga

MANILA BAY

SOUTH
CHINA
SEA

Limay

Mariveles

Cabcaben

Corregidor

0   5   10
MILES

while indicating that we were to start marching. Apparently they were rounding up Americans first, for Filipinos on the opposite of the road were not molested.

One guard was assigned to herd us along while the others continued south to round up other prisoners. Threatening with the bayonet, he kept us moving at a rapid pace—almost a run. I got the feeling that he wouldn't hesitate to shoot us at the slightest provocation. As we moved north we were joined by other small groups of Americans also under guard. Frequently incoming trucks loaded with Japanese soldiers crowded us off the road. By the time we reached the assembly area, our ranks had grown to fifty or more. There we joined at least two hundred other Americans. All looked weary and extremely distressed.

Scanning the group, I spotted Colonel Erwin. His eyes were sunken. He chewed on an unlit cigar and looked worried and in pain. Being twice my weight and double my age, he would have a difficult time under forced march conditions, I feared.

"What do you think we can expect, Colonel?"

"You can anticipate the very worst, Lawton. It's going to be tough. These Japs are running around like crazy men. They are excitable and unreasonable under stress."

"Do you think they will ship us out to Japan, or put us at some place like Fort McKinley near Manila?"

"Who knows what they will do? It's very obvious that they want to get us out of the way and move their troops in for the invasion of Corregidor."

Noticing that his barracks bag was nearly full and that it required some effort for him to pick it up, I commented, "Colonel, you seem to have a heavy load in that bag. What are you hanging on to that is so important?"

"Oh, just some extra clothes and shoes and canned goods and things like that." I tried to pick it up. It must have weighed forty pounds.

"Sir, I had planned to help you if it became necessary, but I wouldn't attempt to carry such a load. I only brought along toilet articles and a change of socks and underwear. Why don't you do the same?"

"Oh no. I may need these things," he answered.

The guards motioned us to the side of the road as a convoy of trucks loaded with Japanese soldiers approached. They were headed south and wore the looks of proud, threatening conquerors. It was not necessary to understand the language to know that they were deriding us. As they passed, some of them flailed us across our heads and backs with bamboo poles, causing pushing and shoving as we tried to avoid the licks. Some prisoners were trampled under foot. It was humiliating, and there was no chance of fighting back. Mollification of pride would have to come later.

After the convoy passed, we again lined up on the road in a column of fours. In groups of one hundred, we set out on what became known later as the "Death March." Eight or ten armed guards marched with each group. Among them I saw none who was taller than five feet four inches. Most of them were short, stocky and hostile looking. Their uniforms were khaki with wool wraparound leggings, and they wore short-visored wool caps with ear flaps and a short flap covering the back of the neck. From the outset, the guards were all business: unsympathetic, unsmiling and ever ready with the bayonet.

It was late morning when the march officially began. The tropical sun was already bearing down intensely. The guards were constantly prodding us to move faster. Passing trucks and horse-drawn artillery churned up a constant cloud of choking dust from the powder-dry gravel roadbed. Small rocks pressed against the soles of my shoes. At times they felt as if they would come through. The ever present dust burned my eyes, clogged my nostrils and throat and made breathing more difficult. Though we were marching along the shore of Manila Bay, there was a total absence of breeze to blow the dust away. Guards on both sides of the column kept ordering "Speedo! Speedo!"

The only stops made during the first two hours were brief pauses while convoys passed. That meant being crowded tightly together along the edge of the roadway until the traffic cleared. In such instances no one was allowed to sit. The only relief was in momentarily not having to push one aching foot in front of the other.

At noon we were halted in a small town for ten or fifteen minutes while the guard changed. We sat erect in place. No one could stretch out and relax. Some were fortunate enough to be near shade trees. Most were still in the hot sun. Guards patrolled the column. Anyone more than three feet out of line was kicked or hit with a rifle butt. Neither food nor water was made available. Those who begged for water were clubbed. Sad-faced Filipino civilians watched from their front yards. Each blow received by a prisoner brought a look of pain to the onlookers' eyes.

In midafternoon the sun's rays bore down with greater intensity. Colonel Erwin, still carrying his heavy load, began to weaken. His shirt, soaked with sweat, clung to his body. Beads of sweat popped out on his face and splashed down his cheeks. He eyeglasses fogged up. I pleaded with him to throw the bag away. He only mumbled, "I will need these things." As his steps slowed and shortened, he gradually lost ground. By three-thirty, I could see him no longer.

I learned later that when he had drifted back to the tail of the column, the guards scolded and cuffed him. That doing no good, one of them pressed a bayonet against his back, drawing blood. By then the Colonel was delirious from malaria, thirst and exhaustion. Finally the impatient and merciless guard pushed him to the side of the road, pressed the rifle to his back and pulled the trigger. Colonel Jack Erwin was among the first of hundreds who were to meet such cruel deaths at the hands of brutal guards who were totally lacking in human kindness and compassion.

The march continued all that day with only occasional brief stops but no food. Hunger, thirst and the intense heat took their toll. Those who broke ranks to drink from a mud hole were shot. By nightfall we reached Balanga. Having started at Cabcabin, I estimated that I had marched fifteen miles. Those who had been rounded up nearer Mariveles had covered twenty.

When the guards completed crowding us into a barbed wire enclosure, it was nine P.M. There was still no food. My last snack had been the small portion of corned beef and fish for breakfast at six that morning. Most of the men had had very little to eat on the day before the march began. In addition to hunger and fatigue, many suffered from malaria and diarrhea. My fever seemed to have broken, for no chills came on as the evening grew cooler.

After standing in line for more than an hour, I got to the one water faucet and filled my canteen. Just as I settled down to get some rest the guards came among us kicking our prostrate bodies and ordering us to move out. It was then midnight. The march began again. Rain began to fall and a strong wind blew. The cold moisture felt refreshing to our exhausted bodies. We tilted our heads back to catch some of the pelting drops in our mouths. Soon we were soaked and the chilling wind made us cold. Even our shoes filled with water, making walking more difficult.

The guards at the head of the column rode bicycles and set a rapid pace. The ones along the side and at the rear kept yelling "Speedo! Speedo!" Soon we were running. Our rain-filled shoes seemed to stretch and become too large. Some slipped off and were lost, leaving raw, bare feet pounding the wet, pebbled road. No doubt the well-fed energetic guards chose to run in order to keep warm; for us, it was an added agony. After a half hour the rain stopped and we were allowed to march at a normal pace again.

As the sun rose over Manila Bay, we reached Orani, having covered ten miles since midnight. Here the column was halted. At first the morning sun felt good to our wet, chilled bodies. By mid-morning we were steaming again in another filthy, crowded pen. All day long we sat baking in the sun. There was no shade.

At noon we were fed one rice ball about the size of an orange. Those who had lost their mess kits took the rice in dirty hands and devoured it like starving animals. It was a pittance, but it helped. This was my first food since the light breakfast of thirty hours earlier.

It was now April 10. I had marched twenty-five miles.

We spent the night at Orani. Though we were exhausted, sleep was fitful and very little rest was possible. There was an uneasiness and tenseness among us as we huddled together on the hard ground. Though we were outdoors, the air was fouled by human waste in and around the open pit latrine. It seemed that throughout the night half the group was milling around in search of water or the latrine. Those who tried to sleep were constantly being stepped on or stumbled over.

When we were aroused the next morning to begin marching again, many did not get up. They had died in their sleep. Perhaps they were the fortunate ones, for more torment lay ahead for those who marched out. Further, it is more dignified to slip away in quiet slumber than to be crucified under an unbearable burden.

The Japanese never bothered to tell us in advance when we would start or stop, or what our ultimate destination would be. There seemed to be little plan or organization. The guards' only words were "Speedo! Speedo!" and their only gestures were threats with the bayonet. At times we were allowed to get water to drink. It is hard to fathom how any of us endured. No doubt a strong will to live, measured against the proven price of faltering, spurred us on beyond predictable human capacity.

At Lubao we were crowded into another filthy, foul-smelling barbed wire enclosure. Again there was the usual long wait in line for water. Before the night was over, most men got a drink and were able to fill their canteens. The evening meal of rice was a little more than the last feeding, but far from adequate. Even with nothing to go with it, not even salt, it tasted like a banquet dish to starving men. Small portions spilled on the filthy ground were scooped up and eaten.

Just as at the last overnight stop, sound sleep or even relaxing was impossible. There was constant milling around by those going to and from the lone water faucet, and cursing from those trying to rest who were being trod upon. In little clusters here and there, bewildered, frightened men sat discussing, in low tones, their terrible plight. Occasionally, a prisoner gone berserk from the horror of it all jumped up and yelled curses at the Japanese, calling them a race of inhumane, low-down bastards. He had to be subdued by those around him. I longed to sleep, so that I could dream of something better than this; or better still, to awaken and find that this had been only a nightmare.

Finally I slept, but only briefly. Guards shouting "Bango! Bango!" aroused us at dawn. When we stood up, thousands of flies buzzed around our heads like swarms of bees. At least fifty men did not stir. Most of them were dead; the balance dying. Large blue flies crawled in and out of their open mouths and nostrils. Some of the struggling living wished that they, too, had not awakened.

As we filed through the gate, a small rice ball was issued to each prisoner. It was now April 12, the fourth day of march. Conditions were no different: dust, intense tropical heat and ruthless, impatient guards. Our already weakened condition grew worse. Three days of hard marching with not enough food for one day's needs had dissipated our reserve of strength. More frequently now, men fell behind and were shot. No doubt had the same guards marched with us all the way they would have tired too, and possibly would have been more reasonable. But such was not our luck. The guard was changed several times a day. The fresh detail would speed up the pace and vent its anger on the prisoners with clubs and rifle butts.

The bedraggled column reached San Fernando, Pampanga, at midday. Japanese staff officers and off-duty soldiers watched our approach with evident pleasure. San Fernando was the largest town through which we had marched. It appeared that the Japanese intended to display us as physical proof that they were the conquering, superior race. Our humiliation was designed to warn the civilian populace that Nippon now ruled supreme.

As far as I was concerned such humiliation was accomplished. I felt shame and remorse for having let our Filipino allies down. But the expected adulation from the onlookers did not materialize. Instead of cheering their new masters, the bewildered witnesses shed unhidden tears of sympathy and love for the vanquished.

Our stop in San Fernando was brief. No food was issued, but those who happened to be near a flowing well were allowed to get water. Breaking ranks was forbidden and we could not even sit down in place. We stood there to be stared at and derided by off-duty Japanese soldiers bunched along one side of the street. For them the spectacle was pleasing. For the horrified Filipino women and children on the opposite side it stirred no pleasure, and neither did it engender allegiance to the Japanese, for the bizarre spectacle of bleeding, dehydrated, abused men before their eyes included some of their own loved ones.

From Main Street we marched to a nearby railroad station where rail cars awaited us. As we climbed into the small freight cars, I thought it would be a great relief to ride for a while. How wrong I was! The rail line was of the narrow gauge type; consequently the boxcars were small—seven feet high, thirty-three feet long and eight feet wide. Figuring two square feet per person, fifty men could have sat pushed tightly together. The Japs crowded nearly three times that number into each small boxcar and closed the doors. We stood with our bodies jammed together. There was no fresh air and the sun's rays bearing down against the steel sides intensified the heat. Many of the prisoners fainted; some died. Pathetic pleas for water went unheeded, for there was no one to listen. The Japs had loaded us in like so many tons of cargo and shipped us out. Other guards would receive us at our destination.

The two-hour train trip from San Fernando to Capas seemed interminable. It was worse than the march had been, for on the road there was at least fresh air, though dust-filled. On the march, we could see and encourage each other. Here there was darkness and near suffocation. One could not help a friend or even do anything for himself. We were rapidly running out of oxygen, and the intense heat and crowded condition made us feel as if we were in a pressure cooker. In addition, the air was fouled by the odor of sweating, unwashed bodies and the smell of human waste from those suffering with stomach disorders. We were utterly helpless and rapidly running out of time.

At Capas, the train came to a jerking halt and the doors were opened. We gladly piled out. Though the outside temperature was 95 degrees, it felt cool by comparison. The new guards were less brutal. They even seemed sympathetic. Prisoners who fell by the roadside were picked up and given rides into camp by truck. To my knowledge, no one was clubbed or shot in that last eight miles of the Death March.

How any of us made it I have never been able to fathom! I was only twenty-three years old at the time and in generally good health. Senior officers like General Bluemel and Colonel Ray O'Day were twice my age. It is still incredible to me that they were able to complete the march under their own power. I can understand why so many fell behind and lost their lives. Many were suffering from battle wounds or illnesses before the march began. Many had eaten very little food for days prior to the fall of Bataan.

From Mariveles to Capas we had covered 91 miles or 147 kilometers in four days. One hundred two kilometers or sixty-three miles had been on foot, under the most brutal conditions. Forty-five kilometers or twenty-eight miles had been by rail and even worse. As I had struggled to keep going and to live, I could not believe it was real. How could any civilized nation of people in the twentieth century be so brutal and unfeeling? I kept asking myself. I was to learn that what we knew as a Western civilization had not yet reached Japan. The Japanese soldier had been taught that all Americans were enemies forever and that prisoners of war were due absolutely no consideration.

3. Camp O'Donnell

It was late afternoon on April 12, the fourth and final day of the Death March for me, when we reached Camp O'Donnell. The camp was enclosed by six strands of forbidding barbed wire fence. At each corner stood a hastily thrown-up guard tower of bamboo. In each, a threatening-looking guard glared down as if he were looking for an excuse to shoot. Beyond the back fence was a field of brown cogon grass, which always seems to grow in untended land in the Philippines. A bluish-looking mountain range in the distance formed an inviting backdrop for the desertlike plain in which the camp was located.

O'Donnell had been one of the many Philippine Army training camps built just prior to the war. Some of the long, narrow barracks had never been completed. Their construction was of bamboo with thatched roofs. As we marched through the gate, guards herded us toward a platform near the headquarters building. When we had been formed in a semicircle in front of the speaker's stand, the Japanese camp commander, with a lieutenant and a Filipino civilian at his heels, marched across from headquarters. As he stomped up the steps and strode on stage, with sabre dangling and eyes flashing, you could sense that he felt as important as any field general. His rank was captain.

The captain opened with a blast at all Americans in general and he spewed out bitter contempt and hatred for us in particular. At the end of each sentence he paused for the Filipino to translate into English.

"De captin say you are not honorable prisoners of war. . . . You are captives. . . . As captives you have no rights."

The buck-toothed, short, bowlegged lieutenant nodded his head in approval. The small, middle-aged Filipino interpreter seemed slightly nervous and ill at ease to begin with, but as he warmed to his task he became more confident and eloquent.

"De captin say Americans and Japanese are enemies forever. . . . Americans all will be driven out of Asia. . . . Nippon will build a greater Asia for the Asiatics. . . . You will be used as laborers in this project. . . ."

By now the Filipino was imitating both in voice inflections and gestures. "He say if you try to escape you will be shoot kill. . . . Even to go near de fence will be cause for to shoot. . . ."

The guards looked on, with approval for the speaker and threats for us.

After thirty minutes of boasting of the mighty power of Nippon, punctuated with caustic hatred for us, the captain ended his bitter welcoming monologue with the warning, "You will obey all orders of any Japanese soldier. You will salute and bow to even the privates. For failure to do so, you will be severely punished." Apparently satisfied that he had sufficiently established the relative positions of slaves and master, the swaggering, mustachioed little man, as if for emphasis, clicked his spurred bootheels together and abruptly turned and marched off stage. The little interpreter trotted behind him like a puppy.

We were divided into groups by rank and assigned to barracks. My barracks, about fifty feet from headquarters, had an unfloored dirt aisle down the center. On each side of the aisle were double-decked platforms floored with bamboo slats. These were our sleeping quarters. There were no bunks, blankets or mosquito nets.

The Death March had been hell, but O'Donnell was a new kind of torment. Malaria and dysentery were rampant and there was no medicine to treat them. Our medics held daily sick call, but only sympathy was dispensed. Perhaps there was some mental relief in being able to talk to a doctor. With no beds, no drugs or equipment, the so-called hospital was not much more than a morgue.

Hospital patients were housed in two buildings; one for the sick and the other for the dying. The latter was a miserable, depressing, hopeless place. In it men lay in their own filth, being too weak and indifferent to struggle to the outdoor latrine. Being starved and ill, they had ceased to struggle. There was neither hope for life nor fear of death left in them.

I am sure the doctors must have experienced a feeling of frustration and defeat. Their medical knowledge told them what should be done, but the tools with which to do it, adequate food and medicine, were just short of nonexistent.

After the "march" and two weeks at O'Donnell, I was twenty pounds off weight and slowly losing ground. The odds were heavily against us all. The best hope was for a change in command which might bring more food and medicines. I hoped and believed this would happen.

Meanwhile, we continued to witness the shocking daily spectacle of the burial detail hauling away thirty to fifty emaciated corpses. At first we would stand at attention and salute. Soon it became so commonplace that no one seemed to notice. This bothered me for a while, but soon I became indifferent, too. In retrospect, I know it had to be that way.

Each man had to make his own adjustments to the sad and hideous scene around him. That done, he could then concentrate on his own survival. Perhaps that was nature's way of sealing our minds against the hell that was O'Donnell. The human emotions can absorb only so much grief and shock; beyond that point they must become hardened and calloused or else breakdown and insanity will ensue.

I thought back to the dust bowl days in the Midwestern United States during the thirties. Hot sun and drought killed all vegetation and dust storms covered the landscape with sand. There being nothing left for cattle to eat, they were shipped east for contract grazing. My dad boarded several hundred of them. Many died. I remembered seeing the living walk over and around the dead, seemingly unaware of the deteriorating carcasses. Now we too had reached that animal stage where personal survival, for those who wanted to live, was all that mattered.

The food was terrible, and there was not half enough of it. The raw rice issued by the Japs smelled musty and looked like floor sweepings. Our kitchen crew had no knowledge of how to cook it. The finished product was a greenish looking watery paste, resembling glue. Only starving men would have tried to eat it. Even though we were faced with starvation, it gagged us—especially those with malaria. But there was no choice. To live, we had to eat, and to eat meant forcing down anything which could be called food, no matter how unpalatable.

We stayed at O'Donnell for seven weeks. I kept thinking things would get better. "Surely," I commented to the captain bunking next to me, "they will not let us all die of starvation and neglect. Certainly they will soon bring in medicines and more food. This situation will come to the attention of General Homma and he will not want so many deaths on his hands."

"They want us to die," he answered with bitterness. "The more we bury, the less they will have to feed. The camp commander told us on the very first day that we were his enemies forever. They feel that soldiers who surrender should die."

"Maybe so, but I don't plan to die," I said. "Things will improve one of these days."

My hope for better conditions proved to be only wishful thinking. The high death rate continued. At the end of six weeks nearly two thousand Americans had been buried in mass graves. Across the road in a separate camp, Filipinos died at a rate ten times greater.

Robert W. Levering, in his book *Horror Trek*, in attempting to analyze why some lived while others died, had this to say:

It was at O'Donnell we learned that Hell is not a place but a condition. But no matter how bad the condition, everything is relative. The living lived because we were able to adjust ourselves to the gradually worsening situation. A man's spirit is subject to great fluctuations, the extent of which are unknown until put to the test. This test was greater than ordinary fear, love and hate. Many men, in an attempt to avoid the rugged impact of realities against their lives, simply gave up and died, because that was painless, while living was terrible.

How easily they slipped away through inanition, and how violently others struggled to keep within them the breath of life. Cerebral malaria victims went into a coma before dying. A dozen times I saw the swaying head, eyes with a maniacal stare, and thrashing arms held down while the priest administered extreme unction.

Frequently, in the midst of this cross section of humanity, I marveled at the varying degrees of determination with which men held on to the thin thread of life, which seemed to swing over a bottomless pit of despair. In order not to lose it, one had to hold on tight every minute, every hour, and every day throughout the seemingly endless months and years. To want to live with a mad desire was the sine qua non of survival.

The water supply for the entire camp of 9,000 came from a single spigot. Its power source was a gasoline engine in a pumphouse somewhere outside the fence. It frequently broke down for hours at a time, resulting in an intermittent, low pressure trickle. There was always a long line of men waiting to fill canteens. No matter if one went early or late, night or day, the line was there.

To avoid standing continuously in line, the men in my squad agreed on a duty roster. Each in turn would haul water for the others. One day it took me three hours, with ten canteens, to work my way up to the spigot, only to find the pump had stopped working. That meant another hour of waiting in the sun. Bathing and washing of clothing was out of the question. There was barely enough water to drink.

In any large group of men there are always a few who are enterprising and venturesome enough to try something different. I noticed several who were constantly on the prowl trying to catch grasshoppers, rats or dogs for food. The story spread around camp of two who built a trap for the purpose of catching a stray dog which had been seen on the grounds. While one was out on a work detail, the other caught the dog, promptly butchered and cooked it, ate his fill and sold the surplus. The next day, when the partner learned what had happened, a violent argument broke out between them.

"You thieving son of a bitch, half of the money is mine," was the charge.

"I caught the dog. You weren't here. He was mine," came the angry answer.

"We built the trap together. We were partners. Everything was to be 50–50."

A violent fist fight ensued which had to be broken up by onlookers.

Most of the few work details were unrewarding, but the few who drew truck driver jobs were in good position to better themselves. They could make contact with Filipinos and acquire extra food and medicines. Some of the drivers used the opportunity to help their sick friends. Others became black marketeers and sold precious drugs at excessive prices to helpless dying men.

Most of us merely sat around in idle boredom trying to keep cool. In the mornings when the barracks heated up from the tropical sun, we moved to the grass on the west side of the building. In the afternoon we switched to the shade of the east side. Sick men, in order to be quiet and left alone, crawled under the building. Many died there.

Nothing good ever happened at O'Donnell. Food, medicines and water were always scarce and the guards never let up on their cruelty and hostility. It was not uncommon to see a Japanese private slap and kick an American colonel for forgetting to bow and salute him. Seeing early that exercise burned up energy and caused thirst, and that close proximity to guards could be dangerous, I made it a policy to move about little and to stay as far away from the Japs as possible. When there was an assembly, I made an effort to get in the middle of the group, never on the fringes. An angry guard always hit the prisoner nearest him. Throughout my three and one-half years of imprisonment, that proved to be a good policy.

On June 2, it was suddenly announced that we would be

moved to another camp. Of the 12,000 Americans who had fought so gallantly in Bataan, only 7,000 were in this weakened, half-naked remnant. The Death March, with its starvation, exhaustion, beatings and executions, had taken a toll of approximately 1,500. Corregidor had opened its arms to 1,000 or more who escaped when Bataan fell. By sheer will power and determination 9,000 had reached O'Donnell. Now 7,000 were moving on.

As our crowded, standing-room-only trucks hauled us through the gate, I glanced back at long parallel mounds of dirt on the south end of camp, the mass graves bearing the remains of over 2,000 of our comrades whose lives had been snuffed out by utter criminal neglect. Food, medicines and humane treatment would have prevented ninety percent of those needless deaths.

4. Cabanatuan

Our truck ride ended at the rail siding in Capas. There we were loaded into those dreaded rail cars which had transported us once before. This time we were just as crowded, but fortunately the doors were left open. The train ride ended at the town of Cabanatuan. From there we marched eight kilometers to camp. Many fell out along the way. To our surprise, they were picked up by trucks, not beaten or shot.

Camp Cabanatuan lay in a rich valley with a view of the Sierra Madres Mountains. Compared to O'Donnell, Cabanatuan looked like civilization. It was cleaner, the buildings were in a better state of repair, and there was evidence of more organization and order. Drinking water from several faucets was ample, and open wells furnished an abundance of water for bathing and laundry. The prospect of being clean once more was heartening.

An additional morale booster was seeing the relatively healthy-looking men who had come in earlier from Corregidor. They had held on for an additional month after the fall of Bataan, and had not suffered as severe a shortage of food and medical attention. Having missed the Death March and Camp O'Donnell, they were not so debilitated and disease ridden. In time, however, they too would take on the look of skeletons.

At O'Donnell, lacking the energy to move about, I had seen no one whom I had known before. Here, after a few days of rest, I was to find Captains Otis Morgan, Henry Leitner and

Ben Skardon, friends of college days. In a nearby barracks were Major Karl Bauer and Lieutenant Francis Scarborough, officers of my outfit. (Bauer and Scarborough were the only two of nine Americans who served with the Thirty-first Infantry, PA, whom I saw during the three and one-half years as a prisoner. They died later on a prison ship. Colonel Erwin was killed on the Death March. Most of the others either died in combat or were lost on prison ships en route to Japan.)

Major Bauer was seated on a bench in front of his cabin where he and nine other majors bunked together. With a startled look he exclaimed, "Well, if it isn't Manny Lawton! I'm glad to see you made it. So many were lost." His voice weakened and his eyes became blurred.

"It's wonderful to see you, Karl. We must be the only two Americans left of the Regiment," I answered with equal emotion.

"I saw Lieutenant Scarborough this morning. Don't know who else is here."

Bauer didn't much resemble the short, wiry, neat officer with crew-cut black hair I remembered. Before me now stood a weak, gaunt, ghost of the West Pointer of only a few months earlier. His cheeks were sunken and his eyes deep set, but his warm smile was still with him. We sat and talked for more than an hour, reviewing the Death March.

"Karl, did you see many of the atrocities everyone is telling about?" I asked.

"Yes. It's all true. It was terrible. I saw men get shot for trying to get water or for not being able to keep up. There were hundreds of corpses beside the road."

"You must have started on the second or third day. The earlier groups had less actual killings," I observed.

"I had tried to get to Corregidor, so they didn't get me until April 11. I joined those who had withdrawn toward the west coast and then drifted down to Mariveles. That meant at least ten or more additional miles of marching, and then two more days with no food. They were already hungry and weak. Many of them had malaria, too."

As we talked, Sergeant Calvin Graef of Carlsbad, New Mex-

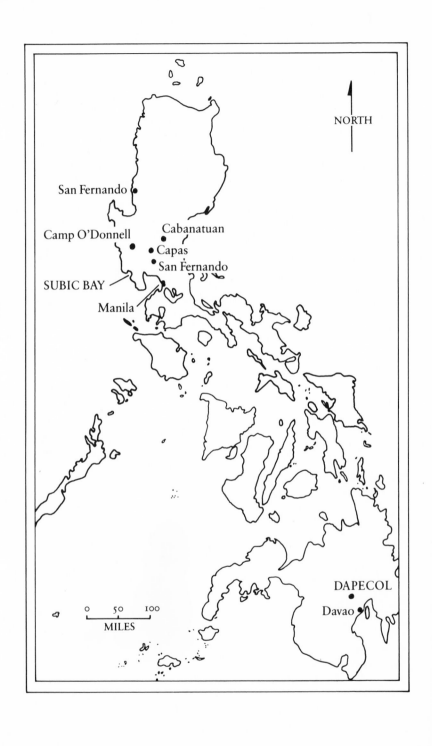

San Fernando

Camp O'Donnell

Cabanatuan

Capas

San Fernando

SUBIC BAY

Manila

NORTH

DAPECOL

Davao

0   50   100
MILES

ico, walked by. Hearing our conversation, he stopped and joined us. Graef was First Sergeant of Battery H, 200th Antiaircraft Regiment, from his state. Being a National Guard unit meant that its ranks were filled with local boys. For a state with less than one million population to furnish so many men, they had to draw from practically every community. It was to mean collective heartbreak, for with few exceptions every family lost a son or relative in Japanese prisoner of war camps. Throughout New Mexico today are to be found monuments, lakes and shrines with the sad word BATAAN emblazened in bold letters—a reminder that there once lived and played some of the state's finest and bravest.

Of the one hundred men in Graef's Battery H, eighty were American Indians. From the outset in prison camp, their rate of mortality was excessively high. When the war ended, it was learned that only nine of the eighty had survived. No one can explain why they succumbed more easily to the malaria, dysentery and other diseases than did Mexican Americans and those of European extraction. Certainly they were tough and courageous fighting men, and surely they were no more subjected to the hazards. Yet ninety percent did not return.

Someone has advanced a theory, though unofficial and certainly unscientific, that being a pure-blooded race, they had no built-in immunity or resistance to the new diseases which those of mixed bloods did possess. Who knows? There may be some logic in the theory. The sad fact remains that our American Indian prisoners of war in the hands of the Japanese had an extremely high mortality rate.

Sergeant Graef was short, erect, handsome and had strong, searching brown eyes. He impressed one as having courage and leadership ability. His speech was gentle and naturally courteous.

"I overheard your conversation," said Graef. "I saw some things on that March which were terrible beyond all belief. Aside from the regular shootings, the most horrible thing I saw was two American airmen being clubbed to death. The poor fellows were exhausted and had to fall out. Those damn Japs literally bludgeoned them to death with clubs. Just plain murder wasn't enough. They seemed to be in a rage, and they kept pounding them until their heads were pulp," he said with passion.

"It was hard to take. We just stood there in shock, cringing and trembling. I have never felt more hate and contempt, and been so powerless to do anything about it."

The hot afternoon sun drove us to the shady side of the cabin. As we talked, I observed other prisoners shuffling by. All had exposed, sun-browned bare backs. Very few still owned shirts. Most were clothed only in loin cloths, which we called g-strings. Their shoes having been worn out on the rock-filled route of the March, most hobbled about on tender bare feet.

It was saddening to see these once proud and courageous men moving with obvious weakness and pain. Some few appeared to have purpose and a destination, but most seemed to be wandering aimlessly about in search of something edible, or of some lost friend who could help them. The great majority had the blank, forlorn look of men who were subdued and saw no hope for the future. Without exception, all had lost a great amount of weight—some as much as twenty-five percent of normal flesh.

Corporal David Peace of Anderson, South Carolina, joined us. Peace was a rough, tough fighting man of the 803rd Engineers. A young career soldier, he had lived in Manila before the war and knew all of its night spots and places of fun. With thick black hair and large brown eyes, he was a handsome young man who had had his share of pleasure, and was determined to take whatever tough blows fate might deal. Though not large, five feet ten and wiry, he had the reputation of being able to hold his own in a scrap. David's indomitable spirit was to see him through some illnesses and torture that would have crushed lesser men.

"David, how bad was the March for you?" I asked.

"Well, to begin with, I had two bullet wounds in my leg which gave me a lot of trouble. Somehow, though, I managed to keep going. But I saw some terrible things. The worst was seeing my good buddy, John Wyatt of Easley, South Carolina, get beaten to death with a rifle butt. That Jap kept hitting him after he was down and out. It was horrible.

"At another place two men, tired and weak, had dropped back from the group ahead of us. They were shot right in front of us and we had to walk over them. They weren't dead yet and were begging for help. It was pathetic, but we couldn't stop and couldn't walk around them."

Peace gritted his teeth and shook with anger as he relived the horror scenes. For a man schooled and practiced in fighting back, it is sheer agony to be a helpless witness to brutalities which cry out to be avenged.

Peace also told of seeing several Americans who had been buried alive up to their necks. He said only their heads and hands were above ground. "As we marched by, they were feebly scratching the dirt with their fingers and pleading for help. We could do nothing for them," he said with tears in his eyes.

Those eyewitness stories, put together with similar ones from other prisoners, painted a hideous picture of savage and inhumane brutality unbelievable in modern times. But they were true; unreal and unbelievable, yes, but definitely true—and unpardonable. In retrospect, it appears that we were considered less than human, and our lives meant nothing to the Japanese.

We didn't expect to be coddled, but we did feel entitled to a reasonable chance to survive. We expected to be marched out of the war zone, which was accomplished in the first fifteen miles. But sixty-three miles for starved, dehydrated and exhausted men proved to be unbearable. For many it was impossible. They and many more who were to die later would have been better off if they had been massacred on the first day of capture. Of the 12,000 Americans who fought in Bataan, half were to meet lonely, cruel, inglorious deaths within the first six months. Wrecked prison ships, which will be dealt with later on, were to claim another 4,000, some of whom were from Corregidor.

Malaria was at first the most prevalent ailment at Cabanatuan. Its accompanying loss of appetite caused weight loss and general debilitation. If a patient could not get relief, he soon became the victim of malnutrition diseases—scurvy, pellagra and beriberi. After I had experienced several attacks of malaria, my skin began to turn yellow. The doctor pronounced it jaundice, for which he had no treatment. "If you could get some canned meats it would help. You need protein," he advised. His advice was good, no doubt, but getting meat was about as easy as acquiring a Japanese rifle.

Having resolved that I would somehow live, I began to look around for some way to get extra food. I saw men stewing rats, lizards and an occasional cat or dog, but none of that appealed to me. I did try some boiled cat once, but it wouldn't go down.

It was generally known around camp that a man named Ted Lowen was operating a black market. The story was that Lowen had been a nightclub and gambling kingpin in Manila before the war and still had his connections. Those contacts were supplying him with goods and money. With American money, he was successful in bribing certain guards to allow selected truck drivers to smuggle in quantities of canned goods. My problem was to get my hands on the cash to do business with Lowen.

All who had made the Death March were penniless. The looting Japanese had robbed us of everything. However, it was known that those captured on Corregidor had been allowed to keep their possessions, including money. Having come into camp at a different time, they were housed in a separate area at the east end of the compound. Inquiring among them, I learned that my good friend Mac was there. Having escaped to Corregidor, he had been spared the hell the rest of us had experienced.

Mac (his full name is omitted for fear of hurting his family), Lieutenant Henry Leitner and I had formed a warm friendship on the boat trip to the Philippines in October, 1941. We had enjoyed the night life of Manila together while awaiting our assignments. When we parted, I felt as close to Mac as I did to Henry, who had been a friend since college days.

During the February-March lull in Bataan, I invited Mac to share my birthday dinner on March 5. (I was probably the only officer in Bataan who had a good supply of food.) We enjoyed together an excellent meal, including jungle fowl, which Alberto had prepared. I remembered Mac saying repeatedly, as he gorged himself, "I can't believe it." Like most others, he had been on half-rations for a month. As my full-stomached, contented friend arose to leave, I reached into the panel truck and took out a bottle of Scotch whiskey. His eyes glowed with excitement.

"Take this along. You may need it in case of snakebite," I had jokingly said.

"Oh, no, Manny. I couldn't think of accepting such a rare gift. You had better keep it for yourself," he halfheartedly protested.

"I want you to have it. Consider it a token of our friendship," I insisted.

With those pleasant memories of the recent past in mind, I felt confident my good friend would gladly come to my rescue. It will not be begging, I reasoned. All I need to do is let him see my condition. Certainly he will offer to do what he can without being asked.

I found my friend, now a captain, seated in front of his quarters with several other officers. Compared to the Bataan crowd, they looked like fresh troops from the States. Each wore neat, clean uniforms and practically new shoes. As I hobbled up on crippled bare feet, weak, thin and practically naked, I detected the annoyed look of a wealthy man about to be bothered by a poor relative. When I called him by name, his response lacked the warmth I had anticipated. There was a guarded coolness.

"How are you, Manny?" he asked in an almost formal tone.

"It has been rough, Mac, the March was terrible," I answered calmly, while thinking to myself what an unnecessary question.

"Too bad. Wish there was something I could do to help you," he replied with noticeable indifference.

"You can, Mac. There is a black market operating in camp. I am broke. The Japs took all my money. If I could buy some canned food, I know I could get well. Could you lend me a few dollars?"

There was an awkward silence. Then he answered as impersonally as a banker turning down a skid row bum, "I'm sorry,

Manny. I only have a hundred bucks and I may need that."

I answered as calmly as I could. "All right, Mac. I understand. You will probably need that much and more."

In shocked disbelief and with pent-up bitterness, I turned and slowly hobbled back to my barracks. With each labored step, I laid bitter curses on him and wished every evil the Japanese could dream up for him alone. To find that a fellow American in fairly good circumstances could, with cool indifference, refuse lifesaving assistance to a friend, seemed unbelievable.

Reaching my bamboo-slatted bay, angry and exhausted, I climbed in and slept for an hour. I was awakened by the noise of two prisoners arguing over the division of a snake they had jointly cornered and slain. One laid claim to a larger portion because he had seen it first. The other contended he was entitled to a full half for helping him kill it.

"You crippled thief," he yelled, "the damn snake was getting away when I came along. You never would have caught him."

"It's my snake. I found it. Consider yourself lucky if you get any at all."

"I'm having half of it or a chunk of your hide."

The barracks leader, stronger than both of them, intervened and divided the reptile equally, giving them both a tongue lashing.

As I listened, I laughed at first. Then it saddened me to realize that two men were willing to tear each other apart over an item of food which neither would have considered edible in better times. The incident demonstrated two sad truths: 1) We had sunk to a terrible low; and 2) friendship is a fragile thing which has little elasticity when survival is threatened.

That new awareness of the reality of our situation even caused me to mellow my bitter censure of Mac. Perhaps, I reasoned to myself, I am being a little too harsh in judgment of him. After all, our acquaintanceship had developed out of a chance meeting on a luxury cruise six months earlier. It had no background in school, hometown, or even regional ties; he being from California and I from South Carolina. At the time neither of us had any unfulfilled needs. We happened to enjoy the same things and had much to make merry over. The dinner and Scotch in Bataan were more than I had need for, and I enjoyed sharing them with him that day.

What happened then, I reasoned, should not be compared with what was taking place now. Then we were carefree and had no need to conserve. Now it was a matter of survival and each man had to think of his own preservation. I came to the conclusion that I was expecting too much of friendship. Friendship, unlike love, is a social thing to be enjoyed for a season, or to be turned on and off as convenient. It is only within the close bonds of a family that one naturally and willingly shares the last sustenance of life. So why should I expect sacrifice from a temporary friend?

Unwittingly, Mac had taught me a very valuable lesson: in a crisis, one must think and shift for himself. He should not expect someone else to help to the extent of lessening his own chances for survival.

That settled, I felt more at peace and began to think more clearly. Cash money was the answer to my problem. I could think of no way to get it short of robbery. Possessing neither the inclination nor strength for that, I ruled it out.

Suddenly a bold plan with a long-shot chance of success crossed my mind. Credit. Why not try to talk one of the operators into taking my check? Who knows? He might do it. The very worst he could do was to say no.

Learning that a sergeant named "Mo" Gardner was a sub-dealer for Ted Lowen, I decided to approach him. His shop was located four barracks away, a distance of one hundred yards. Gardner's barracks was only half-filled with men; consequently, there was ample room to store his wares. Standing around were several well-fed looking cohorts: bodyguards, I assumed. The presence of protectors was well justified, for in plain view were dozens of cans of corned beef, salmon, sardines, luncheon meats and sandwich spreads. I had a sudden urge to grab up all I could carry and dash out. My saliva flowed, my heart pounded, and my legs trembled.

Gardner was a short, square-shouldered, neat looking man, thirty-five, with thick, crew-cut, black hair and a keen, well-groomed mustache. He was all business, yet I detected a glint of kindness in his searching brown eyes.

"What can I do for you?" he asked, with the air of a Main Street merchant.

Nervously, yet with a forced air of self-assurance, I presented my case. "Sergeant, as you can see, I am in a terrible physical condition. In addition to malaria and the other common ailments, I now have jaundice. If I don't get some protein in me I won't make it. I am drawing a captain's pay which is going to the bank each month. If I don't get back to spend it, it won't do me any good. Would you consider selling to me on a personal line of credit and allowing me to pay you with a check?"

He furrowed his brow and scratched his head as if in deep thought.

This was the most important and serious business transaction I had ever made. The stakes, life itself, were higher than any other that I would ever bargain for. I anxiously awaited his answer.

Surprisingly and to my great joy, he answered, "OK, captain, I'll do it for a short while. Under those conditions, though, the prices will be higher."

"Thanks, Sergeant. Prices don't matter. I want to live," I assured him.

We shook hands to seal the bargain and I walked away with one can each of corned beef, salmon and sardines stuffed under my ragged shirt. Clutching my prizes tightly against my body with both arms as I limped back to barracks, I experienced a combination of triumph, hope, excitement and gratitude as seldom hit a man all at the same time. What prompted Gardner to agree is a mystery to this day. I had fully expected him to say no; even to have laughed.

It was surprising what a half can of salmon could do for the horrible soupy rice. Mixed together, they tasted like something good back home. Corned beef and rice delighted the palate like a roast beef dinner. So as not to tantalize those who had no such luxuries, I would slip out behind the barracks with my helping of rice and secretly mix and devour my gourmet meals. Within a week, my yellow skin took on a normal appearance and I gained strength.

This secret good fortune continued for thirty days, during which I made biweekly credit purchases from "Mo." He never complained, and I was careful not to be greedy or extravagant; never requesting more than two or three cans.

At the end of the month he said, "That's as far as I can go. We'll have to settle up now."

"All right, Mo. It's up to you. I knew it wouldn't go on forever. How much do I owe you?"

"With today's purchase it comes to one hundred thirty dollars," he answered.

From his file he took a check-sized piece of paper and handed it to me. I filled in the date, name of bank, payee, amount and signed. We shook hands as I thanked him for his trust in me. "I am confident this food has saved my life. I hope I can do you a favor some day," I said with deep gratitude.

For the next several months I puzzled over what prompted Gardner to do that for me. His was a cold-blooded business. He had never seen me before and had no reason to be sympathetic. Both of us knew that the check was negotiable only if he could get it to my bank after the war. Even then I could refuse to honor it. Besides, he was doing a brisk cash business and had no need to extend credit.

I came to the conclusion that the hand of God must have touched his heart in my behalf.

Over the next three years there were to be several dramatic incidents which meant the difference between survival and death for me. This was the first. Without it, the others would never have occurred, for within a short while I would have died.

Throughout the summer and into the fall of 1942 the struggle for survival continued. As at Camp O'Donnell, the death rate held at between twenty-five and thirty each day. There was little to be optimistic about. Hope was the only sustaining asset. Those who blindly clung to it lived; those who lost it gave up and died. Though it wasn't as simple as that, it is fair to say that there was no room for despondency. I came to understand fully the phrase "the will to live."

The hospital compound was more of an isolation area than a place of treatment and cure. Food and drugs were the solution to most of the health problems; both were in extremely short supply. Of the more than twenty-five hundred who died at Cabanatuan from June to November, most could have survived in U.S. Army or Navy hospitals.

I visited the hospital compound one day to look for some of my friends and to see what conditions actually were. To get there, one had to walk through the area occupied by the Japanese soldiers. My passport to get there was a white flag held on a stick above my head. This, I was told, would distinguish me from some prisoner trying to escape. It was an eerie business, walking that two hundred yards with Japanese soldiers all around, some drilling with rifles and others lounging around off-duty. Suppose, I thought to myself, a group of them decides to have some fun at my expense; or worse, what if one of them should suddenly decide that he needs another notch for murder on his gun stalk? I looked straight ahead and quickened my steps. Several guards on the left looked in my direction, but none made a move. I felt relieved. Suddenly from the right, one crossed my path twenty feet ahead. He hesitated, eyeing me sternly. My heart pounded. I stopped and bowed. He grinned and moved on, having enjoyed seeing me sweat.

Finding the hospital was easy. Had I not been given directions, I could have found it by scent. As I approached the fence, the poignant odors of death and human waste pervaded the air. Getting inside, I quickly determined the source of that repulsive smell: the "death" or "zero" ward. It was the last building down the line, where the hopeless cases were placed to die. Only very few men ever came out of Zero Ward alive. Like its counterpart at O'Donnell, it housed unrecognizable, unwashed skeletons of formerly proud soldiers awaiting death. It was a pathetic, saddening spectacle.

In other wards, most patients showed evidence of severe beri-beri. In some cases it was the "wet" type, causing swelling of the legs and body. Though not necessarily painful, the weight of the extra fluid made walking, or even getting up and down, difficult. Consequently, most such patients just sat around, moving about only when absolutely necessary. Victims of the other type, dry beriberi, suffered severe pain. Their feet became so sensitive and painful that walking was most difficult. It was not uncommon for such a patient to lie on his back with feet elevated for hours without ever attempting to move. By experience he learned that it was better to lie motionless and suffer the throbbing, shooting pains than to move and bring on self-inflicted torture.

On the benches in front of one ward, a small group sat motionless and totally indifferent to what went on about them. They seemed to have no interest in themselves or in each other. I offered a friendly greeting, but got no response. They seemed to have built a shell around their minds and spirits to shut out the hurt, the awesome fear and the bleak reality which threatened to engulf them from all sides. Maybe it was better that way, for the next step for them might be violent insanity.

All patients suffered periodic bouts with malaria. There were also a few cases of diphtheria and perhaps a dozen who had gone insane. In all, it was a depressing, ugly spectacle. There must have been one thousand patients in the so-called hospital. With few exceptions, they had the appearance of doomed men. I came away convinced that all would die unless there soon was a dramatic improvement in conditions.

Glancing back at the frail, ill prisoners as I walked away from the hospital fence, I had a greater hatred for the Japanese authorities than ever before. With each step, the feeling of contempt and desire for revenge were intensified. But the not too distant goose-stepping armed guard detail quickly brought me back to reality; we were the slaves, they the masters. They, who held the guns, would control our destiny. If they decided we would be fed and medicated, we would be; if not, we would continue to bury larger and larger numbers of victims each day.

Though it was a bleak and discouraging existence, life somehow went on for those at Cabanatuan who could withstand the multiple hazards. An occasional gain was always offset by added losses. It was like the proverbial frog trying to get out of the well; he jumped up one foot and fell back two, but he had to keep trying.

It was unpredictable who would be among the survivors. Often the young who had been daring and physically fit were the first to lose hope. Just as surprisingly, older men seemed to be able to ignite and hold on with an uncanny determination to a spark of life. What made it so is hard to fathom. In some instances their mental and psychological strength seemed to be rooted in a deep religious faith; in others it could have been a defiance of death itself. No doubt both were factors. In either case, though, it was evident that remembrance of things back home, where there was love, pride and a strong heritage, made a great difference.

By mid-August, the Japanese were requiring large numbers of men for work details. Those who were strong enough volunteered. They were involved in such projects as wood-gathering, road and airfield construction and stevedore jobs at Manila docks. The incentives for working were extra rations and the hope of making outside contacts with Filipinos. Overall, however, the extra benefits proved to be a net loss; the small amount of extra food was more than burned up by hard labor and long hours. At least, though, they had the mental diversion of getting from behind the barbed wire and away from the depressing environment of sick and dying comrades.

In October of 1942, a group of one thousand officers and men was selected for transfer to another camp. My name was on the list. As usual, no details of where we would go were given. The most consistent rumor was Mindanao, the large southern island, not Japan. It was also believed we would be working on a large farm. That sounded good to me. Growing food would give us a chance to get fresh vegetables and fruit, I thought. Though all of us were undernourished and weak, only the mobile and relatively well were scheduled to go.

5. Move to Davao

On the appointed day, our group marched out of Camp Cabanatuan and headed on foot for the town of Cabanatuan, eight kilometers away. I felt stronger on this march than I had on the incoming trip four months earlier. No doubt the canned meats "Mo" Gardner had sold me on credit were largely responsible. Also, I had sold my class ring for twenty-five pesos ($12.50) and used the money to purchase quinine, which halted my malaria for a while.

As we approached the town, I began to wonder what the Filipinos thought of us now. Since the surrender, I had had no contact with them at all. I recalled a very cordial relationship with the officers and men before and during the campaign. It was also pleasant to remember the warmth and courtesy with which Americans were received wherever they went in prewar days. Now I wondered if that had been genuine, or just a sham, in deference to our superior position. Had the Japanese won their allegiance and turned them against us? I wondered.

Marching again now, I thought back over the nightmarish Death March. A mental picture of women and children in the small towns watching us, defeated Americans, being force-marched under the cruel command of Japanese privates, haunted me all over again. Their expressions had been hard to read. I could detect sadness, shock and fright. But I wondered, then as now, if there were sympathy and loyalty. After all, we had been

48

overpowered and captured by an enemy generally thought to be inferior. Defeated and humiliated, we had been on display as the inferiors. Had we permanently lost face? Would the Filipinos ever respect us again? Japanese bayonets had prevented any open gestures.

For the past six months, those taunting thoughts had torn at my heart. Now as we marched into town they were intensified. As always, when American prisoners were moved, the civilian populace turned out to watch. Searching the hundreds of sober faces viewing us from sidewalks and open doorways, I could read no hint of inner feelings. Keeping their distance, they stared at us in silence. I wondered what their reaction would be if the Japanese suddenly moved away.

At the train station we were crowded into freight cars. It was hot. Though we were uncomfortable, it wasn't as bad as an earlier train ride we remembered. We were not now as sick and exhausted, and the doors were left open. At least those in the middle third of the car could get fresh air when the train was moving.

The train, a freight, stopped at all stations along the way. At the first stop I heard chattering voices outside. Peering through the open doorway, I saw a group of women and children bearing gifts of food—fried chicken, bananas and rice balls. It wasn't much in quantity, but the gesture was heartening. Not allowed to come close, they had to pitch the food in. Only those near the door physically benefited, but all got a boost in morale.

The same thing happened at the next stop and the next. Each succeeding group was larger and more bold. Though our spirits were greatly boosted, I pondered the motivation of the givers. Could it be an expression of the general feelings of the Filipinos, or was this an act of Christian charity?

At the fourth stop, the crowd of gift-bearers was still larger. In addition to their excited talking, I heard a different sound. It was music coming from the opposite side of the train. Glancing down toward the end of the station platform, I saw eight small boys. They hummed a tune. In perfect pitch they rendered their melody over and over until the train pulled out. They hummed; for to sing the lyrics would have infuriated the Japanese. They might have been imprisoned, or shot. Their tune was "God Bless America."

Now I was sure where the allegiance of the Filipino people lay, and I knew with certainty that they still felt respect and affection for us.

The remaining two hours of the hot, crowded train trip to Manila were not nearly so miserable as they might have been. The musical incident had refortified our will to endure. In any circumstance in life, man is always seeking approval and encouragement. To receive it spurs him on to greater effort; to be denied it, or to be derided, can destroy him.

As we trudged over the two miles from the rail yards to Bilibid Prison in Manila, I paid close attention to the faces of thousands of Filipinos who watched us from the sidewalks. Now I could interpret their expressions. They were no different from what I had seen along the march through Balanga, Orani, Lubao, San Fernando and Cabanatuan. They were somber, serious and unanimated. But close up now I could look into their sad, brown eyes. Moistened with tears, they were silently saying "hang in there, Joe, we are with you." Quite frequently I could see a half-hidden, two-fingered V for victory signal flashed for our encouragement. At several points along the way, as we turned corners and came close to the curb, I heard soft utterances of "Victory, Joe. Mabuhay!" (Long life.)

Those expressions of support on that exhausting trip to and through Manila sustained me then, and have lived within me ever since. I found out for sure that they were our friends and that they would never be completely subdued by the Japanese.

Bilibid Prison, built by the Spanish in the eighteenth century, was a large two-storied masonry building with a high brick wall around it. Its heavy, closely guarded iron gate opened as we approached, and then was locked shut behind us. There were no beds or bedding in its large rooms. We slept on concrete floors. There was enough water for drinking and outdoor bathing. The food was the usual insufficient quantity of poorly prepared rice.

Several days after arrival we departed Bilibid on foot for a five-mile march through Manila to the port area. The weather was extremely hot and muggy. It was depressing to see the widespread ugly scars of war in the once beautiful city. Vast wasted areas stood as grim testimony to the destructive force of high explosive bombs. Many masonry buildings were now only charred walls enclosing piles of rubble. Block after block on which formerly stood nipa-roofed bamboo dwellings were now the depositories of heaps of ashes. Very little effort had been made to rebuild. No doubt building materials were nonexistent.

Dewey Boulevard, the former showplace of Manila, had suffered its licks, too. Before the war, with the influence of Western architecture, it had the appearance of a Florida or Southern California thoroughfare. Now its east side, where formerly stood modern bank, store and apartment buildings, lay naked and burned. Surprisingly, we learned later, the Japanese had spared the majestic Manila Hotel, the spacious Army-Navy Club, the High Commissioner's home (symbol of American authority) and the beautiful Malacanan Place, home of Filipino presidents, built by seventeenth-century Spaniards to house their Governor General. Those impressive structures still stood on the artistically landscaped strip bordering on romantic Manila Bay. As we now marched down the great boulevard, hungry, weak, half naked, it was ludicrous to think that only ten months earlier it had been ours to exploit and enjoy with no one to question our oft-committed indiscretions. Now we were lower than peasants, forced to obey every whim and command of any Japanese, no matter what his rank might be.

At the port docks, we were immediately loaded on an ocean freighter. In groups of one hundred we were assigned space below deck. Unlike any other such trip before or after, whether by rail, truck or sea, there was ample room aboard ship. Each man had sufficient space in which to stretch out without being crowded. Though it was hot, the hatches were left open and the air was fresh.

After the ship had cleared Manila Bay and headed out to sea, prisoners were allowed to go on deck. Just before sunset, the evening meal was served. Much to our surprise and delight, the helpings were generous. Compared to the tasteless starvation diet we had been existing on, it was a banquet. Each prisoner got a full messkit of rice and a canteen cup of thick cabbage soup containing tasty slivers of pork. Such flavor had only been dreamed of prior to this, and never in the seven months of captivity had there been a full serving of anything. Sitting on deck after supper, with full stomachs, enjoying the stars and the cool breezes of the China Sea, we felt almost like human beings again. Just to be away from Cabanatuan was good fortune; to have enough to eat made our new situation too good to be real.

With stops at the various ports of call along the way, it took two weeks to sail the inter-island waters from Manila Bay to Davao. The Merchant Marine crew in charge of the ship seemed relaxed and friendly. Even the guards who came with us were almost civil. Meals were served twice daily and were always ample and tasty. On two occasions the menu included corned beef. Our men on kitchen detail said it came from barrels marked U.S. Navy, Cavite, P.I. Each serving contained several hunks of meat. Few prisoners in the hands of Japanese ever ate so well. During the following three years I never did again.

Latrine facilities aboard ship consisted of several opentop five-gallon cans at strategic locations on deck. One morning I noticed the one serving my area was full and would soon overflow. Someone had to take care of it, so why not me? I decided to empty it over the side. Carefully lifting the sloshing can of human waste, I placed it on the rail. No wind was blowing at the time so I felt safe in tilting it forward to allow its contents to flow into the sea. All seemed to be going well until I suddenly felt my legs begin to feel wet and warm. Looking down, I noticed a round hole in the ship's side just in front of me. Outside, just beneath the hole was a bell-like projection extending out about one foot. The contents of the "honey bucket" had fallen on the bell, splashed back through the hole and soaked me from my knees down. At that moment I decided that navy men could handle ships' chores in the future. That was my first of several experiences with "honey buckets."

When the freighter docked at Davao, we debarked and immediately began a twenty-seven kilometer march to Davao Penal Colony, known as DAPECOL. Due to the two weeks' rest and extra rations, that march should not have been bad. Compared to the "Death March" out of Bataan, it could be classed as no more than a brisk hike. But I had a problem. On the last day aboard ship I began suffering with hemorrhoids, a condition which is aggravated by marching or by any type of movement at all. I reported my condition to one of our doctors, thinking surely he could explain to the Japs.

The doctor approached the nearest guard, pointing to his Red Cross arm band. The Jap seemed to understand that well enough. Next Doc motioned toward a group of ailing prisoners, trying to explain that they were too sick to march.

I couldn't understand what the guard was saying, but his actions indicated extreme displeasure. As he hurried toward us, jabbering and pointing his bayonet, I quickly decided that it would be wise to start marching. After only a few steps, discomfort turned to pain and pain to agony. Soon I felt like giving up and refusing to go farther, but the sight of bayonets and the knowledge that Jap guards didn't mind using them kept me plodding along.

At the end of an hour we stopped for a brief rest. Lying beside the road in misery, I felt I just absolutely could not march any more.

"I know you are suffering, but I have no authority. I will try to explain to them, but you know they aren't very sympathetic with pain," said the doctor.

"They will just have to shoot me. I cannot keep going," I answered, fully intending to refuse to get up when the order was given.

It is strange, though, how a strong will to live and the fear of dying can spur a man on to extra effort. As the toothy, bespectacled, mean-looking guard jabbed his bayonet at me and shouted something like "koo-dah," I jumped to my feet as agilely as someone with no ailment at all.

Ten kilometers farther down the road another rest stop was given. This time an interpreter came along and our doctor persuaded him to allow the sick men to stay behind. We were informed that a truck would be along to take us to camp.

Upon arrival at DAPECOL we were taken directly to the hospital. Dr. Davis informed me that he would operate the next morning.

"But doctor," I protested, "do you think I can stand surgery in my run-down condition?"

"Sure you can. It isn't major surgery, you know. Anyhow, you must have relief."

Technically he was correct. The operation was not major, and all went well in surgery and for a while afterwards. What he had no way of knowing in advance was the ravages of chronic malaria, which was to be a part of life for me during the next several months. Weighing 120 pounds upon arrival, I was to soon go down to 100 and then less. By Christmas time, I was suffering with all the ailments of malnutrition which had been so prevalent at Cabanatuan—scurvy, pellagra and beriberi. Soon they moved me into a special ward in a separate building with nineteen others in similar condition. I never did decide whether the move was designed to make us feel that we were getting special attention, or to isolate us from the other patients for the sake of their morale.

I spent three months in that ward. Even now, four decades later, certain people and details there still stick vividly in my memory. The building was small, approximately twenty-six feet by sixteen feet. With a double, screened entrance door and several large windows on each side, it was well ventilated and reasonably cool. The bunks were wooden, except for a few canvas cots. Captain Albert George, my good friend from Aiken, South Carolina, gave me a cot which he was not using. Each patient had a mosquito net, without which sleep would have been impossible. Mosquitos were large and plentiful at Davao, and malaria was a constant threat.

The medical staff was excellent. Lieutenant Colonel Dwight Deter was in command of the hospital. On the staff were Major William R. Davis, who did most of the surgery, Major Weldon K. Ruth, and Captain Andrew Rader. Major Davis had been resident physician and surgeon for Del Monte Pineapple Company in prewar years, and was well known and much in demand as a surgeon throughout the Far East.

The medical corpsmen were especially attentive and helpful. After going through the early days at O'Donnell, where there were no medical supplies and where the general atmosphere was one of helplessness, this new setting of cheerfulness and willingness to serve was encouraging. Corporal Hughes and Pfc. Beaty worked the night shift in our ward. Both handled sick people well and never seemed too tired to do what they could to comfort us. I remember with great admiration Corporal Joe Garcia of Albuquerque, New Mexico, who worked the day shift. He was one of the kindest and most sympathetic men I have ever known. He was always willing to stay on duty an extra hour or so if someone needed him. Always cheerful, soft-spoken and kind, he could cause even the most despondent and discouraged patient to feel that life was worth living. I am convinced that through his kindness and strength of character Joe helped many to live who without him might have given up and died.

Another exceptionally kind and efficient medical corpsman was Pfc. Lee Davis of Pennsylvania. I remember him especially for the broad smile which he always wore, and for his sympathetic tone of voice. Davis assisted in surgery.

Lieutenant Warren Garwick of the Navy, a nonmedical man, performed a volunteer service which was of inestimable value to those of us suffering from beriberi. Every evening, after laboring in the rice fields all day, Garwick would visit the ward and massage our aching legs and feet. To those unfamiliar with the suffering of victims of peripheral neuritis, that may sound trivial. To the patient, it meant soothing relief which no other therapy could give. From time to time, patients would lie head to foot and attempt to massage each other's feet, but that was not very satisfactory, for their hands were as sensitive as their feet. They could only gently stroke each other's limbs—more of a tickling action than a massage.

Lying on our backs with legs drawn up to avoid the pain of feet touching the blanket, we anxiously awaited Garwick's nightly visit. To have had to choose between his relaxing treatment and the meager evening meal would have been difficult for starving men, but I believe I would have foregone the food. Immediately after the daily massage, I would doze off and sleep soundly for several peaceful hours. On the nights our benefactor had to miss, sleep was fitful and slow in coming. What prompted Lieutenant Garwick to give up his rest time and volunteer to help nurse sick men is still a mystery to me. I do know that he was a cheerful, kind and gentle man who possessed a degree of compassion far above the average.

Sunday was a day off for workers. On that day several of my friends would visit me. Among them was Captain Albert George of Aiken, South Carolina. He would usually bring some little gift—a banana, or a mango, or a few coffee beans. Even if the items had been in surplus supply, the thought behind them would have been greatly appreciated. But to realize that Al had smuggled them past the guards at considerable risk to himself made me even more deeply grateful. As a rule, those who ran that risk were not willing to give their contraband away. Al was different. Soft-spoken, rather quiet, completely unselfish and kind, he habitually and naturally responded to the needs of others. Just the reassurance of his visits would have been sufficient, but his sharing what was scarce and dangerously acquired made the attention doubly treasured.

Major Ruth made daily rounds to the ward. With very little medicines to work with, about all that he could do was to comfort us with his presence. My condition grew worse. By February, I must have weighed less than ninety pounds. It was very difficult for me to walk even on the floor, but I forced myself to move around indoors a little each day. Soon my vision was practically gone. Men's faces were featureless through my blurred eyesight. Recurring malaria ruined my appetite. Though starving, I could hardly force myself to swallow the rice and tasteless potato-vine soup.

One afternoon Dr. Ruth made what I felt was a startling announcement.

"Men, I know you are suffering terribly with this beriberi. The corpsmen tell me that you get very little sleep at night. What you need, of course, is food—protein and vitamins. That, as you well know, we don't have. I plead with the Japanese doctor each time he comes in, but so far he hasn't done anything. The other doctors and I have decided to give you narcotics so that you can rest at night. It will be left up to you. If you want it, you may have a shot two or three times a week for a while. Let me know your decision."

At that stage in life, I had never been around drugs, and didn't know how dangerous and destructive they could be. As a child, I knew a woman who acted strangely and was said to be a dope fiend. When the doctor returned later, I questioned him.

"Doctor, what about these shots? What will they do for us? Will there be any harmful effects?"

"Well, our idea is to offer you some way to relax and get some rest. I don't recommend it unless you badly need to have the shots. There is a danger of it becoming habit-forming."

The thought of a full night's uninterrupted sleep was tempting. No one with severe beriberi could sleep soundly for long. Slumber lasted only until he rolled over and rubbed his feet against the blanket. This would bring on such acute pain that the patient would often scream out in the night. One lieutenant developed the ability to lie on his back all the time, with his legs drawn up in a full knee bend. That worked fine for protecting his feet, but finally his knees became locked or frozen in that position and he could no longer straighten them out.

Six or eight of the patients took the morphine. It was administered twice a week. On those nights they slept quietly and soundly from sundown to dawn the next morning. On the off-nights there was groaning and restlessness among them.

Seeing how well it worked and how peacefully they slept, I

decided to give it a try. Within seconds after the syringe was emptied into my arm, my whole body broke out in a stinging, itching rash. Sitting up in bed, I scratched furiously with both hands. In addition to itching all over, I became nauseated. The severe reaction to morphine was fortunate for me, for I never tried it again. Those who took it soon developed a strong craving for the drug. They would cry and beg for it, swearing that they had not slept for twenty-four hours. Dr. Ruth, however, held firmly to his plan and refused to give it more often. All of them survived that camp and some lived to get back home. I have often wondered whether any in later years had a problem with drugs.

The Japanese doctor visited our ward once a week. He was one of the very few Japanese with whom I came in contact who possessed a noticeable degree of gentleness. A tall, handsome, neatly dressed officer, he always politely bowed his head in the Japanese manner of greeting when escorted in by Major Ruth. His large brown eyes reflected a sadness and compassion uncommon to his fellow soldiers. His expression seemed to say, "I am sorry about your condition. I will try to help you." I always felt better after his visit.

There was speculation and rumor among us as to what manner of man this gentle Japanese might be. Some said he was of the noble class, but certainly not of the Samurai military type. Others said he had been educated at UCLA and knew the American way of feeling kindly toward the underdog. His overall appearance radiated a tenderheartedness that was uncommon and encouraging. I never felt nervous or intimidated in his presence.

Dr. Ruth, always alert to any possibility of getting relief for his sick patients, never failed to point out to the doctor that starvation was the cause of our ailments. "If you could get these men some extra food we could have most of them well and back to duty in thirty days," he would plead.

"Yes, yes, I understand. I shall see what can be done," would come the sympathetic-sounding reply.

That persistence on the part of Ruth finally got results. In January of 1943, he came in one morning and announced that we would soon be getting a small daily ration of milk and one boiled egg per patient.

The extra protein did wonders for us. Within three weeks there was a marked improvement in my vision. Having gone through a period of several months of being able to recognize people by voice only, it was good once again to look a friend in the face and see that he had contoured features; before, his face had looked like a shapeless hunk of meat. The other malnutrition ailments soon showed improvement too.

In February, Dr. Ruth informed us that he had found among the medical supplies a drug which had been developed years earlier as a treatment for syphilis.

"The idea was that the drug would create a fever which would fight the venereal bug. I have a theory that it might attack the malaria bug in the same way. There is no guarantee, but it just might work. It's administered by intravenous injection. Anybody who wants to try it can get a shot tomorrow morning."

"Count me in," I quickly spoke up. "I'm willing to try anything that might check this malaria."

Of the twelve patients who agreed to try the experimental treatment, I was the lucky one on whom it was successful. That one injection gave me an immediate and permanent immunity to malaria. Up to that point I had suffered attacks of chills and fever every few weeks for almost a year. Afterwards, I remained in the tropics for two more years and in Japan and Korea for seven months without ever having the symptoms again.

That curing of malaria with a drug which worked for nobody else was the second in a series of mysterious events which meant the difference between survival or death for me. Such happenings reinforced my strong belief that I would somehow get back home someday.

With malaria cured, the supplement of one egg and a cup of milk to the diet began to show dramatic results. The beriberi pains lessened to the extent that I could hobble around by stepping very cautiously and gently on the edges of my feet. I began to get outside and to take daily baths. I gained a little weight. Five or six pounds were so noticeable that Garcia began to call me "fatso." My vision improved to the point that I could read once again—a pleasure I had been unable to enjoy since arrival at Davao.

Toward the end of February the doctors pronounced me well enough to be moved from the hospital to the main compound on a nonduty status. The hospital and barracks #6 were at opposite ends of camp, which meant a distance of two hundred yards to walk. To me, being thin, weak and crippled, it was a major journey. Garcia carried my folded-up canvas cot. My other possessions, wornout shoes and tattered shirt and pants, I wore. For Garcia, a wonderfully patient man, it must have been like exercising a sickly two-year-old who was just learning to walk. We would move about a hundred feet and stop for me to rest. Actually, I was laboriously and painfully learning to walk again.

After fully a half hour, we reached my new home. It was officially designated as Sick Barracks. The building, unlike the traditional bamboo-framed, nipa-roofed Philippine Army barracks at other camps, was made of wood and had a metal roof. Like the other five beside it, it was approximately twenty-six feet wide and one hundred feet long. Its sides, two feet up from the floor and three feet down from the roof, were open. In between, a two-foot band of wood siding gave some semblance of privacy, but did not inhibit the free flow of breezes. The center aisle, three feet wide and one foot above ground, was floored with wide boards. On each side of the aisle was a raised platform, one foot higher than the aisle, floored with similar boards. These platforms or bays were our living quarters. Though there were no partitions, the bays were divided into twelve-man squad groups. Each barracks housed approximately three hundred men.

None of the prisoners in "sick barracks" was ill enough to be hospitalized, but all were disabled or unfit for duty. Most suffered from malnutrition and/or chronic malaria. Captain Belinky of the Medical Corps was barracks leader as well as doctor. Belinky was short, blonde, tended to be chubby, was Jewish and had a good sense of humor. As is customary in any military unit, we lined up for roll call and count early each morning. Instead of counting off in English, the usual one, two, three, four, etc., we counted in Japanese. One morning at the command "count off" I could see a twinkle in Belinky's eyes as the front rank sounded off "Ichi, ni, san, shi, go, roku, shichi, hachi, ku, ju, etc." At the conclusion of the count and report, Belinky inquired with a serious expression, "Now who is the Jew with the itchi knee?"

On another morning when he was feeling jovial, he picked out the most untidy and unwashed looking prisoner and informed him, "Soldier, you need not turn out in full dress uniform tomorrow." To a group of g-string clad, barefooted prisoners, that was real humor. Such men as Belinky, possessed of an easy, natural wit, were a great help in keeping us from growing stir-crazy.

On Sunday nights we were allowed to assemble and have entertainment. As in most of the camps, there always seemed to be a few people with talent who had the willingness and energy to perform. At DAPECOL, Lieutenant William Saunders from Mississippi, Sergeant Yeager of Texas and a third man, whose name I think was Peeples, formed a trio which was little short of professional in quality. Saunders played the guitar accompaniment and sang bass. Yeager, with a clear, true tenor voice, could reach unusually high notes. He was also an excellent whistler and was the only man I had ever seen whistle with his mouth open. Among their favorite numbers were Johnny Long's arrangements of "A Shanty in Old Shanty Town," "If I Had My Way," and "The Girl of My Dreams." Those were all popular songs of the day and seemed to have special significance for each of us. Corporal William Biggs, a sharp comic who usually worked in a solo number of his own, served as master of ceremonies. There were others who performed at times, but basically Biggs and the trio did the entertainment. From Monday morning until Sunday night everyone anxiously awaited the next show. It was the one and only weekly event which could help us forget our ailments and worries and drift into a nostalgic dream of being home again. The service the entertainers performed for the morale of their two thousand fellow prisoners deserves at least a Silver Star decoration.

One had to learn to savor every moment of relaxation and musical entertainment, without letting it make him too homesick. Also, he had to learn to laugh at the little funny things which happened, even if he himself were the butt of a joke. Those without a sense of humor soon grew bitter and depressed and lost the will to endure, for the drudgery, loneliness, fear and helplessness of being slaves were ever present. Guards with loaded rifles and fixed bayonets were always visible just outside the fence to remind us that the slightest infraction of rules could being on instant and severe punishment.

There was ample water from open wells for bathing and washing of clothes, though soap was scarce. The system of bathing was to pour a bucket of water over your body and then soap down, followed by having a friend slowly pour a second bucket of water over you to rinse the soap off. In the tropical heat, bathing was a necessity as well as a luxury. The lack of bodily cleanliness was not only uncomfortable, it was also conducive to skin diseases. Each evening before supper, outdoor public bathing was a standard, enjoyable daily ritual.

At Davao, as in all the camps, there were four kinds of annoying insects: 1) mosquitos bored into our flesh and feasted on our blood and caused itching and malaria; 2) ants bothered our food and stung or bit on occasion; 3) graybacks, or body lice, seemed to get their kicks from crawling over our bodies; 4) bedbugs, perhaps the most repulsive and annoying, were bloodsuckers which worked at night. Unlike the mosquito, the other three didn't seem to be carriers of diseases. Of them all, the bedbugs were the most loathsome and hated.

The defense against mosquitos was mosquito nets. Without a net, sleep at night would have been impossible. Ants could be avoided, as they moved about and fed only in daylight hours. Body lice were controlled by frequent bathing and picking them off the body. But the bedbug seemed to be an unconquerable pest. He multiplied rapidly and traveled and fed only at night. During the day he crawled back into the woodwork and slept on a full stomach of human blood. He was noiseless and his bites did not sting enough to awaken the victim. The bites caused enough itching, however, to make the victim scratch and break out in sores.

There were no insecticides or sprays to fight insects, but someone finally came up with the idea of scalding bedbugs to death. Thereafter it became standard procedure to take all bedding and clothing out of the squad area and douse the wooden bunks and floor with boiling water from the kitchen. Having a canvas cot, I would put it, top side on the ground, in the noonday sun and bake the bugs out. Within fifteen or twenty minutes, the combined heat from the ground and sun would create an unbearable temperature of probably 120 degrees. It got to be a sporting game to watch the dazed little pests come scrambling out of the canvas as I smashed them with a fly swatter. One day I counted fifty "kills."

In the early days at Davao, while I was in the hospital, prisoners on the smaller work details fared rather well in scrounging extra food. The guards would let them gather the plentiful tropical fruits or wild chicken or anything they could find for noonday meals. However, they were not allowed to bring anything into the compound at the end of the day.

Many took the chance and brought in small items which could be hidden in their clothing. Guards at the gate were much stricter than the ones who supervised workers. Periodically, they would have a shakedown. Prisoners found to be carrying any contraband got cuffed around and sternly scolded. If the guilty one had only one banana or mango or an egg, he usually got by with a few hard slaps and a kick or two on the shins. Punishment varied with the mood of the guard on duty at the gate. Also, it was soon learned that what one guard gave you permission to do could be overruled by another. David Peace found that out almost at the cost of his life.

"I was working as a carabao driver in the rice fields," Peace explained. "One day the guard told us we could take some bananas into camp at the end of the day. Thinking that was official, I took a whole stalk. The guard, a right decent Jap, grinned and nodded his head in approval.

"When those guards at the gate saw that stalk of bananas, they went crazy. They snatched the fruit away and started beating on me, jabbering all the while. I tried to explain. They didn't understand English. I looked for my guard. He wasn't there. Next thing I knew they had knocked me to the ground. One was flailing me over the head with the banana stalk and the other clubbing me in the back with his rifle butt. They kicked me in the stomach and groin until I passed out.

"When I came to, they tied me to a post with my hands pulled around the post behind me and tied together. I remained tied up all night and the next day into the second night. When I sagged or slumped down from exhaustion, they beat me some more. Large ants stung my feet and legs. When I moved my feet, the ropes cut deeper into my wrists. All that time I got no food or water. I expected to be shot. At times I wished they would finish me off and be done with it.

"Just before the second night, Father Bauman, a Catholic priest, got permission to visit me. A guard accompanied him. With a distressed and compassionate look he asked, 'What can I do for you, David?'

"In a daze, I mumbled, 'Pray, Father.'

"'God be with you, my boy,' he said with tears in his eyes.

"Two hours later they cut me down. I am convinced Father Bauman's prayers were answered."

When they cut the ropes, Peace slumped to the ground and couldn't get up. His face was blistered and his tongue and lips were swollen from heat and thirst. His throat was parched.

"I felt as if every bone in my body was broken. As soon as the guards left, Sternberg, Day and Gibson came and bodily carried me to the barracks."

6. Davao Penal Colony (DAPECOL)

Compared to previous camps, conditions at Davao during the first six months were not too bad. We were able to keep our bodies bathed and our clothes washed. Inside the compound the guards seldom bothered us. There was ample room inside barracks for sleeping and housekeeping, and sufficient space behind the row of barracks for exercising and for planting small vegetable patches. Food, though far from sufficient, was better prepared. Rice was cooked to a fluffy dryness by our own cooks. That was a welcome contrast to the watery, tasteless "lugau" served at Cabanatuan. To accomplish the desired dryness, the cooks learned to boil the rice in large cauldrons until most of the water was cooked out, then lay burlap sacks over the pots and allow the rice to steam until the proper moisture content was reached. There was also a daily ration of dried fish—a smelly salt and sun-dried trash fish which was boiled, chopped into tiny pieces and mixed into the dry rice. Such a dish would gag most of us today, but at the time it was very tasty. Though the prisoners grew a variety of vegetables on the farm, they all went to the Japs. All we ever received was something resembling a sweet-potato vine. Plentiful tropical fruits, such as mangos, papayas, coconuts, oranges and bananas, went to ruin. The once cultivated groves were swallowed up by the jungle. The Japs, not seeming to care for such foods, chose not to let us have them.

Prisoners on work details fared very well during those early days at DAPECOL. Due to the influence of Japanese Lieutenant Youke, guards supervising work groups were lenient and did not push the prisoners hard. Youke was a Christian, a Roman Catholic, and often came into the compound at night to visit several officers with whom he had struck up a friendship. Of the hundreds of Japanese guards and officers who ruled over us during the three and one-half years of imprisonment, Youke was one of not more than half a dozen who showed any compassion toward us, or who made any effort to try to offset the inhumane treatment we habitually received. It turned out that those few, without exception, were Christians.

DAPECOL had been established many years earlier as a place to confine and work incorrigible convicts. Prior to our arrival, the Japanese had removed all of the convicts except a few trusties, who served as technicians for the general farm operations. Over the years, more than a thousand acres had been carved from the jungle and developed into a food producing plantation for the federal prison system. The land was fertile and highly productive. In contrast to most tropical areas, which had distinct rainy and dry seasons, Davao had a year-round rainfall. Consequently planting and harvesting were continuous. That law of nature was good for our masters, for they needed the produce for their armies. For their rice-planting slaves it only meant no off-season from the backbreaking bogging in muddy paddies as they stuck rice shoots into the muck.

The main farm effort was centered on rice production, with several hundred acres under cultivation by more than a thousand prisoners. An equal amount of land was devoted to other crops or projects. There were groves of coffee, banana, coconut and papayas, Brahma cattle and carabao ranches with a hundred or more head of each, and a chicken farm of ten thousand laying hens. Additional projects which used prisoner labor were the blacksmith shop and sawmill.

Those other projects were of lesser importance to the Japanese and required fewer laborers; consequently, work details for them numbered from twelve to twenty-five men. Assignment to one of them was sought after and hard to get. It was generally known that those groups worked at a leisurely pace and were not closely guarded. At lunchtime they were allowed to scout around in the fruit groves for extra food. On the coffee detail, one man's full morning was devoted to a hunt for food. He usually came up with a wild chicken or a small animal, which he cooked into a stew for the group.

Free from malaria, I experienced a marked improvement in my own physical condition during February and March. I actually gained weight, and was soon up to one hundred pounds again. Noticing that I seemed stronger, Captain Belinky suggested that I go to work on the rope and basket making detail.

"The work is light and you will be inside the compound. You won't have any walking to do and the work certainly will not tax your strength," he said.

I agreed that to be busy at something would be better than sitting around idle day after day. "When do I start?" I asked.

"You will move to barracks #1 tomorrow. The barracks leader there will assign you to the job."

The following morning I got my few possessions together and moved out. In a way it was hard to leave my poker-playing buddies behind. Bert Bank, Arthur Holmes, Tom Patrick and I, along with several others, had been running a game each morning for several weeks. The stakes were low and the Japanese money practically worthless, so no one lost or won much.

Making rope turned out to be a very simple and easy process. All my life I had seen and used what was commonly known as "Manila hemp rope," but up to now had never known its origin or how it was manufactured. Now I was to become a producer rather than a consumer of the product. The raw material, hemp fiber, came from the leaf stalk of a plant similar to the banana tree. The best quality, known as "abaca," is grown in the Philippine Islands. One of the work details spent full time harvesting the fibers, separating them by a simple stripping machine, and placing them on racks to dry in the sun. The cured raw material was delivered to our rope detail in bundles. Within the bundles were groups of one dozen fibers varying in length from three feet to five feet. Each group was wrapped tightly together at one end and tied with a strand of the same fiber.

Two prisoners were assigned as rope starters. The job of a starter was to select bundles of fibers of varying lengths and to bind the even ends, previously bound, together. The number of bundles determined the diameter of the finished product; the varying lengths made it possible to keep the diameter uniform. This preliminary step completed, he hooked the bound end over a headless nail, which projected from a post at the six-foot mark above ground. The rope maker took over next. I was a rope maker.

By twisting the rope in a counterclockwise direction, the rope maker wrapped the bundles of fibers around each other, all the while keeping the rope taut by pulling gently downward against the nail. As the short strands played out, he fed in other bundles. When the rope grew to three feet in length, he slipped the starting end off the nail and hooked the bottom of the new length in its place. This process was repeated over and over until the desired length was attained. Ropes were made to order. They varied from one-half inch to one and one-half inches in diameter and fifty feet to one hundred feet in length.

7. Red Cross Packages

There was great joy in camp on a Sunday in mid-March, 1943. We received our first Red Cross packages. Each man got an individual box of food weighing twelve to fifteen pounds. Included were such items as powdered milk and coffee, lump sugar, cans of sardines, salmon, corned beef, soups and cheeses, jellies, cigarettes and a sewing kit.

I recalled the excitement I experienced as a small boy at Christmas time. My stocking would have an apple, an orange, a bundle of raisins, a pair of socks and a crisp new one dollar bill. How lucky I had felt, for it was hard for Santa to furnish such luxury items during the Depression years. But actually, those treasured gifts had no deeper meaning than that a mysterious, bewhiskered little fat man in a red suit had found his way to my home and rewarded me for being a good boy during the previous several months.

But now, as a grown man, hungry, weak, lonely and beginning to feel that my comrades and I had been written off and forgotten, the packages had a profound meaning. They brought sorely needed nourishment as well as renewed morale and a rekindling of hope. After a long year of no word from home, we now knew that somebody cared, and that an effort was being made to come to our relief. Rumors of American armies on the way suddenly began to seem real again.

Brisk trading developed among the prisoners for items in the parcels. Some naturally placed greater value on certain items over others. For example, those who were not coffee drinkers found they had a valuable commodity with which to bargain. A two-ounce jar of Nescafe would bring four times its weight in powdered milk. One package of American cigarettes frequently traded for two cans of salmon. Salmon and corned beef went about even, with perhaps two cigarettes going with the salmon.

Each parcel was designed to supplement a man's rations for one week. Most prisoners used the items as seasoning or dessert, and rationed themselves so as to make them last as long as possible. Lieutenants Arthur Holmes of Hoboken, New Jersey, Tom Patrick of Chester, South Carolina, and I pooled our resources and stretched them out for three weeks. By dividing a can of meat three ways, we could have something tasty for each meal. Naturally, it was far from enough, but it was at least sufficient to say grace over and gave much cause to be thankful.

Chief Warrant Officer Richard Irby refused to deny himself. He could be seen eating in the middle of the night. "Mr. Irby," I cautioned, "at the rate you are going, your food will be gone in less than a week. You should hold back a little."

"Hell no," he quickly answered. "I'm not tantalizing myself! I intend to eat as much as I want as often as I want until it's all gone. Why not eat, drink and be merry?" As if to punctuate that last remark, he made himself another cup of coffee to go with the quarter pound of cheese and candy bar he was having for dessert, on top of the can of corned beef he had eaten with his evening meal.

The week following the Red Cross shipment, we received our first mail. Those few letters from home brought a different type of joyousness and excitement. Where the food gave pleasure, hope and physical strength, the letters from mother, sister, brother or girlfriend stirred the deep down tender emotions. A letter from home, when you are far away, is a very personal and private thing. Coming from someone who knows you better than anyone else in the world, it bears a message for your eyes and heart alone. It erases the miles and places you in an easy chair beside the fire with family members sitting around, or in church on Sunday in an attitude of reverence and prayer.

I received two letters from my mother. In them I learned that brother Paul was training recruits at Camp Croft in South Carolina, and brother Walter had joined the Merchant Marine. She also said the Reverend Skardon had offered a special prayer for me in church on Sunday. I felt that each of those efforts would have an effect on my ultimate freedom.

Few prisoners were so fortunate as I at mail call. Most got no mail at all. Perhaps the most let down was the recipient of a letter from his home church containing an annual statement showing that he had made no contribution during the past year.

8. Ten Men Escape

The coffee workers apparently enjoyed their light duties and good food so much that they persuaded the authorities to allow them to work on Sundays—normally a day of rest. Their excuse was that they were getting behind in pruning the trees and it must be done if good production were to continue. The Japs fell for the idea and allowed them to go out, unguarded, each Sunday morning. Lieutenant Colonel Arnold Amoroso was in charge of the group and went with them six days a week, but he decided that resting on the seventh would suit him better. So the other eleven went without him.

We could easily understand why those men were willing to work on Sundays. It was a matter of getting the extra food, we thought with envy. In retrospect, though, we should have wondered why they didn't replace the two who were missing from the group; Colonel Amoroso had chosen not to work and the eleventh man came down with malaria and had to go to sick bay for several weeks. It all came to light at sunset on Sunday, April 4, 1943, when the ten volunteers failed to return to camp.

The Japs were excited and furious. We were mustered out for roll call and counted and recounted. Mr. Wada, the ugly, hunchbacked, hateful interpreter, reminded us with a snarl of the rule. "For every man who escape de other nine in his squad wirr be shoot kirred," he railed with bitterness and contempt. "You are arr guilty of herping them escape. De major say you wirr arr be confined to camp untir he decide what other punishment wirr be necessary."

Our American camp commander, Colonel Olson, and all barracks leaders and members of squads of the escaped prisoners were taken to Japanese headquarters for questioning. All others were ordered to return to barracks and stay inside until morning. While we admired the courage and physical ability of the daring ten, each of us pondered the consequences for the two thousand left behind.

"Those dirty bastards," someone said, "don't they know they might get a bunch of us killed?"

"Wait a minute," another answered, "the book says it is the duty of a prisoner of war to escape if he can."

"That's true. But the guy who wrote the book didn't consider that we might be captured by barbarians who refuse to abide by the Geneva Convention rules."

"Yeah, and another thing. He assumed the prisoners would be within a reachable distance of our lines. Those guys know damn well they can't swim to Australia!"

While we debated the ethics of escape and trembled over the sure-to-come reprisals, and the Japanese fumed over their embarrassment and plans to recapture the culprits, darkness afforded the lucky ten an extra twelve hours before pursuit could begin. They had to traverse ten to fifteen miles of vine-entwined jungle, half of which was a dismal mosquito, leech and snake infested swamp, but time was on their side. With ten hours of daylight in which to pick their way and twelve hours of darkness to delay the enemy and to allow nature to cover their tracks, the determined refugees stood a reasonable chance of success. Steve Mellnik, one of the ten, later wrote a fascinating book, *Philippine Diary*, about their daring escape. In the group were: Lieutenant Leo Arthur Boelens, Army, Lieutenant Michael Dobervich, Marines, Captain William Dyess, Army, Lieutenant Sam Grashio, Army, Lieutenant Jack Hawkins, Marines, Lieutenant Commander Melvin McCoy, Navy, Major Stephen Mellnik, Army, Captain Austin Shofner, Marines, Sergeant Robert

Spielman, Army, and Pfc. Paul H. Marshall, Army. We later learned that they all made it to safety and refuge in the hands of Filipino guerrilla fighters.*

Reprisals were swift and severe. Rations, which had been barely adequate, were cut drastically. Several hundred men who had been in squads with or quartered near the escapees were moved out to another compound for a period for "contemplation" and restrictions, where they remained in isolation for two months. Camp authorities and barracks leaders were reprimanded and fined. Religious services and Sunday evening entertainment were abolished. Guards became distrustful, hostile, and quicker to slap, kick or hit prisoners with rifle butts for the slightest infractions of rules. The hours of labor in the rice fields were increased and the workload made heavier.

After that April escape things were never the same at DAPECOL. What could have been, by Japanese standards, a model prison camp, abruptly deteriorated to the typical slave labor camp ruled over by American-hating guards. Our friend, Lieutenant Youke, who had been responsible for the easygoing atmosphere which had prevailed before the escape, was transferred out. We never heard of him again, but it was surmised that his friendship toward the prisoners was the reason for his banishment. From then on, things grew worse. The long work hours and hostility of the guards never let up. It was only after work hours, inside the barbed wire, that we felt any degree of security and relaxation of tension. Such rigid control cowered some prisoners, but it seemed to spur others to more reckless and daring acts. For example, the smuggling in of extra bits of food continued. Though it was known that being caught brought on severe punishment, the culprits persisted.

The Japanese didn't search the returning work groups every day. At times, a week or more would pass with no indication that wrongdoing was suspected. Then suddenly, there would be

---

*After the war Captain Albert George of Aiken, South Carolina, loaned me his diary in which he had recorded details of that escape and other facts and dates of that period.

extra armed guards waiting at the gate as the tired workers marched in from the fields. Those at the front of the column, having no opportunity to dump their contraband, would be caught in the big shakedown. While the offender stood at attention, the sadistic guards seemed to outdo each other in slapping, kicking and clubbing him. When he was finally knocked to the ground, he would be kicked. Often he slipped into unconsciousness and had to be carried into barracks by fellow prisoners. Yet some got by.

One of our men outsmarted the searchers in hiding his loot. Over two weekends he carefully carved out a pair of wooden sandals, the regular footwear, with hollow heels. To each he attached a duplicate bottom with matching hollows. The combined secret hiding places held a quarter cup of rice, which he pilfered from the field each day. By week's end he would have accumulated enough for two full Sunday meals.

Health conditions grew worse by summer. Though there were only sixteen deaths during the eighteen months we stayed at Davao, no one in the entire camp was physically up to standard, all being undernourished and weak. The common ailments were malaria and beriberi. There were always at least three hundred men in sick barracks; another fifty to seventy-five were in the hospital and an equal number assigned to light duty. Most of the chronically sick were from the 1,000 who had moved in from Cabanatuan. The 1,100 who were originally stationed in the nearby islands had come into camp in good physical condition, having missed a death march or a Camp O'Donnell.

No one was immune to the body sores caused by scratching mosquito and bedbug bites. Rice field workers suffered worse from festering sores on their legs. Daily bogging in the mud aggravated the condition, causing tropical ulcers. Sergeant Gilbert Jackson's legs became so infected that he had to be hospitalized for several weeks of treatment. When the infections finally dried up he was left with numerous round scars resembling bullet wounds. Jackson's scarred legs were not unique. Many others were that way.

Anyone suffering with beriberi could easily be identified by his halting, cautious way of walking. Bent forward, standing on the outer edges of his feet with arms held outward for balance, he stepped lightly, as if tramping on nails. Being one of those victims, I knew why. With feet as painful as if the raw nerves were exposed, walking on a wood floor was painful. On the hard ground, where there were coarse sand and sharp pebbles, each step was sheer agony. A common wisecrack from an on-looker was:

"Hey, Lawton, are you afraid you'll break those eggs you're walking on?"

"No," I would reply, "I'm practicing my tightrope act."

Many suffered marked deterioration in vision, due to malnutrition. Malaria, of course, was always with us. With conditions as they were—always bad—it would have been easy to become depressed. To prevent this, I made it a point to cultivate the friendship of optimistic and humorous men. Someone with a sense of humor generates laughter, even out of the most ridiculous situations. Optimists always believed there would be a tomorrow with better opportunities; whereas a pessimist was fully convinced we would never make it and, if you took him seriously, could assure you there was no use in trying.

Lieutenant Colonel Arnold Amoroso, six feet tall, of sturdy build, forty-eight and graying, was the kind, steady, calm type. He had it figured, based on General Staff studies to which he had been privy, that it would take our forces three years' time to retake the Pacific. That knowledge caused me to set my sights on a long-range target date and to cease expecting immediate rescue. The colonel took things one day at a time and influenced me to do so also.

Joe, the dentist, was always good for a laugh. Tall, rather handsome, with a prominent nose and a short upper lip, he was delightful company and a refreshing wit. Though not a clown and somewhat shy, he enjoyed telling about funny little personal experiences, usually of the ridiculous type in which someone was the goat. As often as not, the joke would be on himself.

I am sure that all men in a battle zone are afraid, though few will later admit it. I have known some who would have you believe they were a one-man army who singlehandedly turned the tide of battle. Also I have known some—very few—to admit that in a particularly dangerous situation they were temporarily frightened. Joe was an exception. He freely confessed that even in the rear area he was extremely uneasy. Approaching enemy aircraft caused him to run for cover without even attempting to determine their distance or course.

"I finally dug a big hole right beneath my office window. As soon as I heard a Jap plane coming, I would dive through the window. Once I left a patient sitting in my dentist's chair." Such frankness endeared him to me.

One evening after supper Joe suddenly announced, "I had a good time today." He hesitated for someone to ask how.

"What do you mean, Painless Parker?" I queried. "How can a dentist plying his trade have a good time?"

"I worked on a Jap guard, that's how," he answered with a chuckle.

The Japanese army had no dentists. Consequently when one of them had a toothache, he came to the American dentist for relief. "I pulled the aching tooth," continued Joe, "then I convinced him that there were several more needing attention. The teeth were perfectly good, but I ground three of them out down to the nerves. I used no anesthetic. Pumping the foot-pedaled drilling machine at its slowest speed, and with a dull drill, I bore in with relish. The drill actually bounced up and down as if in protest. The Jap sat impassively, never letting on that it hurt!"

At roll call one Sunday the Japanese interpreter announced that the camp commander wanted us to enter a writing contest. "Prizes will be awarded for the best papers," he said. "You are to write of your most frightening experiences during the war."

Everyone knew the motive; to collect written statements from the prisoners which could be used as propaganda. The prizes would be extra food and cigarettes. All savored the food, but none wanted to produce something useful for the enemy. A great amount of skill and chicanery would be required to write a winning theme and at the same time make fools of the Japs and not be caught at it.

Two weeks later as promised, Mr. Wada, accompanied by two guards pulling a cart loaded with goodies, showed up for awards day. In a rare jovial mood, he was obviously pleased over the themes. There were five winners and four honorable mentions. The latter were recognized first, and then he called the fifth place winner. From there he built up to the grand prize in reverse order. As each name was called, the contestant marched forward to receive his reward of fried bananas, peanut brittle and cigarettes. There was much chiding and some uncomplimentary remarks from onlookers.

Second prize went to the author of an exciting account of how frightening it had been for him to watch Japanese bombers in action. He described the speed and power of the Imperial aircraft and noted that they never seemed to miss their targets. The touching part was his sadness on watching the accurate bombardier lay a bull's-eye hit on poor Chic Sale's house. Of course, the Japanese judges were unaware that the house was a small, one-hole privy pictured in Exlax advertisements all over America.

Art Holmes, Joe and I were seated together on a bench in front of our barracks. Mr. Wada was making a real production of recognizing and awarding his script writers. An air of excitement had built up as we awaited announcement of the grand prize. The hunchbacked Wada looked over the crowd with a half grin on his normally hateful face. His eyeglasses rode halfway down his nose. In shocked disbelief, I heard Joe's name called as the winner of first prize. Joe looked down. His body stiffened but he failed to move. Art looked at me and commented with tongue in cheek, "That has to be a mistake. I know the number one Jap hater hasn't turned to writing propaganda for the enemy."

"A double agent, no doubt," I said.

On third call Art said, "Go forward and get your pay."

Then Joe reluctantly strode forward and bowed. The guards filled his sun helmet with fruit, candy and cigarettes. We failed to sense the extent of his embarrassment until, upon returning, he dumped the loot in my lap and went into the barracks. After eating nearly half of his winnings, we went in and assured him we were only teasing. He never told us what he wrote.

There were no reliable sources of news at DAPECOL. Truck drivers picked up rumors from Filipinos, but they always sounded too good. The standard Filipino message was, "Berry soon now, Joe. You will be free. The Americans are winning the war." Word was that the Japs had been driven out of New Guinea. Later we heard of a naval disaster for the enemy in the Coral Sea. Reports of Allied successes became more frequent in 1944. We began to suspect our Filipino friends of exaggerating for morale purposes.

The Japanese themselves, however, inadvertently confirmed what we had been hearing. At irregular intervals they distributed an English-language newspaper in camp. The issues were carefully selected with the obvious intent of convincing us that the Imperial forces were in control of the war. Their claims of victory were so one-sided that they were farcical. For example, consider this: BIG VICTORY FOR IMPERIAL FORCES IN NEW GUINEA WATERS. The news release claimed the sinking of two American battleships, three cruisers and eight destroyers. In addition, 125 American planes were shot down; Japanese losses, one destroyer slightly damaged and one plane failed to return to its base.

A month later another front page story proclaimed, AMERICAN NAVY ALL BUT DESTROYED IN CORAL SEA BATTLE. As before, the Japanese suffered only minor damage while the American losses were twice the amount of the previous battle.

The real convincer came in the announcement that Imperial forces had evacuated Guam because it was no longer of strategic importance. A look at the map revealed the direction in which the war was going: back toward Tokyo.

On October 25, 1943, two enlisted men, Privates Oscar B. Brown and Robert Lee Pease, escaped. They and a Filipino convict trusty were on a dike repair job some distance away from the other prisoners. Their guard was found dead, his head having been split open by an ax. The three made a successful getaway. For the rest of us it meant tougher treatment and a further cut in rations.

In February of 1944, one year after receipt of the first Red Cross parcels, a second delivery was received. Their contents were the same, but the taste was even more savory, if that were possible. As before, we rationed ourselves so as to make a one week supply stretch into three.

9. Another Escape

Things now went along rather routinely for six months. There had been no escapes, no infractions of the rules, and consequently no severe disciplinary actions against us. Though we were undernourished and continued to work long hours, we had the feeling that the war was going well for our side. Suddenly on March 27, 1944, while out on a work detail, eleven officers were involved in a bloody escape plot. The eleven were: Captain Mark M. Wohlfeld, Captain Wohlers, Lieutenants Hadley C. Watson, Marvin H. Campbell, James McClure, James D. Haburn, Andrew T. Bukovinsky, Mickey Wright and Fensler, all of the Army, and Navy Lieutenant Senior Grade Baldwin Boone and Navy Warrant Officer Carmichael.

Prior to that fateful date Captain Wohlfeld had been planning an escape with two entirely different officers—First Lieutenants Maynard Bullard and Roland Salanier. Bullard had been a psychology major in college. With such a background, he was conscious of some of the mental preparation that they must do in order to effect an escape in the face of the great odds against them. First of all they must take the guards by surprise, and secondly they must be willing to attack and do physical harm without warning and even to kill if it became necessary. (By training and sociological background, Americans normally do not strike another person without warning.)

Wohlfeld, Bullard and Salanier worked on their plans each

day. They even practiced how they would strike a guard and make their getaway. In spite of realizing that it wouldn't be easy, they were determined to take the risk—and soon. But those plans changed when a most unlikely stranger entered the picture. On March 26, Captain Wohlfeld was visiting the latrine at midnight. As he sat there alone rehearsing the possible ways to escape, a stranger came in. In spite of the fact that there were twelve seats, the man sat down right next to Wohlfeld. He wore a bandage on his right eye and one on his left knee and walked with the use of a cane.

"Good evening," the stranger said. "You are in on an escape plan, aren't you?"

"How do you know such a thing?" asked Wohlfeld.

"I just happen to know," the man answered.

"If you know, keep it quiet," said Wohlfeld.

The man began to speak more boldly. "No. You listen to me. The time is tomorrow. I have it all planned. I have food and medicines. Someone will awaken you one hour before roll call tomorrow morning. Be prepared to go."

"Who are you, and what's going on here?" asked Wohlfeld.

"I'm Lieutenant Hadley Watson," came a quick answer. "Don't let these bandages and the cane fool you. I'm perfectly okay. Forget your plans and join us."

Just before daybreak the next morning someone shook Wohlfeld awake and moved on without saying anything. He got up, got his few belongings together and stuffed a dummy in his bed. Soon it was time for roll call and chow. Shortly, work detail leaders were called to report to the main gate and be ready to call their men out for duty. Hundreds of men stood ready for another day of toil. Wohlfeld, still not fully informed of the escape plans, waited nervously.

Suddenly someone eased up beside him and nudged him with his elbow. It was Watson, minus bandages and cane. "It's all eleven members of the fence detail," he whispered. "They are all in agreement and ready to go."

No sooner had he said that than the interpreter called out,

"Lieutenant Mickey Wright, call your fence detail forward." Wright began reading off the names, Watson, Wohlers, Campbell, McClure, Wohlfeld, Haburn, Bukovinsky, etc.

At the front gate each of the eleven picked up a shovel and they marched off to duty accompanied by five guards, four riflemen and a corporal armed with a pistol. The corporal marched ahead of the column and two riflemen on each flank. Their destination was three kilometers away to the west of the camp. The rice fields were six kilometers east.

After they had gone a short distance, Wohlfeld asked permission for the men to sing as they marched. Permission was granted. He chose the song "Mademoiselle from Armentieres" with the idea of working in conversation between the lines to be sure that everyone was in agreement on the plan.

Wohlfeld led the singing. "Mademoiselle from Armentieres, this is a day you will never forget, Watson, parlez vous."

"That is so true, Mark, parlez vous."

"Mademoiselle from Armentieres, Campbell, McClure, Haburn, parlez vous?"

"We are ready to go, parlez vous," came their answers in song.

"Mademoiselle from Armentieres, does anyone want to back out, parlez vous?"

After polling each officer by name in song, there was no doubt as to whether everyone fully intended to make the break. They reached their place of work at approximately 8 A.M. Captain Wohlfeld asked if they might take a break before beginning to work. The corporal agreed.

As they sat closely together, Wohlfeld spoke in a muffled tone, "At the next break we will sit in a tight circle. The guards will then position themselves around us. On signal we will jump up and disarm them. We will not kill unless we have to. Remember, the element of surprise is our biggest ally."

At the end of five minutes of rest the Japanese corporal indicated that work would begin. Their job was to reinforce the fence around a cucumber field by placing a new post between each existing post; hogs had been getting through the fence and eating the cucumbers.

When the corporal signaled five minutes rest at nine o'clock, the group had scattered. Carmichael had lured seven men away, leaving Wohlfeld, Watson and Campbell to themselves. Two guards were now with each group and the corporal had placed himself halfway between. Wohlfeld called and asked why they had separated.

"To hell with you," answered Carmichael. "You're on your own. We want no part of that."

When they went back to work the three decided they would have to come up with another plan. At the ten o'clock rest period they noticed an apple tree in the edge of the jungle twenty yards beyond the fence, and asked if one man could go over the fence and get some fruit. Watson was elected to go. One guard went with him and another climbed the fence after them and stationed himself on the edge of the clearing. Watson convinced the guard that he would need his shovel to knock the fruit down.

No sooner had they gotten into the thick brush than there was a loud whack, whack! as the shovel hit against the guard's head. The guard began to scream for help. Watson hit him several more times, knocking him unconscious, then took his rifle and shot the other guard. That done, he stepped out of the jungle for an instant, waved the rifle in the air and yelled, "Follow me!" He then disappeared into the jungle again.

Meanwhile the other ten prisoners were left with three guards—two riflemen and the other with a pistol. Excitedly the three fired into the jungle where the noise had come from. Soon they had fired all the bullets from their clips. The Jap next to Wohlfeld nervously tried to put in a new one but couldn't.

Campbell yelled at Wohlfeld, "Get up and get him, you yellow son of a bitch."

Wohlfeld froze. He couldn't force himself to move. Campbell hit the corporal in the face with his shovel. Teeth and blood splattered over the ground. Some of it splashed on Wohlfeld.

This shocked him into action. He swung at the guard with his shovel but missed and fell down. As he stood there on hands and knees he expected to have his head blown off, but instead the guard began hitting him with the empty rifle. This angered him as well as making him realize that he had a fighting chance. Reaching up, he grabbed the guard's legs and tripped him. As the guard fell to the ground, Wohlfeld jumped up and standing over him, took another swing at his head with the shovel. The blow missed its mark but cut a deep gash in the man's left biceps, severing an artery. Blood gushed out; some of it splattered on Wohlfeld. Flies immediately swarmed over both of them.

Campbell, having severely disabled the corporal, turned quickly on to the remaining rifleman. With a quick lunge, he grabbed the rifle and snatched it away and, with several blows to the head, knocked the terrified enemy unconscious.

Meanwhile, the shooting and screaming had attracted the attention of guards on the railroad and sugarcane details some three hundred yards away. They began shooting. Now, with bullets flying everywhere, some whizzing overhead, some hitting into the dirt and splitting rocks around them, the situation was more chaotic and dangerous than ever. Monkeys and birds screamed in the nearby trees. It was hazardous to make a dash for freedom and even more perilous to remain pinned down among the wildly aimed bullets.

In panic, the wounded guard, with blood still flowing from his arm, began weakly crawling toward the fence ten feet away. He made it under the bottom strand of barbed wire and ended up in the drainage ditch on the other side. The ditch, two feet wide and two feet deep, had about a foot of water in it covering a foot or more of sticky mud. Too weak to jump across, he stepped in and got mired up to his waist.

Wohlfeld, in hot pursuit, attempted to jump on top of him to mash his head down into the water. This failed and he, too, became stuck in the slime. Looking back to where he had come from, he saw several of his frightened fellow prisoners still pinned to the ground trying to avoid being hit by rifle fire.

"Bukovinsky," he yelled, "come and get this guy's rifle. I'm stuck and he's trying to reload."

"To hell with you. Get it yourself. They're shooting at me," answered Bukovinsky.

"You Polack son of a bitch, they're shooting at everyone. Get up and get that rifle."

"All right! All right," he answered.

Bukovinsky then jumped up and dashed for the fence. However, instead of crawling under, he attempted to climb over and got his clothes tangled in the barbed wire. After a long sixty seconds, during which he was a perfect target, he finally flopped to the ground. He jumped the ditch and grabbed the rifle, but instead of shooting the Jap he made a dash for the jungle. Before he reached safety, however, he flopped to the ground with a bullet wound in his side.

"Good for you, you bastard," yelled Wohlfeld. "You deserve just that for leaving me here." But fortunately it was only a flesh wound and Bukovinsky was able to get up and make a dash for the jungle once more.

Wohlfeld was shortly able to pull himself free from the bog. He then packed mud in the Jap's face and pushed his head under water and held it there long enough to make sure he had drowned. That done, he too ran into the jungle.

All of this action had taken place in less than fifteen minutes. At this point the five guards were either dead or dying and eight of the eleven prisoners had escaped. The remaining three, Captain Wohlers, Lieutenant Mickey Wright and Navy Warrant Officer Carmichael, failed to get away. There is some question as to whether they remained pinned down by enemy rifle fire and could not leave the scene or whether they changed their minds about escaping and chose to give themselves up voluntarily.

Captain Wohlfeld ran as hard as he could go for about fifty paces into the thick vine-tangled swamp. He was then exhausted and could hardly breathe, but he dared not stop. Slowing down to a rapid walk, he continued to pick his way through the dense growth. Even at that pace his efforts seemed futile.

Vines entangled his feet and thorns tore at his flesh. The oppressive heat drained his strength as sweat oozed from every pore of his body. A bullet flesh wound on his left arm, which he had hardly noticed when first hit, was now bleeding profusely.

He was at the point of giving up when he came to a pond of water on which a large tree had fallen. This, he quickly saw, would give him a clear path for one hundred fifty feet or more. Climbing on top of the large tree trunk, he began jogging across. Suddenly it occurred to him that he might hide temporarily beneath the log. Halfway across, he stopped and slid down into the water. At that point the water was no more than a foot deep, but it covered two feet of soft mud.

While the water cooled his hot and exhausted body, the fugitive lay still and listened; no footsteps were in pursuit and he heard no voices. Feeling confident that he had a temporary safe lead, he turned his attention to the bleeding arm. Lacking anything with which to make a tourniquet, he made a mudpack, wrapped it with leaves and tied it with vines. This served to seal the wound.

Partially rested and with the bleeding wound taken care of, Wohlfeld then worked as much of his body under the log as possible, pulled clumps of lilies over and around his face and waited. After fifteen to twenty minutes, during which the stirred up mud had had time to settle back beneath the surface, he heard the enemy calling:

"AMERICO! AMERICO! COME BACKO!" This was followed by a burst of automatic rifle fire and then again the invitation, "AMERICO! AMERICO! COME BACKO!" Then more firing.

Wohlfeld thought to himself: how stupid can they get? Inviting me to surrender and then spraying the area with bullets. I'll never turn in. They'd shoot me on sight.

Shortly the search party drew near, still calling and shooting. When he realized they were following the same route he had taken, a new fear gripped him. What if they have tracked me and will shortly riddle my body with bullets? he asked himself. He stiffened and trembled with dread. The footsteps drew nearer. Soon they were on the log, trotting across the pond. Wohlfeld peeped up through the lilies and counted; twelve Japanese soldiers, like hounds hot on the heels of their quarry, passed above him in single file and kept going. After he heard the last one jump off the far end of the log, he knew he was safe for the time being. His body relaxed and his runaway heartbeat slowed down considerably.

After ten or fifteen minutes, the sound of the Japanese calls faded out completely and the sporadic rifle fire grew more distant. Feeling temporarily out of danger, he pushed the lily pad cover away and sat up and washed the mud from his face and the upper part of his body. Now somewhat rested, he worked his way to the end of the log where he washed his clothes and the balance of the mud from his body. That done, he began cautiously walking in the same direction in which his pursuers had gone.

Fresh signs such as broken limbs, cut vines and foot tracks in wet places made it easy for Wohlfeld to follow the Japanese patrol. After trailing them for about one hundred yards, he came across an animal trail veering off to the left, which he took. There was no way of knowing where or how far the trail would lead, but at least it was headed in a direction opposite from where the Japanese search party was going.

He had gone only a short distance when the ground gave way under his feet and he found himself in a man-made trap. He had fallen into a hole four feet deep, two and one-half feet wide and three feet long that had sharpened bamboo stakes along the side walls to impale pigs or deer that might fall in. Wohlfeld was not impaled, but one of the bamboos did cut his leg slightly.

Climbing out, he continued to move in the same southerly direction for a while longer, then headed north toward the railroad track. It was now about 4 P.M. and as he approached the railroad track he could hear the Japanese talking as they made camp for the night and began cooking their rice.

As he sat from a concealed position watching them, a railroad handcar came into view. On it were two guards and an American. The American was Major Montgomery, the officer in charge within the prison camp. He was calling loudly through a bull-horn, "We know you are in there. Come on out and surrender. You will be given a fair trial and then be allowed to resume your work. Americans! It will be best for you if you surrender now!"

Captain Wohlfeld crawled under a thick clump of bushes and watched and listened from one hundred fifty yards distance. At first he felt a wave of bitterness toward Montgomery come over him at the thought of his trying to persuade his fellow Americans to surrender. On second thought, he realized that it certainly was not a voluntary act.

With darkness now coming on, there was nothing else to do but to bed down for the night. Nearby he found what in effect was a cave in the root system of a large tree which had been blown over by storms. He crawled in and pulled some clumps of ferns across the entrance.

Exhausted, he began to doze. Before falling asleep, however, he tried to review the events of the day. He remembered that Campbell had finished off one rifleman and the corporal and Watson had killed one with his shovel in the jungle and shot another, and that he himself had taken care of the last one in the ditch. He knew that eight of the eleven prisoners had escaped, and yet here he was alone, with no idea of where the others might be. Why? he asked himself. They had all started off together and here he was alone. Why? Not only was the thought melancholy, it was frightening as well. In spite of cramped quarters and insect bites, he soon fell asleep.

The next morning he was awakened just before dawn by the singing of birds mixed with various animal noises. He crawled out of his hiding place and attempted to pull leeches from his flesh which had burrowed in during the night; this effort met with little success.

Wohlfeld knew that he must get to the north side of the railroad somehow, but it was being patrolled by Japanese. He decided to stay in the swamps another day and gradually work his way back to where the whole escape episode had begun; from there he could better orient himself and decide which way to go. Meantime he might find some food; roots, herbs and bamboo shoots were not very strengthening.

He hadn't moved very far when the Japanese spotted him and started shooting. He ran into a pond of water where there was thick, tall grass and burrowed down. The Japanese formed a line ten feet abreast and started combing the area. As they moved through the pond they fired bursts of bullets into the thickest clumps. At one point he thought surely he had been caught; a guard's foot came down just beside his elbow and his other foot missed Wohlfeld's face by inches. But he lay undetected and the search party moved on.

Though he was lying in six to eight inches of water, Wohlfeld thought it best to remain where he was for a while, or until he felt sure the searchers were out of the general area. After an hour, hearing no more shots or movement, he moved out of the pond toward higher ground. After drying his clothes he started walking again.

It was easy going for about another hour on dry ground along the edge of the jungle. Wohlfeld's confidence was beginning to pick up again as he felt that he had finally evaded his would-be captors. But that optimism was soon shattered when he entered a large bamboo patch and almost walked into another Japanese squad. He turned on his heels and dashed for the thickest part of the swamps again. The Japanese began shooting in his direction; one of them threw a hand grenade. But they weren't quick enough. By the time they swung into action he had disappeared into the dark, thick growth once again.

It was now late afternoon of March 28. A full day had passed since the break and he was still not out of reach of the enemy. He found another uprooted tree and crawled in between its roots and bedded down for the night.

Without a compass, one would normally try to determine direction by the position of the sun in the sky. From Wohlfeld's position deep in the woods, that was impossible; the overlapping branches of the tall mahogany trees completely blocked out any sighting of the sun. He decided to work his way back to where they had assaulted the guards and escaped, feeling sure that they would no longer be guarding the area.

Having almost been killed or recaptured three times in the general area in which he had been moving about, he became even more convinced that he must get north of the railroad tracks. Picking his way through the underbrush just inside the treeline, he headed north; out of the swampland, he could now see the sun. It was nearly sundown when he finally reached the railroad. Cautiously he eased up and looked in both directions. Only two guards were in sight and they were more than two hundred yards west of his position and both facing away from him. He climbed up the embankment and quickly slid down the other side. Wanting to get as much distance as he could as quickly as possible between himself and them, he ran for one hundred yards and then kept walking as rapidly as he could manage.

Darkness soon forced him to stop and rest for a while, but as soon as the moon came up he began walking again. Feeling confident that there were no Japanese around, he worked his way to the edge of forest, where there were less underbrush and vines to tangle his feet. All night he kept pushing himself, and into the morning of March 30.

Around midmorning the tired and hungry fugitive came to a stream of running water. After refreshing himself with drink, he took a quick bath and started on the move again. Reasoning that the upstream direction would eventually bring him to higher ground, he splashed along in the water against the flow. By staying in the stream he avoided the thick underbrush through which he would otherwise have to pick his way.

For the balance of the day, most of the night and all the next day he plodded along. It was now March 31, four days after the breakout, and he was still alone and hungry, and not knowing if he were going in the right direction or if he would ever find any of his buddies, or anyone friendly. But at least he felt that he was safe from recapture.

April 1 found him still splashing along in the shallow stream. Every muscle and bone in his body ached, but his feet, swollen and bruised, hurt worst of all. Sitting on a rock, he took off his shoes and socks and put on a fresh pair of socks from his bag. After a short rest, he compulsively and mechanically struggled on, fearing he could not last much longer.

Around midmorning, as he came around a bend, he was startled to find himself face to face with a Filipino holding a spear which was aimed directly at his head. Wohlfeld held up both hands and quickly called out "Friend! Amigo! American!"

The new friends proved to be a fishing party from a village some two kilometers distant. They were in a hurry to get back with the morning's catch and invited him to go along. He couldn't keep up, so two men were left behind to help him along; they fed him delicious rice and bananas, which gave him renewed energy.

After two hours of leisurely stop and go walking, they came to a village of about sixty thatch-roofed bamboo huts on stilts. Wohlfeld was greeted by everyone in the village. He was made guest of honor of the headman and his family.

To show their friendship and hospitality, as is the custom with Filipinos, an abundance of food was brought in by the neighbors. There was cooked rice and fish and a variety of tropical fruit, all of which his hungry body craved but very little of which his starved stomach could handle; consequently his host family had a feast.

Though Wohlfeld now basked in his good fortune of being free from the Japanese and pampered by friendly Filipinos, he could communicate only by sign language and gestures; they spoke no English, and he was totally ignorant of their dialect. On April 2, that handicap was remedied by a seven-year-old girl from a neighboring barrio; she had learned English at a Catholic school in a distant town. With the young girl acting as interpreter, he found out that there were many Americans in faraway places on the island serving in the guerrilla forces. He asked for guides to take him there, explaining that he was ill with malaria and dysentery, the leech bites and sores on his skin were infected and he must have medical attention. This was agreed upon.

After two more days of rest, Wohlfeld, with two guides, set out on the first leg of what was to be a long, long journey. It took them a full day to travel to the neighboring barrio; his feet were still swollen and sore and he still was unable to wear shoes. After a night's rest they marched for another day and stopped over for the night. As they moved along a trail during the third morning suddenly they were startled by the command, "HALT!"

From both sides of the trail rifles were pointed at them. Observing that the riflemen were dressed in American-type uniforms, Wohlfeld assumed they were guerrilla fighters. Raising both hands in surrender, he asked, "Where is your commanding officer? Take me to him."

A young second lieutenant came forward smiling, extended his hand in greeting and introduced himself as Lieutenant Marakit. He apologized for his men having frightened Wohlfeld and ordered them to unload their rifles. Another four hours of march brought them to a clearing in the woods which was company headquarters for the local unit.

Lieutenant Marakit assigned him a place to stay and an orderly to see after his needs. Shortly someone came in with a cup of hot broth. After he had rested for an hour or two, the orderly brought in a tub and buckets of hot water. Following a luxurious hot bath, he went back to his wooden bunk for more rest and another cup of broth. Late in the afternoon he was given another hot bath and a shave and haircut. In addition, someone cut his toenails and fingernails and a medic drained his infested wounds and bites and applied medication.

Meanwhile, Lieutenant Marakit, who spoke English fluently, informed him of the progress of the war. In so doing, he confirmed the rumors and newspaper stories we had been getting in prison camp; the Japanese were taking a terrible beating and the Allied forces were advancing rapidly toward the Philippines. There were copies of *Life* magazine and American newspapers to support the report.

Wohlfeld was amazed to learn that after a week of steady though slow movement, he was only nine kilometers across the swampy jungles from Davao prison camp. It seemed as though he had traveled fifty miles.

Among the items of equipment in the field camp was a radio transmitter and receiver. The operator contacted guerrilla headquarters and informed General Fertig that certain prisoners had been recovered. The general ordered them brought to him. Meanwhile, Wohlfeld was pleasantly surprised to learn that Lieutenant Hadley Watson had been picked up and was on the way in. Watson had no information on anyone else.

Watson got the same hospitality and care that had been accorded Wohlfeld. After several days of rest, during which they both got their systems accustomed to eating again and their wounds and sores taken care of, their long journey to headquarters began. From start to finish, the trip was to take twenty-one days. The party included about thirty guerrilla troops, who were to be dropped off for duty at various points along the way. First they marched for several days and then, upon reaching the Agusan River, took borotas (outrigger canoes) for the rest of the journey. Wohlfeld had to walk with only socks on his feet as his feet were still too swollen for shoes. At one point along the way the party had to stop for two days while he got treatment for a stomach disorder from a local doctor.

Upon arrival at Talacogan, the guerrilla headquarters, Wohlfeld and Watson were given a somewhat less than cordial welcome by General Fertig. He let them know that he had some doubts about the usefulness of a person who had been a prisoner of war. He feared that they would have suffered certain psychological damage which would make them unreliable and incapable of leadership, he said. However, he would think it over and give them an answer the following morning.

When they reported the next day, an aide to the general did give them their assignments. Lieutenant Watson's post was to be nearby, and Captain Wohlfeld would be sent to a distant headquarters. It was now early May, 1944, nearly six weeks after their escape from prison camp, and it was another five or six weeks before the two officers built up their health and strength sufficiently for full duty. In the interim they studied maps and familiarized themselves with the roads, rivers and general terrain and the positions and tactics of the enemy. The guerrilla forces on the island of Mindanao were very active in dynamiting bridges and passes and ambushing enemy convoys. As did those on other islands, they made a great contribution to the war effort.

In October, when it was known that General MacArthur's forces had landed on Leyte, Wohlfeld became impatient to be where the real action was. After many attempts, he finally found a Filipino who agreed to take him there. At night they secretly stashed food and water in a hidden outrigger sailboat and soon set out on a two weeks' journey. By the time he finally got to American forces the island had been secured, but there was still fierce fighting going on.

Wohlfeld located the commanding general, told him of his background and experience, and pleaded that he be given command of a combat unit. "Sir, before this fight is over I'd like to have a fair crack at the enemy. I have many scores to settle, both for myself and for the thousands of my buddies who died in their hands."

The general could see that Wohlfeld was itching for a fight and was speaking in dead earnest. Without hesitation, he issued an order giving him temporary command of the First Squadron, B-Troop of the Seventh Cavalry Regiment in Tunga, Leyte. As commander of that rifle company, Wohlfeld was engaged in numerous successful fire fights with the Japanese. Over the following three weeks they overran several strong enemy positions, inflicted heavy casualties and took numerous prisoners. Captain Wohlfeld said he then felt a certain well-earned peace within his restless being. Revenge for all the hurts, hunger and abuse had finally become his. No doubt it was worth every bit of the agonizing effort he had pushed himself through to get to that point.

Wohlfeld stayed with the Seventh Cavalry in Leyte and Luzon

in the Philippines and went with them to Japan in the army of occupation. In Japan he joined the reorganized Thirty-first U.S. Infantry as executive officer of the Second Battalion, with the rank of major. I asked him how he felt toward the Japanese after having lived in Japan as a superior rather than a slave. He said, "I never hated them. I just disliked them. But now my score with them is squared off."

It is confirmed that Navy Lieutenant Senior Grade Baldwin Boone was cornered and killed by the enemy on the second day. Three officers, Captain Wohlers, Lieutenant Mickey Wright and Lieutenant Carmichael, for reasons known only to them, did not get away. Lieutenant Fensler is unaccounted for. Lieutenant Hadley Watson speculates that he may have been hit by a stray bullet, and his body never recovered.

Six made the long trek through the merciless jungle and lived to fight another day. Captain Mark M. Wohlfeld, Lieutenants Hadley C. Watson, James D. Haburn and James McClure eventually joined up with General Fertig's headquarters. Lieutenants Andrew T. Bukovinsky and Marvin H. Campbell joined guerrilla forces in Zamboanga.

Following the March escape, conditions grew much worse for us at Davao. Guards grew tougher and more intolerant. Food allotments were reduced. Practically all productive work stopped. All efforts seemed directed toward closing the camp. Farm tools were crated for shipment. Carpenter and machine shops were closed and tools crated. Only the rope makers remained in production. We worked under a large open shed just inside the main gate. The shed was eighty feet long and fifty feet wide and stood twelve feet high at the eaves. There was ample room for fifty men to work and there was usually a cool breeze.

The lone guard posted himself about twenty-five feet from the nearest prisoner. Near him was a charcoal burner where we could light our cigarettes. After several weeks the guard became relaxed and informal. At times he would even engage various individuals in conversation. He liked to be shown snapshots of wives and children—especially small children. As the work was being performed inside the fence, he probably came to feel that his duties were to supervise rather than to guard the prisoners. Often he would lean his rifle against a post and sit on a stool near the charcoal burner.

One morning in late May, after we had been at work for about an hour, there was a sudden scuffling and screams. It was the guard who was screaming. Major Charles Harrison, a chemical warfare officer and West Pointer from Virginia, had casually strolled over and lit a cigarette. After doing so, he moved around behind the seated, unarmed guard and pounced on him. Hooking his left arm tightly around the Jap's neck, he commenced beating him over the head with a short length of half-inch iron pipe. The terrified guard screamed and flailed his arms wildly, but could not free himself. Blood gushed from his gashed head and streamed down his face.

At first the rest of us, in shocked disbelief, froze in our tracks. Harrison undoubtedly had gone mad, I thought. Fearful that other guards would rush in shooting, several of us dashed over and rescued the helpless guard. Harrison then grabbed the rifle from the post and took aim at close range. There was only a snap as he pulled the trigger. The rifle was empty. The freed guard, still yelling, ran out through the open gate. Harrison, thwarted and frightened, ran into a nearby barracks.

Before armed reinforcements arrived, our group leader had us lined up and standing at attention. Such quick thinking on his part probably prevented mass slaughter. Shortly, ten excited, threatening-looking Japanese soldiers rushed in with rifles and bayonets at the ready. The infuriated Japanese lieutenant immediately began slapping our leader and threatening all of us. Mr. Wada, the interpreter, in his most bitter and emphatic manner, informed us that the guard reported having been attacked by ten prisoners. Our leader tried to explain that only one had made the attack, and that the others moved in and saved the guard's life.

In a high-pitched, impassioned voice, Wada yelled, "You are a riar. Many of you attacked Japanese guard. You wirr arr be shoot."

Again the lieutenant slapped our spokesman repeatedly, this time knocking him to the ground.

After fifteen minutes of threats and abuse and holding conferences among themselves, the Japanese ordered us to sit in rows at attention. That meant sitting erect with backs straight, legs crossed at the calves and heels drawn up tightly against the buttocks. "You wirr sit rike dat untirr we find out who the guirty ones are. One at a time you wirr be taken to headquarters for questioning. Unress you confess, arr wirr face firing squad," Wada informed us with anger.

For the rest of the morning and into the afternoon we sat in physical agony and with the mental anguish of condemned men. Armed guards patrolled among us, up one row and down the next. If anyone relaxed his rigid position he was kicked in the spine or clubbed over the head. An additional worry was the thought that one of our number might crack under the strain and do something which could cause the nervous guards to gun us all to death. It was like being in death row, except that a condemned man so situated can stretch his legs, have a smoke and a last meal. We had nothing but the dim hope that our story would be believed.

One by one our men were marched under guard to headquarters two hundred yards away for questioning. Since we were not allowed to speak among ourselves, we could not learn what had been said or whose names were mentioned to the interrogators. It was a long, frightening, miserable day. As the hours dragged slowly on, the odds for survival looked smaller and smaller.

After two hours of sitting rigidly upright my back ached, my leg muscles were tied in knots, my feet, for lack of blood circulation, tingled as if being stuck by pins, and my ankle bones burned as if the hard ground were gnawing into them. Suddenly I was startled to notice blood stains on my g-string. They had splashed there from the guard's bleeding head as we broke up the fight. Knowing the blood spots would be sufficient evidence to convict me, I trembled in fear.

The bright red splotches, which could neither be hidden nor rubbed off, seemed to grow larger and more glaring. I prayed the Japs would get their answer before my turn for questioning arrived. That was my only hope. By quick estimate I determined there were twenty more to go for questioning ahead of me, since I was in the third row. The questioning dragged on for six hours.

Finally, at 3 P.M., Wada informed us that we were free to go to barracks. "De major has decided you are terring the truth," he announced, with neither thanks or apologies.

At that point, though anxious to leave, we were almost powerless to move. In order to get up we had to lean forward, place our hands on the dirt, slowly untangle our cramped legs and push up to a kneeling position. With stiff joints, knotted muscles and legs and feet throbbing from the sudden free coursing of blood through veins, standing was torture. In pairs, leaning on each other, we slowly hobbled back to barracks.

No one ever cleared up the mystery of Harrison's action. It was assumed he had an accomplice who feigned sickness that morning and remained in barracks. Their probable plan was for Harrison to finish off the rope detail guard by hand, seize his rifle and shoot the lone sentry at the gate. At that point his fellow conspirator would rush from barracks with a bag of supplies, and together, armed, they would make a dash for freedom. Though foolhardy, it might have worked if the first stage had succeeded. Unfortunately the Jap had a tough skull.

We never saw Major Harrison again. Screams from the guardhouse during the quiet of night communicated his bitter fate; hours of merciless torture before execution. Two days later the Japanese camp commander issued an official report stating that Major Charles Harrison had died as a result of wounds sustained in a fight with a Japanese guard.

Rope making was resumed two days after the Harrison incident, but there were some noticeable changes. Now there were two guards in place of the one. They were much more vigilant and unfriendly than the hapless victim of Harrison's freedom attempt. Additional security measures were evident at the gate, where four sentries replaced the former one. Also, each fence corner guard tower had two riflemen where formerly one had stood watch.

The sudden increase in military police surveillance was more significant than we could know at the time. Later historical information revealed that local guerrilla activity had become more aggressive and bold, and that American forces were closing in on the Philippines. The Japanese were uneasy. The local commander was under orders to deliver all prisoners to dockside in the near future for shipment north.

June–October, 1944

10. Back to Cabanatuan

At lunchtime on June 5, we were informed that the camp was
being closed and we would be moved back to Cabanatuan
on Luzon. Even though conditions were bad at Davao, the
thought of long marches, another boat trip and a terrible train
ride were discouraging. Worse still were the haunting memories
of starvation, disease and deaths during the early days at Cabanatuan. But prisoners have no choices. They move when told
to move.

Shortly after dark a fleet of open bodied army trucks arrived
and parked in line along the road leading from the compound
gate. There must have been twenty of them. Their presence indicated we would ride rather than march the twenty-five or thirty
miles to town.

Everyone was up most of the night making preparations for
the move. Not that there was much packing to do, for after
being prisoners for twenty-six months our possessions had become fewer and fewer. It was the excitement and fear over the
journey that kept us from sleeping. The Japanese truck drivers
outside the fence had little fires going to warm up their evening
meal. They talked and laughed and appeared to be having fun.
Out behind barracks little clusters of prisoners squatted around
fires stewing up the last of their vegetables from their small garden plots. Here and there other small groups sat around, spec-
ulating on what lay ahead. We knew our forces were closing in

and suspected that submarines were prowling the waters among the Islands. Added to the fears of all the hazards involved was the realization that each hundred miles northward would put us that much farther from possible rescue.

Before dawn the following morning, June 6, we were awakened, fed and issued an extra messkit of cooked rice for the journey. By sunup everyone had been loaded into trucks. In spaces ample for twenty-five standing bodies, forty to fifty men were crowded. After boarding we were instructed to blindfold ourselves with the strips of white cloth we had been issued as we approached the trucks. Also, we were to remove our shoes. That done, guards climbed aboard each truck and tied us together with hemp rope—some of which we had made with our own hands.

As the convoy bumped eastward along the pitted gravel road, I pushed my blindfold up slightly for a peep at the countryside. Not surprised, I noticed riflemen stationed at regular intervals along the way. That sight, in addition to blindfolds, bare feet and being guarded by two armed soldiers on each truck, emphasized the Japanese determination to prevent further escapes.

By five in the afternoon we were passengers aboard a dirty, greasy cargo freighter in the Gulf of Davao. It was hot and crowded in the hold. Crew members were still busy loading cargo. They looked at us with curiosity. One smiled. After settling in our assigned spaces in the semidarkness below deck, we were allowed to come topside. The ship remained in port for six days, probably waiting for convoy escort. Meals of rice in ample quantity were served twice daily. Each prisoner was issued a Red Cross parcel, our third in over two years. It was encouraging to see fresh water being pumped aboard from a barge anchored alongside. As days passed we learned that our portion was only slightly adequate for drinking, with none left over for bathing.

Weighing anchor on June 12, the rusty freighter headed north. Under aircraft cover, it traveled during daylight hours only. It was obvious that the skipper feared aircraft or submarine attack. After two days of stop and go movement, we pulled into Moro Bay in Zamboanga. It was here that the Moros lived; devout Mohammedans, they were widely known as skilled sailors, successful fishermen and fearless warriors.

It was late afternoon when the anchors were lowered at the north end of the Bay. Most of the prisoners were on deck. As I faced south, the city was to the left and the golden setting sun to the right. In between were dozens of outrigger fishing boats returning with the day's catch. Gently rolling waves nudged the bancas homeward as soft breezes billowed their red, yellow and blue sails. Green-fronded palm trees along the shore swayed as if beckoning. It was a scene of peace, calm and beauty—rare and unforgettable. For a fleeting few moments the harsh reality of our prisoner of war status slipped from my consciousness.

After sunset darkness came on quickly. All was quiet except for the sound of crew members chattering back and forth as they went about their duties. Prisoners above and below deck bedded down for the night. Al George and I chose a spot on deck near the rail on the seaward side of the ship about twenty feet from the bridge. On the deck above, directly forward of our position, four guards manned an antiaircraft gun. On the opposite side of the ship a similar crew was on station. Stars were out but no moon was shining. A few clouds drifted overhead. It was cool and, in spite of the hardness of the metal deck, I soon drifted into a sound sleep.

Around midnight I awoke, stood up and looked around me. I noticed the ship was now facing south, and realized the changing tide had swung her around. The current must have been strong and swift, for items of debris raced by as if motorized. Looking toward shore some three hundred yards away, I had an urge to jump overboard. However, realizing that my strength was limited and that I had no knowledge of the terrain or the people ashore, I dropped the idea. Suddenly I heard a splash followed shortly by bursts of rifle and machine gun fire. I thought for an instant the guards had read my intentions and were firing at me. Shocked and frightened, I dropped to the deck and huddled tightly against Al. After what seemed like an eternity, I realized no bullets were hitting near us. They were going into the water below.

Word quickly spread that a man had plunged overboard. It was reported to be Lieutenant Colonel John H. McGee. Word was that he had been stationed in Zamboanga before the war and knew the territory well. We learned after the war that McGee made it safely and joined the guerrilla forces.

On June 17 we arrived in Cebu. All prisoners were unloaded and marched to the former site of Fort San Pedro de Cebu, where one thousand of us were crowded into a metal warehouse building. The remaining three hundred were left outside on the dirt, enclosed by a wire fence. It was hot and suffocating inside. Outside, the hot sun, flies and mosquitos took their toll. When it rained all of us were packed inside. There was much diarrhea and malaria. Rice was ill-prepared and inadequate.

After three days of cramped misery there, we sailed on another ship. This one was smaller, and no prisoners were allowed on deck. Five days later we tied up at pier 7 in Manila, the point from which most of us had departed eighteen months earlier. It had taken nineteen days to make the 800-mile trip, a distance which normally would have been covered in three.

Of the approximately 2,100 prisoners who had worked at Davao Penal Colony in Mindanao during 1943–44, 1,330 of us marched wearily into Bilibid Prison in Manila on June 25, 1944. Of the original number, twenty had escaped, eighteen had died and 750 had been moved to another camp in Mindanao. After a three-day layover, 900 of us were moved to Cabanatuan on June 28. The others were left behind, under the leadership of Colonel Stubbs, to be sent to Japan. Those of us going to Cabanatuan felt more fortunate than they.

The camp at Cabanatuan looked practically deserted. In the early days its population had numbered 8,000 or more. Now there were less than 700 fellow prisoners to greet us. For the most part they were in very poor health, which accounted for their still being present. All able-bodied men had been shipped out on permanent work details, most of them to Japan to work in coal mines and steel mills. Only a small number had been kept as cooks and drivers for the Japs. A few doctors and corpsmen remained with the sick.

For a week or two our group was quarantined in a separate area of camp. From the outset, war news came in regularly. Authentic-sounding reports of Japanese defeats and American advances were almost daily bulletins. Also sprinkled in was news of guerrilla activity throughout the Islands. Once again we had cause to hope. In spite of inadequate rations and substandard living conditions, morale was high.

In early July I began working in the rice fields for the first time. Even though it was backbreaking labor under the hot sun, I wanted to try it, both to keep myself occupied and to learn how the crop was grown. The field we worked contained approximately thirty acres. It was divided into small paddies of one acre or less, which were separated by dikes or mud walls.

In preparation for planting, the ground was flooded in order to soften it and make plowing possible. Being in a valley, the ground was level, which made flooding by gravity easy. It was a very primitive operation, with no machinery or modern equipment. The wooden plow was pulled by a carabao, or water buffalo. One prisoner controlled the plow by holding onto its handles, while another led the lumbering carabao. After the soil, while under water, had been plowed back and forth and crisscrossed several times, it was then leveled by dragging a wooden-toothed harrow over it. That done, it was ready for planting.

Straight rows were marked off with cords stretched across the paddy ten inches apart and anchored to the dike on either end. Standing in water almost knee deep with bare feet bogged in the newly softened ground, the planter punched a hole in the mud with his forefinger, selected a plant from his other hand, placed it in the hole and pressed mud around it. With its top no more than two inches above water, directly below the cord, the new seedling was launched on its growing cycle in a watery bed. Its roots and lower stalk would remain under water until it reached maturity. Then the water would be drained off to allow the rice seeds to dry.

Rice planting could not normally be classed as strenuous

physical labor, but for weak, hungry men it was fatiguing. Bending over continuously was backbreaking, and pulling the feet from the stiff mud tired the leg muscles. Stepping on unbroken clods of dirt was hard on tender feet, too. The sun was hot; so was the water. By midmorning, we felt as if we were in a steam bath.

Twenty-five men working in a small paddy should have planted it in two to three hours. Knowing that we would not get to eat the finished product, and not desiring to aid the Japanese effort, we took all day. The guards, standing on the dry dikes, at intervals yelled "Speedo! Speedo!" Knowing that they would not come into the mud to kick or club us, we murmured to each other "Slow down." Rice planting is normally slow work, but ours must have been a record for movement with little forward progress. A pack of snails would have left us behind. I should judge that four Filipinos would have done as much in half a day.

Throughout the months of July, August and September, our group of approximately two hundred labored in the rice fields. Once I became adjusted to working with head down and back bent, it wasn't so bad. It beat sitting around camp all day doing nothing. The small extra portion of rice which workers received each day was also an advantage.

Each night after supper I visited around camp and renewed friendships with men I had known in college, or had identified as being from my home state of South Carolina. Captains Henry D. Leitner, Beverly N. (Ben) Skardon, William (Bill) English and Lieutenants Francis Scarborough, Otis Morgan and Martin Crook had been students with me at Clemson College. Lieutenants Jack Leonard, Alton Bryant and Wilson Glover were graduates of The Citadel in Charleston, South Carolina. There was much optimism among us at the time. News reports indicated that the war was going favorably and that we would soon be free again. We talked of home and food and beautiful girls we had yet to meet, of football games and hunting trips and vacations at the beach. Of all subjects discussed, however, none held the attention or stimulated the imagination as did food. It was the thing dreamed of most, and for which we felt the need most personally and strongly.

Henry Leitner and I became very close friends during that period at Cabanatuan. Six feet, blond and broad shouldered, Henry normally made a striking appearance. As a prisoner he became thin and gaunt, but his blue eyes still sparkled and his sharp wit remained refreshing. We shared what little extras we would get and had long discussions about the future. Henry had been married just ten days before sailing for the Philippines. The trip to San Francisco had been the Leitners' honeymoon. I had met his wife at the wharf, where she watched him board ship. A beautiful and courageous brunette, she had stood waving until the *USS President Cleveland* sailed beyond view toward the Golden Gate Bridge.

In addition to having a brilliant scientific mind, Henry was also a deep thinker on things aesthetic. He often jotted down descriptive nature poems and themes on man's struggles and dreams. His written verse revealed intense thought and feeling, balanced with warmth and tenderness. Henry's friendship and strength often gave me reassurance when I needed it most.

On September 21, 1944, around midmorning, as we worked in the rice field, we suddenly became conscious of a distant faint rumbling. At first it sounded like the close up droning of a swarm of bees on the move. It gradually grew louder.

"That sounds like airplanes," commented Henry.

"And it's different from the rattling, labored strain of the Jap planes," observed Alton Bryant.

The sound grew louder as it rapidly moved nearer. Everyone stopped work and faced north toward the Sierra Madre Mountains. The buzzing changed to a clear, high-pitched drone, then to a smooth, powerful purr. Suddenly many clusters of small specks came over the range. Quickly the specks grew to bird size, then larger and larger as their powerful thrusts closed the distance. We waited tense and breathless, feeling certain they must be ours, but after so many years of frustration, daring not to admit it.

Lieutenant Wilson Glover, one of the few who still had good eyesight, shouted "Look at those beautiful stars on the wings! They're ours. Americans!"

My heart pounded as every nerve in my body tingled with excitement. "American planes! Our planes!" I repeated. "Thank God! They've come at last."

No one could hear me, for they all cheered at once. They shouted, they yelled and they screamed. There was alternating laughter and tears as the excitement exploded into exhilaration. Some sat down in the mud and pounded the water with their palms, splashing those around them. Henry and I turned toward each other with unseeing tear-filled eyes. Pounding each other on the shoulders, we fell into the mud.

As the planes swiftly passed one mile to the east, headed south toward Manila, we counted five groups of bombers of six to eight, each flying in V formation. To their right and left and above them, darting in and out of the clouds, were groups of protecting fighter planes. Out front, faster flying scout fighters crisscrossed the sky, as if leading the way and egging them on. It was the most beautiful sight we had witnessed during the entire war; the first actual proof that our side was winning.

Our Japanese guards looked frightened, shocked and indecisive. Recalling how, three years earlier, we had helplessly watched their planes swoop in and gain mastery of the skies, we knew the anguish with which they contemplated their impending doom. But we felt no sympathy and they knew it. Remembering their boast of "Ichiban Nippon hikoki" (Japanese plane number one) when Japanese planes flew over, someone shouted "Ichiban American hikoki." All of us took up the chant, "Ichiban American! Ichiban! Ichiban!"

The guards, though armed, seemed powerless to act. A wrong move on their part probably would have cost the lives of some prisoners, but it certainly would have meant death for them. Fortunately, in the midst of their consternation and our revelry, a runner came from headquarters with instructions to bring the prisoners back to the compound.

Marching in, though weak, hungry and half naked, we held our bodies erect and stepped with a quick cadence, singing "God Bless America."

After being dismissed, we stood around in small groups, happy and excited, discussing our imminent freedom. There was no question in anyone's mind; we would soon move out of Cabanatuan unrestrained and unmolested. It was only a question of how soon and by what means—airlift, truck convoy or on foot. Regardless of how or when, we knew it would happen soon.

We had hardly settled down from the excitement when the drone of airplanes could be heard again; prrr . . . Zooommm . . . ZOOOMMM, closer and closer, louder and louder, until the whole earth around us seemed to tremble—beautiful, comforting, reassuring. When they arrived at a point two miles opposite the prison camp, one fighter peeled off and made a strafing run on a nearby empty airfield. Then it leveled off and headed straight for us at low level. Directly overhead it dipped its wings in salute as if saying "Hello, fellows. We know your location. Hang on. We will be back." Everyone waved and cheered and uttered prayers of thanksgiving.

That evening detailed reports of the raid swept the camp. It was said that Clark Air Field had been hit by Navy bombers, resulting in heavy damage to Japanese aircraft and facilities. Also we learned that Manila Harbor had been pounded and a dozen or more enemy ships were destroyed. I wondered how details of a bombing raid which took place at noon could have filtered in to us so quickly. Years later, while attending an Ex-Prisoner of War convention in Albuquerque, New Mexico, I learned that the reports were not only authentic, but they were being received live over a clandestine radio. The one responsible was J. Harold Harveston, a career Navy enlisted man. This is his story as told me years later. "Yes, the news reports were more than rumors. They were hot off the wire each night," he said with a twinkle in his bright eyes. "I had a hidden radio. Only one other man knew about it."

"How did you ever get a radio into camp?" I asked in amazement.

"One piece at a time," he answered with the satisfied grin of one who knows he has accomplished something which few would have possessed the nerve to try. Sensing that there was some doubt mixed with my surprise, he quickly added, "Let me explain. Being a machinist, I was skilled with my hands. As a hobby, I had learned watch repairing some years earlier. The Japs learned of this and put me to work in a little shop behind headquarters repairing watches for them. Soon they began bringing in radios to be worked on. With access to radios, I began listening to the news, but could only listen to the Japanese station. When there were no Japs around I would turn the volume down low and tune in on the "Voice of Freedom."

With the self-assurance of one who knows he has his audience spellbound, he continued, "One day I thought to myself, why not just steal enough parts to build my own radio. It took many months to accomplish. This is how I did it.

"Often when a set came in to be fixed it only had a loose wire. I'd tell the Jap he needed a set of tubes. When he left to order new ones, I'd slip out the perfectly good old tubes and hide them. The next one I would diagnose as a bad condenser, and so forth until I had accumulated a complete set of parts.

"I had a close friend who worked in the small camp library. Swearing him to secrecy, I told him of my plan. We decided that the ideal place to operate the radio would be beneath the floor in the library. Since he always closed at sundown, there would be no one coming in at night.

"While everybody was out at work during the day, he made a trap door in the floor and covered it with a straw mat. For the next several nights we worked at scooping out a small pit in the ground beneath the trap door. That completed, I assembled the stolen parts and got my radio in operation. I used an old car battery for power.

"From then on I became a great student. Each day after work I would go to the library, select a book and sit in a corner reading until closing time. When he closed up for the night, I'd crawl into the pit and put on the headset and get the news. To avoid having our fellow prisoners trace the source to me, I let the news out each day as truck driver rumors."

"How long were you in operation?" I asked.

"For more than a year. It must have been mid-1943 when I started receiving."

"Did anyone else ever know about this?"

"Only the two of us. It was the best kept secret of the whole three and a half years."

"It was a courageous thing you did. Had it been discovered, you probably would have been shot," I observed.

"The Navy later thought well of it," he said with pride, as he took an official document from his briefcase and handed it to me. It was a Navy citation for the useful and daring service he had performed for his fellow prisoners.

After a two-day layoff, work in the rice fields and on other projects resumed. Food and living conditions showed no improvement, but the attitude of the guards was somewhat better. They seemed a bit less demanding, and not as quick to kick us around. News bulletins, or rumors, became more and more encouraging. We heard of Allied bombings and ship sinkings throughout the area, and of a great naval battle to the south in which our side was successful. It was evident that our forces were getting closer.

On October 20, 1944, we heard that there had been a big landing on the island of Leyte, not more than 300 miles to the south. General MacArthur was even quoted as having said over radio, "People of the Philippines, I have returned."

There was joy and gratitude in camp both over the historical event and the words of General MacArthur. Upon leaving Corregidor in March, 1942, he had made the solemn pledge to the Filipinos, "I shall return." Now, having led an invasion force to Leyte, in the very center of the Philippines, he had fulfilled that promise, and in doing so was tightening the noose around the very throat of the Japanese supply lines. That being true, we were confident that the Japanese could not now ship us out to Japan. In addition, we felt that even before the battle for the Philippines was over, MacArthur would send in troops to rescue all prisoners of war.

11. Tragedy at Sea

On the very day of the Leyte landing, two hundred miles to the north in Manila Bay, the Japanese slipped a convoy of several ships out to sea, bound for Japan. Among the ships was a medium-sized freighter called the *Arisan Maru*. Two of its cargo holds were reserved for prisoners of war being transferred to Japan to be slave laborers in the coal mines and factories. In one of the two compartments was Sergeant Philip Brodsky, of the U.S. Army Medical Corps. Many years after the war Brodsky told me his story of survival, and let me have the use of his personal diary.

Sergeant Brodsky and 214 prisoners who had been working at the construction of an airfield in Palawan boarded a ship at Puerto Princesa one week and moved to Manila. Left behind at Palawan were 150 other American prisoners who continued work on the airfield project.

Had Brodsky known the horrible fate which was to befall those men, he would have felt lucky as his ship lay at anchor in Manila Bay taking on more cargo and additional prisoners. It was learned after the war that the Japanese guards, at the sound of an air raid alarm, had herded the prisoners into an underground shelter, poured in gasoline and set the bunker afire. Eight of the terrified men managed to escape through a small tunnel at the rear end. One hundred forty-two others were either burned alive or were mowed down with machine gun fire as they attempted to dash out the entrance. That beastly event was later exposed as the "Palawan Massacre."

But Brodsky didn't feel so lucky that day as more and more prisoners were jammed into the hold of the *Arisan Maru*. It was hot down there, and bodies kept crowding in. When the *Arisan Maru* was ready to sail, she had 1,800 prisoners jammed into space insufficient for half that many. The prisoners were about equally divided between the forward and aft part of the ship. The additional prisoners had come from various camps and work details.

Sergeant Calvin Graef of Carlsbad, New Mexico, a member of the 200th Coast Artillery, Antiaircraft, was in the forward hold. Sergeant Graef and 430 of his companions had been at Bilibid Prison in Manila since June. Prior to that time they had been rice planters at Davao Penal Colony for eighteen months. As in the aft hold, more prisoners were added until the 430 increased to approximately 900.

From the outset, the journey was a horror story. Men were so tightly crowded together that there was scarcely room to lie down. With the hatch covers closed, there was no way to get fresh air, and the humid, sweltering 120-degree atmosphere soon became fouled with the stench of unwashed bodies and human waste. In their frightening, helpless condition, many men panicked; some went mad.

The skies were overcast when the prisoners and cargo were being loaded. The next day the convoy sailed out into a typhoon. It was October 20, 1944, when the *Arisan Maru* left Manila Bay. As the ship rolled and tossed in the rough China Sea, yet another misery, seasickness, was heaped on the wretched prisoners. The odor of vomit, added to the stench of human excrement (many had uncontrollable diarrhea), made the sweltering hold unbearable. Many prayed that a bomb or torpedo would strike and bring their maddening ordeal to a quick end; some had reached that point at which the prospect of dying seemed a welcome alternative to the tortured struggle to live.

The same conditions continued for the next two days. The

men grew weaker from dehydration caused by sweating, the lack of water, and the miserable diarrhea. Some died of heat prostration. There was a complete breakdown of discipline. The only thing which brought back some semblance of reality was the twice daily serving of a small amount of rice and water.

Philip Brodsky normally was not a big man. At best he carried 170 pounds on his five-foot-seven-inch frame. Now his weight was less than 120. Rather quiet and gentle, he was never one to pick a fight. But there are times when even the mildest of men will swing his fist in anger. Such a time was on October 24, 1944.

"At around 3:00 P.M., we had just received our meager second feeding of the day. The fellow on my right called to me and I turned to see what he wanted. When I turned back the fellow on my left had reached into my mess kit and stolen my rice. Enraged, I swung with all my might and punched the thief in the face."

Of course Brodsky didn't get his rice back and he ended up with a broken hand, but he did prove a point well worth noting: A starving man's food is not to be tampered with.

"Before some of the men had gotten their rice, there was a terrible jolt as three torpedoes tore into the side of the ship," Brodsky says.

Brodsky was in the aft hold, where approximately half of the 1,800 prisoners were crowded. As far as he could see, none were injured by the explosion, but he felt sure that some in the forward hold must have been killed. Surprisingly, no one panicked.

"One of our officers took charge and urged everyone to be calm and wait for orders to evacuate. He said the ship was damaged but was not sinking. He said he would be given the word when to go topside. We stayed there; things were quiet and we just waited."

It is hard to picture men calmly sitting and waiting in a level headed manner when their ship is on the verge of sinking to the bottom of the China Sea 300 miles offshore. But when you consider the nightmarish conditions under which they had sailed for four days and nights, it is believable. Men had gone mad from the heat and stench and thirst. Some had perished. Now, through the gaping hole ripped by the torpedo, light and fresh air were drifting in and the sweltering heat had suddenly dropped to a comfortable 80 degrees. So they waited.

Above them, through the now-open hatchway whose covers had been jarred loose by the sudden impact, bewildered armed guards looked down on them, apparently more frightened than the prisoners. Though the guards did not threaten them, their presence discouraged any attempt to climb out.

After about thirty minutes, the guards moved away and the prisoners began to stir. Several of them leaned a hatch cover against the bulkhead to serve as a ramp for them to climb up. That set off a mad scramble in which everyone tried to get out at once.

"I didn't get in that shoving contest. With my broken hand I knew I couldn't compete. So I just stood aside and let the others out," said Brodsky.

"It was a relief to be on the outer edge and I didn't care whether I drowned or not, because I was in a daze and sick and tired of it all anyhow. Everyone got out. An officer and an enlisted man gave me a hand and I finally scampered up to topside."

There was a pile of life preservers on deck, Brodsky says, and everybody got one. Some of them weren't very good and the one he got didn't have a tape on it, and later that proved to be a lot of trouble.

"A fellow named Lash was the only one I saw on deck I knew well. A lot of the officers and men ran to the rear of the deck and started jumping into the water right away. I persuaded Lash to wait with me and see what happened. They were swimming toward a Japanese ship, hoping to be picked up. I didn't believe they would pick up any survivors and as it turned out, they didn't," he said.

He said those who didn't jump into the water made a dash for the galley in search of food and drink. They were like rampaging animals.

"In retrospect, it was hilarious," he said. "They stuffed hot rice in their mouths and washed it down with two or three bottles of catsup. Some were smoking two cigarettes at a time. It looked like madness, and I guess we were a bit demented. It was a case of starving men gorging themselves, knowing that this was the last chance."

The men who had overeaten paid for it later. When they got into the water they became sick and vomited. Their last meal proved to be a detriment.

"Lash and I ate our share of rice and sugar. After we had enough, we decided to just sit tight. We noticed that the ones who had jumped over and made it to the other ship weren't being picked up. The Japs were rescuing only their own. Prisoners were being left to drown."

Three torpedoes had hit the ship—one forward, one aft and the third at midship. It was taking in water at all three places, but slowly. For two hours or more it remained afloat.

"I didn't know much about ships," says Brodsky, "and I couldn't estimate whether it would stay up ten more minutes or ten days. I told Lash that they were bound to come and pick us up and maybe an American ship would come. If not, the Japs might send a repair crew and try to save the ship."

It was now nearly sundown. Most of the prisoners had gone over the side, but there were still several hundred on deck. As Brodsky remembers it, the stern began to rise up out of the water and the other end went down. Several hundred men were standing on deck, probably wondering what to try next.

"I didn't make any attempt to get a raft and I didn't see any lifeboat. My broken hand was hurting quite a bit.

"Just about dusk the ship started to go down fast. We were sitting on the starboard side, near a big hole in the side of the ship, and it was tilted over in that direction. The typhoon had about ended, but there were still ten- to fifteen-foot swells in the sea.

"I thought I would stay with the ship and if it went down the suction would pull me under and it would be over and I would have no more worries.

"Finally the ship went under, but there was no suction at all and I just stayed where I was and I couldn't figure it out. I floated up; I had a life preserver but it had no cord and kept bouncing up against my chin."

Seeing that he wasn't going down, Brodsky swam away. In the interim he lost Lash. About one hundred yards out he turned to look back. By then the end of the ship was pointing straight up.

"There were about thirty people still on it. It went straight up and then straight down. In about thirty seconds there was a loud explosion and a great number of men started dropping around. I didn't think anyone was hurt, but I didn't look around to see, to be truthful."

Brodsky then began looking for Lash. He called several times and soon Lash answered. Together they found a benjo (a one-hole wooden toilet shack) which had been secured to the rail of the ship for Japanese use, and got on top of it. It was a substantial piece of wreckage and served to keep them afloat until about 4 o'clock the next morning (October 25). By then a dozen more had joined them and more were trying to get on.

"With everyone grabbing and trying to get a better spot, the thing finally tore apart, so Lash and I decided to hop off and try to find something better.

"We next found two hatch covers, each about two feet wide and ten feet long. Also, I found a piece of board four feet long and six inches wide. I laid the board across from one hatch cover to the other and draped my body over the board. Lash got on one of the covers. I gripped my arms across both covers to keep them together. This way we had more support, but the motion of the water kept flapping the board up and down and it pinched me and it skinned my arms to shambles. Soon they were bleeding."

Brodsky weighed about 125 pounds by now, having lost fifteen pounds thus far on the trip, and was fifty pounds below his normal weight. Lash, normally a small man, barely weighed 100 and was weak.

They stayed together until about sunup the next morning, when Lash said he thought it would be best if they separated.

"I wanted to stick together just for the company, but I figured maybe he thought I was a hindrance to him with my broken hand and then maybe he thought he was a hindrance to me. I would rather have stayed with him, but I didn't say anything and we separated.

"In the distance I could see thirty or forty people. They were widely scattered. I could see Lash until about sunrise, and then I never saw him again."

Still clinging to the inadequate hatch cover, Brodsky drifted and looked and wondered where he was and if he would ever be rescued. Glare from the early morning sun pained his sleep-starved eyes, but the warmth of it relieved the chill which had shaken him throughout the night.

He was in a daze for the next hour or so and didn't worry too much. Then about midmorning the full impact of his helpless plight hit him; he was alone in hundreds of miles of rough green sea, whose every wave seemed to be trying to swallow him alive.

"I began looking around again and calling, but no one answered. There was nobody to hear me. I couldn't think anything out. My mind was blank. I just hung on."

Around 10 o'clock a Japanese cruiser approached where Brodsky was drifting. He waved and pleaded with them to pick him up. Sailors lined the rail and stared at him, but the ship passed by.

"After the ship sailed on past me I lost a lot of hope. All I could see around me was the horizon. I thought at least they would want to pick me up for questioning. I was so far from land I knew I didn't have a chance. All I knew about geography wasn't much. I remembered that the sun set in the west and rose in the east, and had my direction from that. In the daytime I seemed to drift eastward and during the night the direction seemed northeast."

Around noon Brodsky spotted another fellow about one hundred yards away. He called to him and asked if it was okay to join him. The fellow answered, "Sure, come on over."

"His name was Glenn Oliver from Wisconsin. He had two hatch covers which were tied in with some other wreckage. We tied our three hatch covers into a triangle with the little bit of line he had."

The triangle seemed like a good idea, but the ropes kept working loose and they spent the next several hours trying to keep them tied together. They were never out of the water completely.

"Around midnight, when we were about to give up struggling with the hatch covers, four rafts drifted by. They were about four feet by six feet flat wooden rafts tied one behind the other with long two-inch ropes. We immediately abandoned our flimsy hatch covers and made for the rafts. Oliver climbed aboard one and I took one. It was the first time in the thirty-six hours since shipwreck that we could stretch out and rest."

In the forward hold, where Sergeant Calvin Graef was, conditions were equally as bad up to the time of the torpedo strike—terribly hot, crowded and unbearable. His description of what happened follows:

"It was horrible. There was a thunderous explosion. Hundreds of men died instantly. Bodies and bits of bodies flew everywhere. The vessel lurched a quarter turn sideways as if rammed by a giant tug.

"The second torpedo hit the aft section and the freighter lurched an offsetting quarter turn. The third shot was a bull's-eye at dead center which brought mass carnage and destruction and split the ship in half. Mysteriously, the two halves drifted apart and remained afloat for nearly two hours before sinking."

Graef, stunned and disbelieving, was still alive and uninjured. The splotches of blood and bits of flesh smeared on his face and body belonged to others; he was unscratched. The powerful force of concussion had pushed him upward and through the open hatchway.

Graef was not the typical burly, tough-looking first sergeant type. Short, weighing a mere ninety pounds at the time, normally gentle and deliberate in speech, he didn't appear to be one who could flex his muscles, grit his teeth and stare death in the face with a cool confidence. But that he did, and more. The

story he told me of his survival is one of raw courage and un-
yielding resolve.

After being forced up, he stood on deck and looked down
into the gutted hold. Below, where he had been moments before,
large waves lashed against the still firm bulkhead and, their fury
spent, flushed out lifeless bodies as they receded. The sight of
countless mangled corpses stirred up a fury within him which
demanded revenge. Many of the victims were his close friends;
men from his home town or county, men he had led in battle. If
only the Japanese had put the proper markings on the ship this
never would have happened, he told himself over and over.

Seeing no life down below, he turned and headed for the
bridge area, hoping to find food. That effort proved to be fruitless; the galley was on the other half of the ship. He did, however, find a tank of fresh water from which he quenched his terrible thirst. Before moving away he filled two Japanese canteens
to take along, thinking he would have at least one defense
against the salty sea.

A half hour after shipwreck the half ship was still successfully
riding the high waves. Graef decided he still had time for another look around. Turning a corner, he almost bumped into a
Japanese soldier. Graef's penetrating brown eyes nervously
searched him up and down. The soldier was unarmed and trembled with fear. Graef shook with anger. The numerous atrocities
committed by the enemy over the past three years flashed before
him: the merciless Death March, the declaration of eternal hatred by the Japanese major at Camp O'Donnell, starvation, untreated diseases, crowded ships and now the nearly 1,800 killed
on this unmarked prison ship. He thought to himself, if I must
die I will take at least one of them with me.

Pouncing like a marauding jungle beast, he grabbed the
frightened soldier by the neck and wrestled him to the deck.
Holding a strangling grip on his windpipe with one hand and
pounding his head against the steel deck with the other, he soon
beat him into unconsciousness. Feeling the body relax, he knew
the guard was dead. Satisfied that he had partly avenged the un-

necessary deaths of so many fellow Americans, he got up and slowly walked over to the rail.

It was now late afternoon. Threatening black clouds obscured the setting sun. Shortly darkness would be all around him. The other half of the ship had already sunk. The forward half, of which he was the lone occupant, would soon go under. Graef knew that he must jump overboard and swim clear to avoid being sucked under with it.

A Japanese destroyer was standing by off the port side as if waiting to pick up survivors. The less than two hundred left alive were swimming toward it. Though he dreaded the thought of being taken prisoner again, there was no choice; the sea was rough and there was no land in sight. With the hope that life with the navy would be better than it had been with the army, he plunged overboard and swam toward the warship.

Upon reaching the destroyer, he felt a sharp blow on his head. He thought he had bumped into the hull. When the second lick nearly severed his ear, he realized the poles extending from the deck into the water were being used to push the struggling prisoners under rather than to pull them aboard. Japanese sailors were making a sporting game of trying to drown the survivors.

Angry and still determined to try to live, Graef paddled out of range and began searching for something to hang onto. As darkness fell, the destroyer pulled away, leaving the Americans with no chance of rescue. Originally 1,800, their number had dwindled to less than one hundred and most of them were already exhausted. Fifteen-foot waves tossed them about, and the storm winds were chilling.

With items of debris set adrift from the shipwreck, Graef and several others attempted to make a raft. While one held to a plank, the others swam out in search of more material.

That seemed to be working until Graef, who was a good swimmer, ventured out too far. When he returned he could find no one. Now he was alone in a storm-agitated sea hundreds of miles from land. It was dark and cold. The ten-foot bamboo pole he had found would not support his weight, but it was a help. Another hour went by before he bumped into another pole of about the same size. With his g-string, his only item of clothing, he tied the two together. (It had been so hot aboard ship most men had abandoned their clothing.)

Later during the night a live human being drifted by. Graef reached out and caught him by the arm. It was Corporal Don Meyer of Los Angeles, California.

"Come on and join me," invited Graef, encouraged to have company.

"I'm finished. Let me go on and die," said the exhausted Meyer.

"Oh, no!" said Graef. "You're not leaving me out here all alone."

So together they hung on, not knowing where, how, or why, except that they determined to try to see another day. There were times during the night when neither, without the other, would have survived. The waves grew rougher and the winds chilled them to the bone. To have surrendered to the pull of the angry sea would have been effortless; to keep struggling was exhausting and painful. And if they should see another day, what promise would it hold? Certainly no American ships would come on the scene; these were Japanese waters and the Japs had already demonstrated no inclination to pick up American survivors. Tomorrow could only mean thirst, hunger, and perhaps madness, and yet they hung on. Maybe it was the dread of the depth of the sea which made them refuse to give up; maybe it was the hope that in the light of day they would find enough timbers to build a raft on which to rest and drift to some yet unseen island.

Once during the long night they thought they saw a lifeboat. But on second thought they decided it was a mirage. Certainly had one been around they would have seen it before dark.

At dawn, incredulously, Graef's now dim vision caught sight of a shiny, white lifeboat bobbing up and down with the waves. His heart pounded. But fearful that his mind had cracked, he said nothing for a moment. Then Meyer saw it and unhesitatingly yelled in a hoarse voice, "My God! Do you see what I see, Calvin?"

"It can't be," said Graef. "We must be dreaming."

They stared in disbelief. First it was there in plain view, then a huge wave hid it again. Alternately it rode a towering swell and then disappeared behind it in a valley. Their spirits rose and fell accordingly. They hesitated for awhile, wishing not to lose the vision and fearful it might be an illusion. If it were real, there was hope. If it proved to be a fantasy, their fourteen hours of agonizing struggle would have been in vain.

Finally Graef and Meyer became convinced that there was a boat, and with great effort began swimming toward it. Reaching it, they were too weak and exhausted to climb over its four-foot sides. Attempts to grasp a handhold proved fruitless and neither was strong enough to boost the other up high enough. Just as they were making a final desperate effort, three heads popped up from inside the boat: Corporal Anton E. Cichi of New York Mills, Minnesota, Sergeant Avary E. Wilburn, Naverino, Wisconsin, and Robert S. Overbeck, a civilian engineer, looked down on them in astonishment.

"Where did you characters come from?" asked Wilburn.

"Don't ask stupid questions," said Meyer. "Just give us a hand."

Once aboard, the two new passengers collapsed, exhausted. After a brief rest, Graef remembered his canteens of water. Unscrewing the cap on one, he passed it to Wilburn who was seated next to him.

"Just one swallow," warned Graef. "It may have to last us a long time."

A quick gulp turned Wilburn's happy smile into a deep frown, followed by gagging and spitting; salt water had fouled their modest supply of drink. Still thirsty and overcome with fatigue, the five flopped over and fell asleep. But at least they had a boat.

Sometime later they were awakened by the noise of something bumping against the side. Peering over, they saw a five-gallon wooden keg being tossed by the waves. They hauled it in, and to their amazement found it full of water. Fresh water. Free of salt.

Feeling better and more hopeful after a rationed drink around, they sat in a tight circle and began to assess their situation. Compared to the afternoon before, their assets were much improved: they now had drinking water and a boat, but the boat's rudder was broken and there was no mast or sail. Also missing were the oars. Still they were fortunate; the fear of drowning and the horror of being eaten by sharks had been eliminated. Cloudy skies protected them from the sun, and the high sides of the lifeboat held off the chilling winds.

Meyer and Graef, still exhausted but more confident, fell into a deep sleep. Wilburn, Cichi and Overbrook scanned the waters for usable items of debris. Having come aboard soon after dark the night before, they had slept well. They assumed Japanese officers had used the lifeboat in getting from the stricken ship to the destroyer and, once aboard, left it adrift.

As they watched, someone noticed a pole drifting by. With their combined limited energies, they worked it aboard, thinking there might be a use for a pole. Exhausted from the exertion and still hungry and weak, they settled down for a nap.

Meyer had been awakened by their noise in pulling the pole aboard. He took over the watch. Suddenly, in a hushed, horrified voice, he said, "Look men, it's over for us. There comes that darned destroyer again."

In the distance, what appeared to be the same warship that had pulled away the afternoon before was approaching rapidly. The frightened men quickly decided that their best course of action lay in inaction. They would play dead, thus making it fruitless for the Japanese to pick them up or to shoot into their boat.

With bodies crosscrossed, motionless, and each facing in a different direction, the five awaited their doom. The destroyer, at some two hundred yards distant, swung to the right and circled the area. Japanese officers could be seen on deck inspecting them through field glasses. Trembling with fear, the prisoners saw machine guns trained on them. Thinking, This is it, they tensely awaited the blast which would end it all. Just as someone said the last amen, the warship mysteriously turned and sailed away.

Soon after the frightening incident, there was another bumping against the side of their boat. This time it was a wooden box two feet square and one foot deep, the top of which was screwed on and tightly sealed. They hauled it in.

After another brief period of rest, they began to examine the items which the ceaseless waves had brought their way. The pole proved to be more than an ordinary piece of timber. It was a mast, the very mast which had been shaped to fit their boat. The box, when broken open, revealed a sail, ropes and pulleys. It was fortunate for them that the discovery hadn't been made before the destroyer came on the scene, for had they been under sail they certainly would have been fired on and killed.

The next project at hand was to repair the broken rudder. The only wood available was that on the wall under the front deck. With the mast pole they pounded the door open. Inside the storage area they found a tightly sealed tin box which contained biscuits (hard tack). After a series of unbelievable happenings, the five spunky survivors began to feel they had a reasonable chance to endure. Now there was hope, whereas twenty-four hours earlier there had been nothing but despair as they tossed about in a cold, angry sea.

So equipped, and with Overbeck's knowledge of astronomy, they set sail by the stars for the China coast. The storm was subsiding but the winds were still strong.

Later advice from seafaring men revealed that only fools or novices would have rigged a sail in a typhoon. But they did, and it worked. Within three days the powerful winds pushed them more than 300 miles. Before setting sail they scanned the area carefully for other survivors; there were none around.

At this particular time in history, with a few isolated exceptions all the thousands of miles of China coast were occupied by the Japanese. As if guided by an unseen hand, their navigator landed them in an enemy-free area. Disembarking, the five physical wrecks from the shipwreck walked down the main street of a city of 150,000 people just as they had come into the world—naked, hungry and weak.

The Chinese were friendly, but fearful of punishment if caught harboring Americans. After feeding, clothing and providing temporary lodging for their uninvited guests, they insisted that the former prisoners move on. For the next thirty days, with guides, they worked their way into the vast interior of China. Their modes of travel varied from bicycle to small riverboat and on foot. Eventually they reached an American airbase, where they feasted, rested and made merry over the luxury of being free Americans once more. From there, by way of India, Egypt and Spain, they were flown to the United States, reaching home eight months before the war ended.

To their knowledge at the time, they were the only survivors of the 1,800 who had been aboard the *Arisan Maru* on that day in October when it was sunk by torpedoes from an American submarine. All the others, one thousand seven hundred and ninety-five, they believed, were swallowed up by the angry China Sea.

Philip Brodsky and Glenn Oliver relaxed for about two hours on their newly found rafts. As long as they remained in a prone position with their weight evenly distributed, the boards kept them just even with the water's surface. When they sat up the rafts submerged to the point that they were waist deep in water.

"I figured that if we stacked the rafts one on top of the other they would hold us above the water completely. I suggested this to Oliver. He didn't seem to want to make the effort," says Brodsky.

"I undertook to do it myself, but my broken hand, now pretty swollen, made it pretty rough. I would get one end over and a wave would bang them together and separate them again. I guess Oliver finally felt sorry for me and pitched in and helped. We worked all that day and finally got them on. It was now October 26, two days after shipwreck."

With the wearisome job completed, they found that the vertical stack of rafts would support the two of them just above water. Exhausted, they stretched out on the small platform and rested and dozed for a while.

Nightfall brought relief from the scorching sun, but parching thirst and gnawing hunger remained with them constantly. But they felt safe from the threat of sharks and the possibility of drowning, if they had remained in the water much longer. As the night progressed, strong winds increased the chill of the cold water lapping over their weary bodies. Brodsky slipped into the water occasionally to move about and circulate his blood, but Oliver, unable to swim, remained in place and shivered.

As on the previous day, early morning brought temporary relief from the night's agonizing cold, but they knew the noonday sun would parch their hides once more. Frequent visual searches revealed only an empty sea all morning long. Then around noon they saw a body floating in a life jacket some one hundred fifty yards away. Brodsky decided to swim out to it in hopes of finding a canteen of water.

As a precaution against being separated from the raft by the high swells, he took off his undershorts, his only clothing, and tied them to a stick for Oliver to hold up for him to sight on when he started back. The corpse slipped through the life jacket before he reached it, but he recovered the life jacket. It had no canteen. They used the life jacket for a pillow.

They kept looking for another corpse, but saw nothing else that day. "We didn't say much about it, but each of us was thinking if we found one we would eat it. Three days had passed since our last meager meal. Neither had we had any water to drink.

"During the day it would get so hot I would slip into the water for about twenty minutes at a time to cool off. Oliver never would do that. He just lay on the raft and kept pretty quiet. I knew crazy things were going through his mind just as they were through mine. But we had an understanding soon after we got together that we weren't going to get any silly ideas about one guy knocking the other off or anything like that. You know it happens sometimes. We came to an agreement that no matter how tough it got one wouldn't try anything on the other; wouldn't shove the other over and eat him.

"One morning Oliver found a dead minnow on our raft. He ate the head part and I the tail. We sucked on it for about an hour. Actually, thirst bothered us more than hunger."

And so it continued for three days and four nights, the wishing for nightfall in the relentless heat and praying for daylight as they almost froze in the darkness. Though tortured by the elements and driven to near madness by thirst, their will to survive remained constant.

"Early on the morning of the 28th, just about sunup, I thought I saw smoke in the distance toward the west. Oliver saw nothing. Then the smoke was gone. I feared my mind was cracking. Earlier I had heard a whistle which he didn't hear.

"About ten o'clock he jumped up all excited and said he saw six columns of smoke. I looked and saw them too; they were as plain as day. We just watched and watched.

"We were drifting in an easterly direction and the smoke was coming toward us. It passed us to the north and then a little later it would be headed our way again. Then it would pass and be directly behind us. Every time it would pass we would feel awful. We kept telling each other we hoped it was an American ship, but didn't care if it was Japanese as long as it picked us up.

"Finally we saw the smoke stacks and then the hulls. It was a convoy and was zigzagging; that's why they would first come our direction and then turn and go away. Finally one of the ships pulled out and headed for us. It came pretty close and I started waving the stick with my shorts on it.

"The ship came within twenty yards; obviously to see what we were. It slowed down and I swam after it. There were sailors along the deck. I was afraid they would do what the cruiser had done before—sail away and leave us. But someone threw over a tie-line. It was about two inches out of my reach and I swam like mad until I was exhausted. I yelled in my best Japanese for the guys not to play around. I feared they were just playing games and had no intention of rescuing us.

"The ship was going slow. Finally a sailor dropped a heavy line to me and I grabbed it, but I couldn't shinny up with one hand—the broken hand was useless. I asked them to pull me up, but they let me hang there for a while. Seemed like a long time, but I guess it wasn't more than a minute."

When they were finally hauled aboard, barnacles on the hull of the ship tore into their sunburned flesh. This caused additional misery, but at least they had been rescued from the sea.

Once aboard they were questioned, but the Japanese wouldn't believe their story. "We told them that we were prisoners of war aboard a Japanese ship which had been sunk by an American submarine, but they preferred to think that we were sailors from an American sub which had been hit by their navy."

The two rescued prisoners had no clothes on at all. The Japanese finally gave them each a loin cloth (g-string) but that was all. They were terribly thirsty and kept begging for water. Finally they got about a demitasse full for the two of them. They kept begging for more. After about an hour they were given some steaming hot broth in small cans. "I knew it would burn me, but I drank it anyhow," said Brodsky. "It burned all the way down, but it helped."

It was about 1:30 in the afternoon when they were picked up. After about two hours they were fed some rice and water. All this time they had been standing on deck. At intervals they were questioned all over again. "We told the same true story over and over; that we were prisoners from a Japanese ship and that we had been drifting around in the sea for four days without food or drink. They would shake their heads and wander off.

"Late in the afternoon it grew cold and I began to shiver," said Brodsky. "I shook and my teeth chattered worse than ever in my life. When the petty officer saw that, he must have taken pity, for he gave us some woolen sailor uniforms.

"Our bodies were caked and scabbed and cracked from sunburn and salt water. Some of the scabs were as big as my hand and the raw spots ran pus and blood. The heavy wool uniforms made our hides burn all the more, but we were cold and had to put them on. We couldn't stand up, sit or lie down with any comfort at all. However, our fatigue overcame the discomfort and we stretched out on the steel deck anyhow."

In spite of their extreme discomfort, they finally went to sleep and slept until dawn. Then they got out in the morning sun to get warm once more. Shortly after sunup they were fed another meal of rice and water. By then they could see land. Their ship, a destroyer, headed for a harbor. They dropped anchor about 7 A.M. The prisoners learned that it was Takao on the island of Formosa. There they were taken ashore and turned over to military authorities. Miraculously, they had survived over a hundred hours in the water without food or drink and an additional eighteen hours of misery on the steel deck of a destroyer with very little attention.

At the end of the ordeal, Brodsky weighed about eighty pounds, less than half his prewar weight, and Oliver much less than that.

Once ashore, the prisoners had to go through questioning all over again. Oliver explained who they were and what had happened to their ship. The Japanese didn't believe the story. They seemed to want to believe that the two were sailors from an American submarine which had been sunk by the Japanese. When Oliver stuck to his story they cuffed him around, evidently not liking the idea that one of their ships had been torpedoed by Americans.

When Brodsky asked for water the guard brought them cups of hot tea. He asked for more and they refilled the cups four or five times. A little later the guard brought in a generous portion of rice and squash soup and they got full stomachs for the first time in months.

Soon a high ranking officer came in. He jabbered with the guard in Japanese for a while and then the questioning started all over again. The officer didn't accept their story. He rattled his sabre in a threatening manner. Both prisoners were blindfolded and led down the hallway. Without warning they came to a stairway. Brodsky says when he hit the first step it nearly jarred his teeth out. The guard was holding to the back of his jacket and kept him from falling. He was forced down two or three more steps and then turned around and marched back to the office.

In the office the blindfolds were removed and the officer took out his sabre and made threatening gestures. The guard unsheathed his knife and pressed it against Brodsky's throat.

"No doubt these antics were intended to scare us into saying what they wanted us to say," said Brodsky. "But I wasn't too frightened. Being as miserable as I was at the time I guess it just didn't matter too much one way or the other. I really didn't think they would cut my head off."

The guards began pushing the prisoners around some more and one said, "How about if we kill you now?"

Brodsky raised his chin as if to say "Go ahead and do it."

"He told us to sit down and the two of them walked away jabbering. Oliver and I talked a little, wondering if they really would kill us. He thought they might. They returned and put the blindfolds back on us again. They then led us out and down the hall where they met some other Japanese. They stopped and chatted for a while and then turned around and brought us back.

"When they took the blinders off this time there was another American prisoner in the room. His name was Charles Bender. He looked about as emaciated and scabby as we, and I could tell he had been afloat for a while, too. He had a heavy growth of beard and said he was Navy."

The three prisoners were then blindfolded again and led to the bottom of the stairs. They were then told to turn around and line up.

"We then heard rifle bolts clicking, but I still felt it was a show. Bender believed the worst and it did sound serious," said Brodsky.

Again nothing happened. Brodsky was then told to start walking. After a short distance he was halted. While he waited the other two went through the same thing.

Back together again, still blindfolded, they were marched for about fifteen minutes on a gravel road. A truck drove up and they were loaded into it. "I was hit in the stomach and dragged into the back of the truck. The dragging scraped our sores and it hurt like hell," says Brodsky.

"We rode for quite a distance sitting in the middle of the truck bed. We couldn't tell whether it had sides or not, so there was the worry of falling off. As we rode along, Bender grabbed my arm and began calling me 'Chaplain.' The guard told us to stop talking. We fell silent. Oliver was very quiet all the while. He seemed to be all right and to have all his senses," said Brodsky.

After about twenty minutes of riding, during which railroad tracks were crossed several times, the truck stopped and they were taken into a building. There they were ushered into an office where an officer sat behind a desk. From there they were taken down a hall and had their blindfolds removed. Now they were in front of cells which had bamboo bars.

Brodsky's cell was five feet wide and twenty feet long. At the back was a straddle trench for a latrine. Two Japanese or Formosan coolies were in the cell. They had heavy blankets. The coolies were told to give him one, which they did.

It was extremely hot. Brodsky took off his jacket. The guard outside poked a bayonet at him and ordered him to put it back on, which he did. He ordered Brodsky come forward and reached in and began slapping him. Brodsky backed away.

"He ordered me again to come forward. I wouldn't. He then made me kneel and had the coolies pile blankets on top of me. I was made to kneel for the rest of the night. The place was filled with mosquitos. It was a miserable, hot night."

The following morning the prisoners, one at a time, were handcuffed, blindfolded and marched up three flights of stairs to a room for questioning. There were two civilians in the room, one an old man who acted as interpreter and the other who appeared to be an investigator. The old man spoke English fluently and was very understanding and sympathetic. They wanted to hear the whole story from start to end and seemed satisfied.

After the questioning session they were brought back to the cell row and fed a breakfast of rice, a slice of cucumber and hot tea. By now there was a fourth American prisoner. His name was Hughes. He came from somewhere else and had not been on the *Arisan Maru*.

Their hot woolen uniforms were now exchanged for light Japanese army cottons. Next they were blindfolded, handcuffed and marched out to a truck again. After a short ride the truck stopped and the prisoners were told to step down. Brodsky stepped but his feet didn't touch bottom. Two men caught him and lowered him the rest of the way. He was told to sit.

"I could hear the others being handled in the same rough way. When we were all down, I heard a motor start up and I knew we were in a small boat. After a ten-minute ride our blindfolds were removed.

"We were alongside a merchant ship. It was the one which had left Manila October 1 and detoured by way of Hong Kong and took thirty-nine days to get to Formosa. It was now docked in the harbor at Takao awaiting clearance to sail on to Japan."

The four prisoners were taken from the small boat and put on the deck of the freighter. It was very hot as they sat in the sun. Glancing down into the hold, they could see American prisoners.

"While we were sitting there an American came by with a bucket of rice," said Brodsky. "His name was Fox. I remembered him from Palawan. A few minutes later I saw another one named Henderson. They were on chow detail. I could tell they recognized me, even though they said nothing. I, too, was afraid to say anything or to give any sign with the guards watching."

They sat there in the hot sun until noon. An American officer came up and got permission for them to move to a shady place. He warned them that they were not to speak to anyone who came up to the latrine or to show any sign of recognition. If they did, he warned, the Japs might shoot them.

They stayed on deck for four or five days without any communication with the other Americans below. A doctor and medical sergeant were allowed to come up and check them over, but didn't do much for them.

"After we were there about six days, the Japs decided to try to make it to Japan. In spite of our not having been allowed to speak to anybody all that time, they now sent us below in the midst of all of them.

"The hatch covers were put in place and tied down with cables. There was only two to three inches of space between the planks. If anything had happened we could never have gotten out," says Brodsky.

The ship sailed out of port that afternoon and continued underway for about twenty-four hours. Evidently considering the waters too dangerous, the captain turned around and returned to port.

After two more days at anchor, the prisoners were unloaded, taken ashore and loaded on a train. Enroute they were organized into groups and placed in three separate camps.

"Doctors and sick men were to go to a camp at Skirakawa. The only one of the four of us who had boarded ship at Takao to go there was Hughes, whose condition had deteriorated badly. We learned later that Hughes died in that camp. Oliver, Bender and I, along with four hundred others, went to Taihoku in central Formosa. There being no officers, Bender, who was a Navy warrant officer, was placed in charge."

A twenty-four-hour train ride brought the group of four hundred prisoners to a camp near Taihoku in central Formosa. The place was clean and there was ample room. There was straw on the floors for bedding and each man was issued four blankets.

Though there were no doctors, one building had been fixed up as a hospital. Brodsky, Oliver and Bender were assigned there. There was no medicine, so their only treatment was rest. But at least they didn't have to work for a while. After three weeks of rest, Brodsky was returned to duty. There being nothing to do as a medic, he joined a carpenter crew.

In December, 1944, American planes began bombing the area quite regularly. Often the raids were so frequent that it was not possible to prepare meals. The camp was never hit, but the threat was always present. In late January, 1945, the Japanese decided to move the prisoners at Taihoku and ship them to Japan. This entailed another long train ride to a port up north. Brodsky, Oliver and Bender hated the thought of another dangerous and horrible sea voyage, but worse, like all the others, they knew that being moved to Japan would end the hope of freedom until war's end.

At the dock they were joined by men from other camps. Once loaded aboard ship, they waited for several days before sailing. Meantime, forty men came down with encephalitis, a very contagious brain disease. The Japanese decided to move the ill men ashore. One doctor and three medical men were chosen to go with and care for them. Brodsky was among the three medics and Captain Coons the doctor.

Most of the sick men died at the quarantine station where they were isolated. Those who recovered and the medical staff were moved to another camp near Taihoku, where they remained until May. This camp was populated with British military prisoners from Singapore.

In May, Brodsky and two other Americans were moved to a coal mining camp in the mountains. The work force was made up of British. Altogether there were six Americans in the detail: two doctors, Captains Snyder and Kern, and four medical enlisted men: Bob Paradise, Alexandro Ensinus, Joe Candrasowitz and Sergeant Philip Brodsky.

For a month or so Brodsky worked at building huts. Later he was changed to farm duties. The work was hard and the hours from sunup to sundown. Treatment was rough and the food scarce and of poor quality. The death rate was high. With that strong determination to survive, Brodsky plodded along, until suddenly on August 18 work details were called off. The Japanese gave no explanation.

"We figured the war was over, for planes had been flying over and bombing the area frequently, unopposed. Finally the camp commandant told us that peace negotiations were underway." The camp was at Tinsen, Formosa. They were marched to a place near Tishoku and quartered in a compound fenced with bamboo and barbed wire. There the food rations improved considerably and the prisoners were no longer required to work. Physical treatment was much better.

"Eventually, American planes flew over and dropped drums of food, clothing and medicines. In some cases the parachutes failed to open and the drums plunged through the roof of the barracks, killing a few men and injuring others. Being a medical man, I had a right busy time taking care of the injured," says Brodsky.

On August 28, the Japanese authorized the removal of the injured to a hospital. Brodsky went with them. Only a few Americans were in the hospital.

On September 7, 1945, an American plane came in to rescue the prisoners. Seven men on litters, accompanied by Brodsky, boarded the transport plane that day and five hours later landed in Manila, free men once again.

12. Ordeal by Water

Just before the escape of Captain Wohlfeld and eleven others at Davao in March, 1944, the Japanese camp commander had called for 650 volunteers to go out to another location on a permanent work detail. Only 50 signed up. The other 600 had to be drafted. Air Corps Private Victor Mapes of St. Cloud, Florida, was among the volunteers. He figured that food and working conditions might be better in a smaller camp. At any rate he was tired of bogging in the mud day after day holding a carabao-pulled plow preparing ground for rice planting. His subsequent adventures, related to me after the war, contribute one incredible story of human endurance.

Mapes and his fellow prisoners soon found themselves hard at work building a military airfield for the Japanese. The location was near Davao City and not more than thirty kilometers from DAPECOL, from where they had moved. It was soon evident that there was a great urgency on the part of the Japanese to get the airstrip in operation. The work, being of the wheelbarrow, pick and shovel type, was hard and the hours were long. The prisoners were closely guarded. The food ration was neither more nor better than at DAPECOL and the strenuous labor caused more weight loss by the men.

With trees and brush cleared away for some distance around the field and guards posted around the perimeter, there was no chance to escape. To make it even tougher, additional guards

First Regiment Staff,
Corps of Cadets,
Clemson College,
1940. Manny Law-
ton is second from
right.

Lt. Henry D. Leitner
and bride of ten
days, San Francisco,
1940.

American prisoners being marched in captivity by their Japanese conquerors, Philippine Islands. *Courtesy NBC-TV.*

American and Filipino troops carrying some of their comrades in blankets during the Bataan Death March. *Courtesy NBC-TV.*

Three American prisoners, hands tied behind their backs, during Death March. *Courtesy Stan Sommers.*

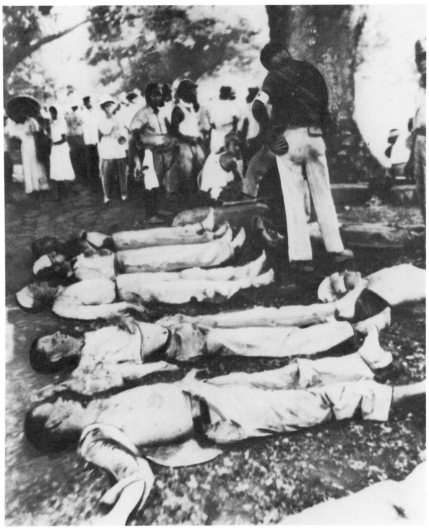

Dead American soldiers lying alongside road during Death March. *Courtesy NBC-TV.*

POWs in Philippines. *Drawing by Ben Steele.*

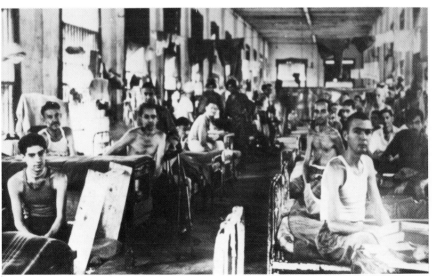

American prisoners in hospital ward, Bilibid, Philippines, 1943. *Courtesy Stan Sommers.*

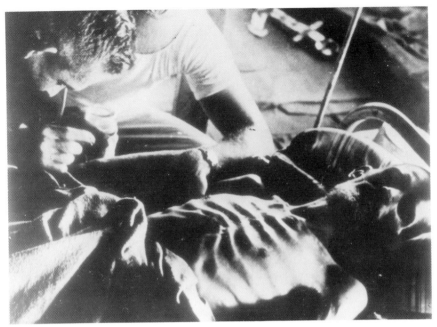

POW suffering from dry beriberi, Bilibid, 1943. *Courtesy Stan Sommers.*

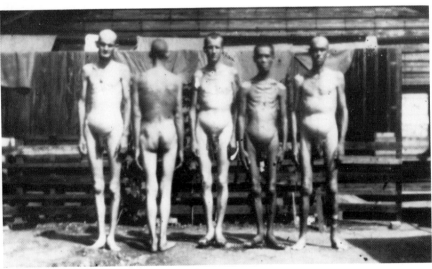

American and Filipino prisoners in Philippines. *Courtesy Stan Sommers.*

Five American ex-POWs immediately after the surrender of Japan, August, 1945. *Courtesy NBC-TV.*

Manny Lawton, three months after being released from captivity and seventy pounds heavier, November, 1945.

Bataan Defenders medal being placed around neck of Manny Lawton by mayor of Manila, 1982.

Manny Lawton standing by kilometer 67, on route of the Death March forty years earlier, Philippines, 1982.

circulated among the prisoners urging them on to greater production. This not only taxed their strength, it also prevented any opportunity to loaf and delay the project. At noon the tired and sweating prisoners sat in the dust under the sweltering sun to eat their small portions of cold rice. It was a tough and miserable existence.

Mapes soon began to regret his move. He longed to be back at DAPECOL driving his carabao in the muddy rice fields. Though he had cursed every mud-laden step he took in preparing the water-covered paddies for rice planting, he could now appreciate that there had been no clouds of choking dust and that the splash of murky water had been cooling to his skin.

Technician 4th Class Cletis O. Overton from Rolla, Arkansas, a member of the Air Corps, was also among the 650. Overton soon realized that work on the vegetable farm at DAPECOL, by comparison, had not been so bad. At least the dirt stirred up by his hoe furnished a cool spot for his feet as he chopped grass from around the plants, and every now and then he could snitch and hurriedly eat a radish or onion when the guard wasn't looking. The guards had been fewer and less strict on the farm and the prisoners could rest in the shade at the end of the row. Here on the airstrip there was no shade and the guards were numerous.

Captain William P. Cain, an infantryman from Columbia, South Carolina, and Captain Eugene P. Dale, a flyer from Enid, Oklahoma, breaking sod and pushing wheelbarrows in the hot, dry dirt, remembered how they splashed water on each other in the rice paddies for its cooling effect, and longed to be doing it once again. They also recalled that the few guards stayed on the dikes to keep their shoes dry while watching over their laborers—a practice which left the prisoners out of reach of cuffing by the guards.

In spite of close surveillance and frequent urgings of "speedo!," the prisoners soon developed the art of appearing to be busy while actually accomplishing very little. It was at a snail's pace that the airstrip gradually took shape. At the end of four months it was far from ready to accommodate aircraft, though its identity could be determined from the air.

One morning in early August there was an air raid alarm. Everyone, including guards, dashed for the woods as the sound of approaching aircraft drew near. Jubilantly the prisoners watched as a flight of American Navy planes made a swoop over the airstrip, unleashing bombs and bullets. No one was hurt, but large craters were blasted into the runway. The Japanese, angered and chagrined, took out their frustration on the prisoners with slaps and kicks as they marched double-time back to barracks.

As a consequence of the air raid, the project was closed down and the prisoners were put on reduced rations for the next three weeks. Finally, just as suddenly as work had been stopped, it was announced that everyone would be shipped out. The following morning, as they stood in formation awaiting marching orders, they were surprised to see guards with long lengths of rope come forward and begin tying the prisoners together. The rope was tied securely around the waist of the lead man of the right file, then looped around the waist of each man behind him in turn, then across the back of the column and up the other outside file and across the front. In this way the two outside files were tied together and the two inside ones boxed in. In this bound and closely guarded condition they were marched to the port several miles away. At the docks they were joined by another group of 100 prisoners from another work project, making their total now 750. Together they were marched into the cargo holds of a Japanese freighter, where it was crowded, dirty and hot.

The ship seemed to sail south for several days and then turned north. Progress was slow. With the ship hugging the irregular coastline by day and anchoring in coves overnight, forward movement was barely perceptible. At the end of ten days they reached Zamboanga, hardly more than two hundred miles from their starting point. There the prisoners were switched to another ship on which conditions in the holds were equally as bad—filthy, sweltering and with little fresh air and light.

After two days at anchor in the harbor, the second ship began its cautious, slow movement northward. It had traveled only a short distance when disaster struck. With a sudden deafening, blinding explosion, one torpedo and then another tore into the side of the prisoner-carrying merchant ship. In the terrible holocaust, bodies were hurled through the air. A few were forced upward by the inrushing water and somehow went through the small hatch opening and ended up above water. Another small number were pushed outward through the gaping holes torn by the blast and found themselves swimming around on the sea's surface. Most of the 750 were either killed instantly by the blast or drowned and went down with the ship. For those who died on the scene, death was quick and merciful. For some of the less than two hundred who surfaced, the struggle for survival during the ensuing twelve to twenty-four hours was hell.

Cletis Overton was fortunate: only slightly dazed from concussion of the exploding torpedoes, he found himself swimming around in the sea with no broken bones or cuts. He had drifted up through the hatchway. Victor Mapes, on the other hand, had serious troubles. In wriggling out through the jagged hole torn by the incoming torpedo, he ended up with a badly mangled leg. Bleeding and in pain, he found it hard to swim at all. Land was more than two miles away. It was late afternoon and darkness would soon erase the sight of it. But like the other floundering survivors, the thought of possible freedom spurred him to almost superhuman effort.

For a while chances looked good. Clinging to hatch covers and bits of debris, the shipwreck survivors paddled in the direction of the distant shore. But soon it was dark. Then, with no moon or stars to guide them, they had to depend on a collective sense of direction. Those with sound limbs did the kicking to propel the makeshift rafts, while the wounded hung on.

There were four or five with Mapes. In spite of the darkness, they were confident that they were making progress toward land. Then suddenly there was panic, as they realized the Japanese were spraying machine gun bullets at them after having picked up their own survivors. Terrified and defenseless, they scattered. It was now every man for himself. As Mapes pulled away, he called to Colonel Colver to join him.

"I'm a doctor," the colonel replied. "These wounded men need me. I must stay with them."

What a courageous and unselfish man, Mapes thought to himself. He has no equipment or medicine, yet he is thinking of duty rather than trying to look out for himself. He was never to see the colonel again.

In the blackness of night, the dispersed survivors, some wounded, most deafened from the explosion, all of them thirsty, hungry, weak and frightened and in a state of shock, paddled off with the determination to reach land. Most didn't. Of the approximately two hundred who surfaced after the shipwreck, only eighty-three touched shore. Of those, one died several days later from wounds and loss of blood. Cletis Overton drifted in during the night to a rocky beach where several buddies welcomed him. He crawled into a cave and slept until dawn.

At dawn, a small group of plucky survivors who had landed nearby and slept in the cave set out in search of food. Things soon began to look brighter, for they found a banana grove and a field of mutton corn and there were no Japanese around. They knew that raw corn and green bananas weren't the ideal diet for empty stomachs, but starving men don't have much willpower when any type of nourishment comes their way; they gorged themselves and later paid for the luxury with upset stomachs. After eating their fill, they returned to the cave, planning to sleep until dusk.

The entrance to the cave was small, hardly more than four feet wide and three feet high. On the inside it widened considerably and ran back about one hundred feet. It was dark and cool; an ideal hiding place. They had no more than settled down for a long rest when their feeling of security was shattered by voices calling to them from outside: "Americans! Americans! Come out. We will help you."

Assuming the visitors to be either Japanese or collaborators, they were frightened and dejected. With no weapons and no secret exit through which to make an escape, there was nothing to do but surrender. Fully expecting to be shot, they straggled out with hands up, feeling like doomed men.

To their great surprise, the strangers proved to be friendly Filipinos whose intention really was to help. A short hike brought them to a home where there was food, drink and a great show of hospitality. Their rescuers were sons and nephews of an elderly lady, who became their hostess and benefactor for a while. The old lady told them that her men had already rescued many of their comrades. Their system was to feed them and to render whatever first aid they could and then to farm them out in groups of two or three to other families; the people were poor and no family could care for a large number. The island was small, so there were no Japanese occupying it. Overton and his comrades now felt secure.

Victor Mapes, after avoiding Japanese machine gun bullets, drifted off into the darkness. Alone and in great pain, he clung to a piece of timber. His ordeal was to be of longer duration and much more agonizing than that of some of his comrades. The broken and painful leg made swimming impossible. He could only hold to the plank and drift with the tide, estimated to be three to four miles per hour.

He hadn't drifted very far when a Japanese launch, searching the water with spotlights, approached. Mapes knew that to be detected would mean sure death for him. Yet to cut loose from the support of his plank would end his chances of reaching shore. He had to make a decision and make it quickly. Which would it be? Death by execution or by drowning?

The searchlight's piercing beam made the decision for him. Just before its rays cut across his location, he relaxed his grip and ducked under the surface of the water. After staying submerged until it felt as if he would suffocate, he popped to the surface to find that the boat had passed.

Now it required great effort to merely stay afloat. After a short interval, which seemed interminable and during which Mapes almost lost hope, he bumped into another piece of debris from the shipwreck. This time it was a board approximately two inches thick, twelve inches wide and ten feet long. Determined to make good use of this second chance, he grasped the plank with both hands, resolving never to let go, no matter what happened.

Exhausted by the frantic effort to keep his head above water while he was without support, Mapes decided to hang to the plank with one hand and let his body float to the surface, relaxed. He soon found that to be unsatisfactory, for the mangled leg, dangling out of control, began to throb and ache. He decided that lying full-length on the board would be better. That, too, proved to be less than completely satisfactory, for before he had worked his body halfway on top of it he found that the board had numerous nail points sticking through both sides. When he attempted to stretch himself out full-length on top of it, the nails tore at his flesh as the waves tossed him about; when he slid back into the water his leg throbbed and pained. As painful as both positions were, he dared not relax his grip on the plank.

For fourteen more hours he was to change back and forth, choosing between the sheer agony of living and the forbidding prospect of dying. Mapes had made his choice and was determined to stick by it; no matter what, the cost would be paid in extreme suffering. Unable to propel himself because of his injury, he had no control over time or direction. Almost like a lifeless object, he could only drift with the flow of the ocean. For several hours at a stretch, the tide nudged him gradually toward shore, and then, for an equal amount of time, it pushed him seaward.

Miserable in any position, he alternated between lying on his barbed bed of nails to rest and hanging in the water until the throb of the dangling limb forced him up again. At times he wished fervently that a shark would come along and tear the offending limb from his body. It was the pain of it, no doubt, that kept him awake and trying throughout the chilling night and into the merciless heat of the following day.

With the bright light of sunup, he could see the distant palm tree-lined shore once again. It seemed no closer than at sunset the day before. A glance around him in every direction revealed nothing else afloat—no life, no boat. Before the sun was two hours high, it seemed that its rays began to pierce his skin like needles. The glare on the water forced his eyelids almost shut. Soon his skin and eyes began to burn. Easing from the board into the water gave no relief. Then he realized he was in the middle of a large oil slick. When he finally drifted out of it two hours later, he was severely blistered.

Fortunately for Mapes, the coastline jutted out seaward ahead, in the direction in which he was going. Otherwise he might have perished within sight of land without ever having reached it. Even so, it was nearly noon before he was close enough to attract attention from the beach. To his great relief, two fishermen came out in a small outrigger sailboat and rescued him.

Although grateful for having been saved from a miserable death, he had some doubts about the intentions of his benefactors. He couldn't understand their language, and they spoke no English. Since he was aboard ship for nearly two weeks, he feared that it might have been in Japanese waters when sunk and that the fishermen were taking him in to turn him over to the Japs. As they neared land, he had an additional shock; a Jap flag fluttered in the breeze atop a tall pole.

"My God!" thought Mapes. "After all that ordeal, here I am back where I was before, a prisoner all over again!"

Upon reaching shore, he was greeted by a small group of friendly people, some of whom spoke English. They assured him that they were Filipino allies and wanted to do anything they could for Americans. "There are no Japanese here. We fly their flag to fool them in case they do come around."

When informed where he was, he estimated that he had drifted approximately thirty miles in his eighteen-hour ordeal at sea.

Just as other Filipinos had done for Overton and his friends at a different location, so did these do for Mapes. They moved him to the village headman's home where he was the guest of honor.

They bathed him and rubbed coconut oil on his parched body. An abundance of food was brought to him—bananas, mangos, papayas, boiled eggs, fish, rice. He ate and drank like the starving, dehydrated man that he was. He thanked them and he thanked God.

The small village was isolated from the populated centers of the island; consequently it was of no importance to the Japanese. Mapes learned that the Japanese seldom came there, and when they did they arrived by boat and could be seen well in advance of actual landing.

Well fed and out of reach of the enemy, he felt secure, but his leg grew worse. The broken bones ached and the ugly gashes became infected and filled with maggots. A Filipino doctor from a neighboring town came to see him. His medical knowledge seemed adequate, but his supply of drugs was extremely limited. With common sense and home remedies, the doctor did what he could. Hot soaks seemed to help, but nothing brought about a cure. The doctor even tried intravenous injections of mother's milk, hoping it would combat the infection. Finally he decided the leg would have to be amputated, but Mapes wouldn't agree to that. In thinking about the ordeal later, Mapes is convinced that nourishing food and the untiring efforts of the Filipino doctor saved his life by slowing down the advance of gangrene.

Approximately one week after being rescued by their Filipino friends, Mapes and 81 other survivors were taken aboard an American submarine one night. They were all who remained alive of the 750 aboard the Japanese freighter when the torpedoes hit; 668 had perished.

During a five-day underwater trip to New Guinea, a Navy corpsman doctored Mapes with hot soaks and sulfa drugs, but that, too, seemed to be only a delaying action; pain and infection remained with him and the odor of gangrene was extremely offensive. At New Guinea, Mapes was hospitalized, while the others continued on their homeward journey. He felt he was left there to die. But that was not to be. Within a few days his despondency was replaced by new hope. Where mother's milk, hot soaks and sulfa had failed, the new wonder drug, penicillin, worked like magic. The infection soon began to subside. The doctors cut away the decayed flesh and cleaned up the wound. Within three weeks he was on the way to Australia by air.

In Australia, where the military had the best of modern equipment and drugs, the doctors operated on his leg twice over several weeks. Each time they removed fragments of chipped bone, and each time they advised amputation. Mapes refused to give his consent. The thought of having a part of his body cut away was frightening. He was determined, no matter the pain, to go home a whole man.

Those two operations marked the beginning of more than a half-dozen which would extend over a period of several years. Mapes left Australia around Thanksgiving of 1944. It had been two months since he drifted ashore in Zamboanga. His shipmates reached home a month ahead of him. In San Francisco, the doctors removed the cast, cleaned the wound, took out more chipped bone, and recommended amputation. Mapes stood by his decision to save his limb, and would not consent.

For the following three years Mapes was in and out of hospitals in the Washington, D.C., area. With the same dogged determination which had gotten him ashore after shipwreck, he clung to the hope that his leg could be saved. The bones eventually knitted back, but certain spots of the flesh continued to drain and refused to heal.

Finally in 1947, one of the doctors who had worked on him in Australia came on the scene. "There is a chance that I can cure you with a skin graft," said the doctor. "It will take a year and will be painful and annoying. If you are willing to go through with it, we will try."

"That's the first encouraging news I've heard yet," said Mapes. "When do we start?"

It did prove to be painful and slow and nerve-wracking. First the doctor peeled a thin layer of skin eight inches square from his stomach. This he rolled into a sausage shape, leaving the two ends attached to the stomach until they began to grow naturally into the flesh. Then he took one end loose and attached it to the palm of Mapes' hand, allowing several weeks for it to knit. Next, the other end was detached and grafted to the upper leg, as far down as Mapes' hand could reach comfortably. By that slow and tedious process, skin from his stomach eventually replaced the leg flesh which would not heal. The graft proved successful and the patient eventually went back to full duty.

Mapes retired from the Air Force in 1971 as a master sergeant. He had completed twenty-two years of active service. During those years he completed his education at the University of Maryland, traveled extensively, and learned to savor every minute of life given to him. Few men have been or will ever be called upon to face the agonies, the horrors and discouragements he has known. And if they should, few would possess the courage and the tenacity to overcome them.

13. Hell Ship #1—The *Oryoku Maru*

Those of us at Cabanatuan continued to work in the rice fields with high spirits and great hope. We were confident that the war would soon be over or that a rescue team would be sent in to rescue us. Though there was always the fear that the Japanese would slaughter us rather than let us be taken away from them, our optimism overrode that fear. After all, optimism was what had kept us alive for the past three years.

On October 7, 1944, those hopes were suddenly dashed. We received orders to prepare to move. Everyone was stunned and frightened.

"What are they trying to do?" asked Henry in shocked disbelief. "With American planes flying everywhere, don't they know that a convoy will be hit along the road?"

"Maybe they're afraid that guerrilla forces will raid the camp and free us," I said. "For some strange reason it's extremely important to them to keep us under their control."

"Well, at any rate," observed Bill English, "Manila is as far as they can take us. All the bombers we've seen in the past few weeks have certainly finished off their merchant ships."

Morale sank to the lowest point since the fall of Bataan. In spite of hard labor and the scarcity of food, we had been cheerful during the past several months. The war news was becoming increasingly better. The Japanese were on the run, and their days of dominance and brutality were rapidly drawing to a close. Freedom seemed to be within our grasp. Now those dreams vanished.

When we had left Cabanatuan before, I was glad to go, for any move held hopes of improvement. Now, travel itself was dangerous, and prospects for better conditions bleak. With the enemy losing the war, food would become more scarce, and, facing defeat, the Japanese would become more irrational and unpredictable. Even now there was the frightening possibility that they might be taking us out for a massacre.

It was deathly quiet as we sat around idle the next day contemplating the hazards which lay ahead. Cabanatuan, the hated, death dealing pesthole with its ugly, defying barbed wire, suddenly seemed not so bad now. If only we could remain there for another month or two, things might end happily.

Bill English, usually cheerful, appeared noticeably blue and downcast. His striking blue eyes, framed by dark hair, stared into the distance as if seeing things beyond our ken. His brow furrowed and his lips tightened. "We are doomed," he said sadly. "We'll never make it."

Japanese guards stared down on the camp from the corner towers. At the gate and along the fence the complement of sentries had been doubled. It was always that way before a move; escape must be prevented.

The following morning at dawn, everyone physically able to travel was crowded into trucks and shipped out. It was late October. Left behind were approximately five hundred hospital patients who looked as if they were destined to join the nearly three thousand already buried in the prison cemetery. A seven-hour ride, with much discomfort but no mishaps, terminated at the gates of Bilibid Prison in Manila. Strangely, there were no American aircraft in the skies. The sight of the old prison was depressing. Having been there twice before, I knew well its scarcity of food, its walled-in isolation, and the discomfort of sleeping on hard cement floors.

Upon arrival, we found several hundred other American prisoners and a small number of Dutch and British, the latter from shipwrecks, the Americans from various work details. Most were in very poor physical condition. From them we learned that all of us were to go to Japan.

Everyone became increasingly depressed as the weeks dragged by. Food, one teacup of boiled rice twice a day, was far below subsistence level. Weight loss and further weakness were very noticeable. The thick, ten-foot-tall brick wall enclosing the prison made seeing out or even hearing the city noises impossible. Had we not seen it on the way in, we would not have known that a crowded metropolis of over a million people existed just beyond the walls. Isolation, boredom and anxiety crowded in on us as never before. Idleness made it worse.

Other than talking of home and food and praying that no ships could get into port to take us to Japan, the main pastime was swapping recipes. From that developed a daily lecture series. At ten o'clock each morning all hands assembled in a large second story room. Sitting in a semicircle on the floor with pencil and note paper, we listened entranced as some expert reviewed the tantalizing details of preparing, cooking and tasting a savory dish. We heard and made note of palate teasing delicacies from every land and every region of the United States: Italian, Polish, Greek, French, German, we eagerly heard them all. Never tiring of listening, we firmly believed we would spend the rest of our days, once home, ceremoniously preparing and gluttonously devouring gourmet dishes. Had the compound been divided into various places of amusement for the benefit of prisoners, I am sure that not even a girlie show would have distracted anyone's attention from the dream world of food.

For several weeks there was no aerial activity, then suddenly the wail of sirens warned us of an air raid. The Yanks had returned! From second story windows we had grandstand seats from which to watch dive bombers roar down in screaming attacks on enemy shipping in Manila Bay. One after another, from an altitude of 5,000 feet, they peeled off and went into dives which took them below the city's skyline. ZZZZZMMMMM went the high-pitched engines; KRUMPH! KRUMPH! the thunderous explosions. So steep and so long were their dives that we feared they would not pull out in time, but they did. It was the first time we had witnessed our Navy aircraft in combat action. It was a beautiful and heartening sight. From our vantage point ten blocks away, we applauded as each steel-nerved hero reinforced our hope that there would be no ship left to transport us to the enemy homeland.

As if their mission was completed and there were no more targets to be hit, the Navy discontinued its flights around December 1. For two weeks all was quiet in the air. Though still facing the doubtful possibility that the Japanese might get a ship in and out of the harbor, we felt reasonably secure. There were various opinions. Optimists firmly believed the day of liberation was imminent; pessimists dared not build themselves up for another disappointment.

"It would be foolish for them to attempt maritime movement, even if they have anything left that will float," observed Lieutenant Commander Frank Bridget. "We haven't seen a Japanese plane in the air for months. Our boys have complete control of the skies."

Bridget was small, short, had black hair and a full mustache. Energetic, nervous and quick of movement, he spoke with conviction. A Navy flyer with combat experience, his opinions carried weight. I was sold on his line of reasoning until Colonel Dave Hardee, a tall, lean senior officer from Raleigh, North Carolina, spoke up. "Don't sell those Japs short on recklessness and stupidity," he said. "They are famous for attempting wild things. Remember how they would send a whole platoon of men charging into a machine gun nest?"

Bridget proved to be entirely wrong. On December 13, 1944, a group of 1,619 of us, including Bridget, found our names on the list to go. The announcement was both heartbreaking and frightening. To go now would mean many more months, or even years, before we would be free. The trip itself would be hard and hazardous, with a more than fifty percent chance of being sunk at sea.

At the last minute before departure, I stopped by the sick ward to say goodbye to several friends who were too ill to make the trip. Among them was Colonel Hardee. Remembering that his home was no more than 300 miles from mine, I asked him to forward a note to my mother. With tears in his eyes and a prayer for my safety, he said with deep feeling, "I'll be glad to, Manny. But let's hope they don't get you out and we will all get home together." (Colonel Hardee was among the three hundred rescued by American Rangers only six weeks after our departure. He delivered the note to my grateful family six months before I returned.)

We left Bilibid Prison for the last time on December 13, 1944, on foot. Stumbling over broken pavement of war-scarred streets, I felt like a condemned man walking the last mile. Filipinos along the sidewalk, silhouetted against burned buildings, attempted to flash signs of hope to us. There was little hope in my prisoner's heart. Our destination could only be worse than the miserable place we were leaving. Ahead of us lay 1,500 miles of submarine infested sea and skies constantly patrolled by American bombers. All of us hated the thought of going to Japan, but more than that we knew that death would stalk every mile of this reckless attempt to reach its inhospitable shores.

A hot, fatiguing four-kilometer march through war-ravaged Manila brought us to pier 7 on the waterfront. With its long row of steel warehouses and loading platforms, pier 7 had been known as the million dollar pier in prewar days. Nearby Manila Hotel, in all its majesty and beauty, still stood undamaged. Cargo buildings and docks were only slightly damaged, suggesting that both sides had spared them for their own future use.

Manila Bay, with scores of ghostly looking wrecked ships, told a different story. Both nearby and far out into the twenty miles of blue water could be seen bomb-blasted, rusting hulks of transports and warships, some listing heavily, some upright with water washing over their decks, while others could be identified only by smokeless stacks reaching helplessly toward the sky. It was not unlikely that many more lay hidden below the surface.

At pier 7, we were marched into a large warehouse of metal construction and told to sit and wait. A cool breeze flowed in through the open doorways, giving us relief from the body heat generated on the march. Some of the men overflowed onto the pier. Fortunately the hot sun had begun its descent, leaving us on the shady side of the building.

As I sat there uneasily waiting but much cooler, I kept looking at a ship tied up to the dock in front of our position. It was a passenger ship with the name *Oryoku Maru* printed on its sides. The thought struck me that with a little crowding, there was sufficient room for our entire group of 1,619 to be loaded into the first and second class space aboard. If this turned out to be true, it would mark the first time in all of our travels that we had been treated so well.

Soon, however, those hopes were dashed as we watched other passengers being loaded into the upper decks. In family groups, hundreds of Japanese began loading. We assumed they were diplomatic personnel and wealthy business people, for the ship's captain and all his staff were bowing to them and escorting each group to their quarters aboard. The exodus of so many important people meant that Japan was losing the war.

Prisoners began loading around 1 P.M. Guards hurried us across the deck and down a stairway into the holds. Those who didn't move quickly enough, whether crippled or not, even the obviously ill, were given severe clubbings, in spite of the fact that they should have been hospital cases.

Once on deck we were herded toward a small open hatch, down from which a stairway extended some thirty feet into a darkened hold. At the bottom of the stairway four guards were busy crowding reluctant prisoners into the inadequate space. One, who seemed to be in charge, was armed with a sword; the other three wielded brooms. The sword bearer waved his weapon in the direction in which we were to move; the other three, swinging their brooms energetically, nudged us tighter and tighter into space which rapidly became overcrowded. On the partially shaded dock the temperature was 90 degrees; on the sun-drenched steel deck, 100; halfway down the ladder it was hotter still and in the hold it felt like 120. Body heat from the crowded, sweating men made it even worse. Enclosed by thick plate steel on all sides, we felt as if we were trapped in an oven. On the western side of the ship where the afternoon sun bore down, the metal was too hot to touch. Save for the eight-by-ten-foot open hatch through which we had descended, there were no openings for light or air to get in. The air soon grew foul and its oxygen diluted. Breathing became difficult.

The loading process was slow. It took an hour and a half to fill hold #1 alone. In the semidarkness, it was hard to estimate how much space there was. My guess was forty feet by eighty feet, making 3,200 square feet on the floor. In addition, a deck or platform five feet above the floor extended from the sides inward nine feet toward the center. This increased the floor space by less than fifty percent, bringing the total to around 4,000 square feet. In that amount of room two hundred and fifty men could have had room to lie down simultaneously. Into it eight hundred gasping, sweltering prisoners were jammed. Most were officers. Their ranks ranged from Army and Marine lieutenant colonels and Navy commanders to lieutenants and ensigns. But rank and authority lost their meanings as tempers grew short and men became desperate for space to stand and even for air to breathe.

Henry and I stuck together, holding onto each other so as not to be separated by the crunch of bodies. Hot, sweating bodies, recoiling like panic-stricken animals from the blows of Japanese guards, pushed us tighter into the darkness. We ended up at the very back end of the ship. Both the upper and lower bays were crowded with exhausted bodies laboring for breath. We found a small space on an upper bay and sat with our legs dangling down.

"We'll all suffocate if they don't pump some fresh air into this place," said Henry, with short, halting speech. Sweat dripped from his face. His clothes were soaking wet.

"Just hang on, buddy. Don't move or talk any more than necessary. We will make it somehow," I tried to reassure him. I, too, was weak and wet and laboring for breath, but I knew that anxiety would only increase our problems. The lack of oxygen soon affects the human brain as well as the rest of the body; aside from making breathing difficult, the lack of it causes one to think less clearly. Some of us passed out, some began to talk incoherently, and others stared blankly.

Sweat drained from every pore in my body. Within minutes I was drenched, as if sitting in a pool of water. Instinctively I reached for my canteen, but fortunately came to my senses before gulping it all down. Knowing that the prospects for getting more water were slight, I cautioned Henry to drink sparingly.

While the eight hundred were shifting and jockeying for space in #1, the guards shifted their attention to #3, the forward hold, where they crowded in six hundred junior officers and enlisted men. Conditions there were equally as terrible. Into the center hold, #2, much smaller but with better ventilation, slightly over two hundred enlisted men and civilians were loaded.

Our ship was the *Oryoku Maru*, a fairly new passenger liner converted to troop transport. In prewar days it had been a luxury liner catering to the leisure class. On this day its passenger quarters, though somewhat crowded, probably had such an atmosphere. In its staterooms important families were quartered. Below deck, in stark contrast, 1,619 crowded, thirsty, miserable prisoners of war struggled for life. Ahead for them lay agony, terror and madness undreamed of; for many, death became a welcomed relief.

Around 5 P.M. the *Oryoku Maru* weighed anchor and began its cautious exit from Manila Bay. The ship's movement brought no improvement in air or temperature. Instead of decreasing as hoped for, the heat seemed to build up. Prisoners began to yell and beg for water. Mr. Wada, the hunchback, leaned over the hatch opening and ordered us to be silent.

"There is no water for you," he shouted. "If you do not remain quiet I will close the hatch!"

His threat brought no cessation in the loud chant "Water! Water! Air! Water!" It became a deafening defiant roar. We should have remembered that the hateful interpreter was a vengeful man, but desperate men are seldom ruled by reason. The hatch cover was dropped over the opening with a loud bang. This brought near panic among us.

The cry for water continued as bodies steamed and voices grew hoarse. Tempers flared as frightened, unreasoning men pushed, struck, and cursed one another. No single voice was strong enough to be heard or commanding enough to be heeded. The situation became chaotic and dangerous. Suddenly two courageous officers rushed up the stairway and pushed the hatch cover slightly open. That brought some relief, but the noise continued.

Again, the voice of the sadistic Mr. Wada was heard; this time with an even more drastic threat. "You are disturbing the Japanese women and children. If you do not shut up I will order the guards to shoot into the hold!"

That startling announcement brought relative quiet. Commander Frank Bridget, a decorated Navy pilot, took advantage of the lull and made his move to restore some semblance of order. Standing halfway up the stairs, he pleaded, "Gentlemen, we must all settle down. If each man remains calm and still it will be better for all. The more you move, the more energy you burn. That weakens you. The more you talk and yell, the more oxygen you use up. That hurts everybody." Everyone listened calmly to his cool-headed logic.

As often happens in times of dire emergency or great public need, someone standing in the wings can step forward and take command. Often he may be the most unlikely prospect. So it was now. I personally never cared much for Bridget before. He had always appeared too nervous and intense and eager. Perhaps my lack of esteem for him traced back to Davao, when I overslept one morning. Bridget was barracks leader. At roll call he was one man short. Excited and frightened, he rushed into the barracks shouting "Roll call! Roll call! Is anybody in here?"

The noise awakened me. As I sat up he stood over me bellowing, "You stupid S.O.B. Get the hell out of here. Are you trying to get me killed?" I dashed out to formation just as the Japs entered the compound. The incident was never mentioned again, but until this moment I had harbored a feeling toward him less than kindly. Now, in an instant, his moment of greatness had arrived, and he handled it with calmness, courage and authority.

"Now hear this," Bridget continued in the traditional Navy call to attention, "The men in the far corners are suffocating. Take off your shirts and fan the air toward them."

Many responded. With caps and shirts swaying back and forth, they stirred the air, pushing that which was less foul toward the back bays. It helped.

With that degree of progress accomplished, Bridget became more confident and aggressive. Climbing to the top of the stairs, under the very muzzles of Japanese rifles, he practically demanded relief for his dying men.

"Mr. Wada, the lack of air is killing men down here. We will all die if you don't do something immediately. Let us put the worst cases on deck for a while."

Wada no doubt remembered Bridget as a good barracks leader in Davao. After consultation with Lieutenant Toshino, he surprisingly agreed. "You may bring four at a time," he informed Bridget. "Any who attempt to escape wirr be shoot," he warned sternly.

Guards removed the hatch cover. A ray of light from the sinking sun pierced the darkness of our floating dungeon; with it small whiffs of fresh air drifted down. Those around the base of the stairs could smell the difference. In the far corners the absence of darkness was the only improvement.

Bridget: "Pass the unconscious men toward the center so that they may be moved topside."

As if by magic, things calmed down and there was a mood of cooperation. Gasping, almost lifeless bodies from the back bays were handed forward to waiting upraised hands which eased them to other hands. The near dead victims of oxygen shortage drifted across the heads of seated comrades like caterpillars with hundreds of feet. A dozen or more, mostly senior officers, were in that way moved to the center. The four worst cases were handed to men seated on the stairway who eased them up to the hatch opening; there two prisoners dragged them to the center of the deck. A few minutes in the fresh air revived them and they climbed back down into the hold so that four more could take their places. Not only did this save the lives of some who surely would have died, but it also served to make Wada and Toshino aware of what was happening below.

Just before darkness swept away the last dim rays of light, a meager ration of rice and seaweed soup was lowered into the hold in buckets. Prisoners with mess kits scooped out a small serving. Those lacking utensils palmed what they could with their bare hands. Many got none. Most of the soup was spilled.

The end of day brought ink black darkness. Seeing was impossible. Sound became magnified. Fights broke out. Angry threats of the offended and pained screams of the tortured filled the air.

"Don't touch me!"

"Keep away from me, you bastard!"

"Somebody help me! He's going to kill me! Oh, God, no!"

Eerie rantings of maniacs could be heard from men crazed by the heat and frustration of it all. Above the individual pleadings for mercy, the loud collective chants, "Give us air! We need water! Let us out!" made our seaborne prison a maddening pit of torture and horrors.

Al George, normally calm and softspoken, spoke to Henry with anxiety in his tone, "Some fool is clawing at me. I think I'll move."

"If he keeps on, brain him with your canteen," said Henry. Al moved away in the darkness. We heard no more from him during the night.

In the total darkness there was no way of knowing fully what was happening, but it sounded menacing. Henry and I had stuck closely together for companionship and reassurance up to this point. Now it became obvious that a man could not survive this madness alone. We made a pact to look out for each other to the bitter end. During the nightmarish hours and days which followed, that mutual commitment was to see us through some ordeals which alone we could not have endured. Even before this terrible night was over, each of us at separate times was to slip into a stupor and awaken to find the other shaking him and talking him back to rationality. The heat, thirst and lack of oxygen did strange things to us.

It wasn't until the dim light of the following morning that we were able to assess what went on during the night. Some men, crazed by thirst, became vampires and slashed others and attempted to drink their blood. Some drank their own urine. Some murdered to satisfy their lust for liquid.

We found Al George near the center of the hold. His bare arms were covered with cuts and scratches. He told us that he had fought off a blood sucker until he was exhausted. Finally, just in time, two men sensed what was going on and came to his rescue. "With their canteens," said Al, "they beat him on the head until he was dead."

Fifty men had perished during the night; mostly victims of heat prostration and suffocation. Some, however, had lost their lives to fellow prisoners who, crazed by the lack of water, had decided in their lunacy that human blood would quench their terrible thirst.

The *Oryoku Maru* steamed slowly northward, clinging cautiously close to the Bataan coast. During the night it followed an irregular course, as if dodging submarines. By early morning American planes, absent for two weeks, could be heard in the distance. They were attacking the convoy. Commander Bridget, now seemingly immune to fear and danger, sat near the top of the stairs. As cool as a tennis match referee, he reported the action.

"A flight of American Navy planes headed this way. Two peeling off to attack a freighter . . . another hitting a tanker . . . several burning ships in view."

We could hear the loud drone of multiple aircraft engines as they went into and pulled out of dives. Praying that they knew we were aboard, we waited tensely.

"Here they come," yelled Bridget. "Everybody duck."

Everyone who had been standing fell prone on the filthy, slimy floor. Henry squeezed my arm as we both cringed in fear. There was a breathless silence as we trembled and waited. The engines of the diving planes sounded as if they would tear out of their frames. Thumph, thumph went the bombs as they exploded in the water.

Japanese antiaircraft guns, firing rapidly though ineffectively, were answered by machine gun fire from the planes. The roar of engines, the rattling of guns, the splattering of hot bullets and the loud explosions of bombs were blood chilling, yet welcome. Though such sounds signaled the potential for death, they also carried the prospects for freedom. Suddenly there was light and fresh air; a bomb which had missed the target but exploded close by in the water had ripped a hole in the *Oryoku*'s side. It was less than twenty feet from where I sat. Several officers were killed instantly.

Having unleashed their bombs, the planes circled and returned for a strafing run. With wing guns blazing, they splashed multiple streams of bullets against the steel deck. It sounded like riveting guns in a metal building.

"Pour it on," we yelled, knowing the Japanese were being slaughtered and believing that the bullets could not curve down into the hold.

"My God! One got me!" groaned the man sitting tightly against my left side. Blood gushed from his shoulder. A bullet had hit the forward edge of the hatch opening, ricocheted thirty feet and torn into his shoulder muscle at the base of his neck. After the initial searing by the hot lead, his shoulder and arm grew numb.

The planes left and returned several times during the day. The last attack came at midafternoon. Crippled, with holes in her side and a broken rudder, the *Oryoku Maru* limped into Subic

Bay. At approximately 4 P.M. on December 14, she ran aground off Olongapo Point, ending a voyage that lasted three hours less than twenty-four and got nowhere.

We could see now. Through disarrayed hatch covers and two holes in the side of the *Oryoku*, beams of light focused into the hold. It was a hideous scene which met our eyes; wounded and bleeding men stumbling over those too weak to move; twisted corpses with eyes and mouths open as if their last gesture was a scream, dazed men oblivious to the ugliness around them and to the hell of the preceding hours. Amazingly, though, the majority seemed relatively calm and functional.

While Bridget and Commander Portz tried to organize some degree of order, doctors did what they could for the wounded; broken limbs and wounds needed attention, and the dead had to be gathered up. We knew we would be evacuated, but no one dared make a move up the stairway until orders were received; the Japs would be angry and quick to shoot. Guards remained posted at the hatch.

With relative quiet in the hold, we could hear much scurrying about by Japanese on deck. From the sound of urgency and excitement in the barking of orders, we knew there was confusion and chaos. Mr. Wada summoned American doctors to come up and attend to Japanese wounded. Two, Lieutenant Colonels Jack W. Schwartz and William North, went on deck where they were joined by several doctors and corpsmen from #3. When they returned several hours later they reported finding mass bloodshed and death. Among some two thousand Japanese civilians and soldiers they saw hundreds of dead and scores of injured. In one compartment, Schwartz saw a group of ten civilians huddled together, all dead. Such scenes were common throughout the first class passenger compartment; there was no protection from bullets. The ship's antiaircraft gun crews were wiped out.

With the approach of darkness we faced the prospect of another miserable night in the hold. Though the air was better, it was still hot, and there were still men with deranged minds roaming around. Also, there was hunger and thirst, for no meal had been served since the evening before. Additionally, there were corpses among us; victims of thirst, murder and the air raid.

At around ten in the evening, the Japanese began discharging their dead and wounded. It seemed to go on for the rest of the night. Below we waited, hungry, thirsty and filthy. Though there was a restlessness and considerable anxiety among us, the madness of the previous night had abated. The insane had either snapped back to reason or been brought under control. Major Houston Parks Houser, a tall, husky West Pointer from Perry, Georgia, took the job of security officer. With the help of four strong enlisted men selected by him, he confined the troublemakers to one section in a corner and guarded them. Men still milled about, but conversation was muted.

Latrine facilities consisted of the usual five-gallon cans. Two or three were placed near the center of the floor. Sometime after midnight I set out to find one. With careful, easy steps I worked one foot down between two prone bodies, then raised the other and eased it gently forward and down. Inevitably someone would get mashed and push me aside. After several such shoves, I lost my bearing. Not knowing I was anywhere near the "honey bucket," I stepped into it with my left foot. On the return trip, lost and turned around, my other foot plunged into it nearly up to the knee. Now, in addition to being pushed aside, I was bitterly cursed by those whose faces I stepped near. Repeatedly calling to Henry, I was guided to my place by his answering voice.

Early the following morning, upon hearing American planes returning, the Japanese frantically called for prisoners to come on deck to be seen by them. Clad only in g-strings, several officers raced up the steps and ran across the deck waving their arms. Seeing the white bodies were Americans, the pilots pulled out of their dives, circled and dipped their wings in recognition. More prisoners went on deck. After several passes the pilots, satisfied, turned and headed south.

We cheered and gave thanks to God. Had they renewed their attack, with the *Oryoku* a still target and its guns silent, we would have been blown to bits.

With the planes gone and no guards at the hatch, it was quiet, an eerie, menacing kind of quiet. I thought of terrible things which might be going through the hateful minds of Wada and Toshino. Frightened out of their wits by the holocaust unleashed on them by American planes, they might vent their anger on us. Thwarted in their apparent determination to see us die by neglect, they might nail down the hatches and let us perish by starvation and thirst. Wada had earlier threatened to order guards to shoot into the hold. Would he now, in his madness, unleash machine gunners and grenade throwers to murder us, as a final gesture of his hatred for Americans?

Such fears were not without reason. We had seen prisoners murdered on the Death March merely for the inability to keep up. We had witnessed executions for attempted escapes. In previous harsh punishments the Japanese had been in the position of victors, killing as a demonstration of authority. Now that authority had been seriously challenged. They were battered and bleeding, wounded by allies of the enemy whom they had so harshly scourged. We waited in agonizing fear.

It was a relief when Wada called down in a voice slightly humbled and noticeably lacking its previous venom, "Prisoners wirr disembark immediatery. Commander Bridget come on deck for instructions."

Bridget's orders were that everyone was to take off all clothes and shoes and swim ashore. No one was to leave from the starboard side of the ship. Anyone getting off course or leaving the wrong side of the ship would be shot.

"They mean what they say," warned Bridget. "Machine guns are set up on the beach. It looks like about 300 yards. Let's get moving."

Prisoners immediately began swarming on deck from all three holds. Though we were weak, hungry, dehydrated and filthy, our morale climbed with each step. To walk into the sunshine and fresh air and to move about uncrowded, made us almost feel free. The prospect of having the grit and slime washed from our bodies by the Bay's cool water was exciting. The immediate luxury, however, was sticking our heads up from the fetid hold and breathing fresh, clean air. I watched prisoner after prisoner upon reaching deck take repeated gulps of the heavy, humid unfouled oxygen as if it were something scarce and forbidden.

In addition to those newly acquired privileges, we were encouraged by the happy thought that the Japanese were less capable of moving us to Japan. This particular raid had not only cost them one of their better transports, the *Oryoku Maru*; along with it a half-dozen other sorely needed vessels had been sunk. Seeing American planes once more patrolling, unopposed, was convincing. Surely, we thought, if the Japanese have any ships left they will need to fill their holds with cargo more essential than prisoners of war.

In their haste to be rid of the blood, stench and filth of the disabled ship, prisoners recklessly took the thirty-foot plunge into the enticing blue waters of Subic Bay. Like insects flocking to a light, they seemed unaware of the hazards concealed by its calm surface; tidal currents and depth sufficient for ocean going ships. Nonswimmers floundered. Some drowned. Many were rescued by fellow prisoners. The few lifeboats and jackets were in use by the Japanese.

It is one of the beauties of the human spirit that man will instinctively come to the aid of his fellow human beings in time of crisis. No one who had endured the debilitating hell of the previous thirty-six hours possessed excess strength or energy. To get himself to land was uppermost in each man's mind. Yet there were some with limitless capacities of unselfishness and heroism.

Navy Lieutenant Ken Wheeler was such a man. He made several trips from ship to beach with someone in tow and then turned around and swam back looking for others in distress. On his second trip, he saw Lieutenant Colonel Jack Schwartz, one of our doctors, standing hesitantly on deck looking at the water far below. He would get to the ship's rail and, trembling, back away.

"Jump," yelled Wheeler.

"I can't swim," answered Schwartz.

"I'm a good swimmer," said Wheeler. "I'll help you."

With eyes closed and holding his nose with two fingers, Schwartz made the plunge. Taking him in tow with one arm, Wheeler pulled the frightened doctor the 300 yards to dry land.

There were others who were equally compassionate and kind, but I cannot recall their names. However, I am sure that those whom they rescued will never forget. Without assistance, many would have drowned.

Henry and I were in no hurry to climb out of the hold. With the hatch covers open and the gaping hole in the port side of the ship caused by the bomb, the air was now fresh and the temperature had dropped to a comfortable 85 degrees. We waited until everyone had gone and then climbed up the ladder.

Assuming that all the ship's company and guards had left the ship, we decided to find the kitchen and get some food. As soon as we got on deck we saw the Captain. Though we were surprised to see him still aboard, we assumed that for him life was to end because his ship had been lost. Perhaps the Japanese tradition of the sea demanded that the Master never abandon ship. Those were things about which we had no knowledge, being foot soldiers, but it was interesting to speculate.

The Captain looked sad, but not as distressed as he might have been. Short, stocky and neat in his clean, white uniform, which no doubt he had just gotten into, he approached us. In broken English and with a not unfriendly tone, he urged us to go.

"You must hurry. Danger to exprode," he said.

We bowed politely in Japanese fashion and moved toward the rail. The Captain returned our bow, half smiled and turned and walked toward where the bridge once was. It was a sad picture, but we couldn't bring ourselves to express any sympathy.

Before jumping into the water, we debated compliance with the order to leave our clothing behind.

"Do you think they'll issue us new clothing?" asked Henry.

"Not a chance," I answered. "There's none to be issued."

"Let's try a compromise," he suggested. "We could take off our shoes, tie the laces together, and sling them around our necks and tie our jackets around our waists."

"That should work," I said. "Then we'd have bare feet and backs and still keep our clothes. When we get near the beach we could abandon them in the water if it looks like the rule is being enforced."

It was thirty feet down to the water. It seemed that I went at least that far under when I plunged in. We bobbed up simultaneously, both spitting and gasping for air. The blue water was cool and invigorating. Both of us being experienced swimmers, we had no anxiety about making the 300 yards to shore. Taking a leisurely pace, we alternately swam and floated. My pores felt as if they were absorbing the clean salt water. It was good to have the encrusted grime melt away from my skin. In the absence of intimidating guards, and having half a square mile of the bay all to ourselves, we felt momentarily free and relaxed. For a fleeting instant my thoughts even flashed back to teenage summers at Bluffton on the South Carolina coast. Subic Bay became the mile-wide May River which I had swum across on several occasions, the giant narra trees became massive live oaks, and the coconut palms swaying in the breeze became palmettos along the shore. But, whereas those carefree summer vacations ended in nostalgic dreams which lasted a winter, this brief reverie was to be terminated by harsh ugliness and the continuing threat of death.

Upon completing our swim we briefly lay in the shallow water and looked across thirty feet of sand beach to a six-foot seawall. We became alarmed at seeing a group of fifty men huddled closely together behind the wall as if they were hiding. As we stood up to approach them, someone yelled "Get down! They have been shooting at us."

Two hundred feet beyond the wall was a hedge row which concealed two machine guns, one at either end. They were aimed toward the beach. Startled, we dashed in a crouched position toward the men. No shots were fired at us.

We were told that some of the early arriving prisoners, in search of drinking water, had wandered beyond the indefinitely defined boundaries and been fired on. Some had been seriously wounded. Periodically, as warning against attempted escape, the gunners had continued to squeeze off a burst of bullets. No one knew just where the off limits lines were, so we waited to be escorted by guards.

The inevitable and familiar "Speedo! Speedo!" routed us from our hiding place and toward the other prisoners. Our new place of confinement was a cement slab about one hundred feet square enclosed by a fifteen-foot-high chicken wire fence. By the white lines marked on it we realized we were on a tennis court; once a place of pleasure and recreation for Naval personnel, it was now to be a slab of torture for American prisoners of war.

Upon being herded into the tennis court enclosure, I was surprised to see so many men practically naked in the relentless tropical sun; very few wore more than a g-string or pair of undershorts. Having taken too literally the order to abandon clothing before swimming ashore, they were now paying the price which unprotected Caucasian skins must in the tropics. Henry and I felt fortunate in being fully clothed. There was no overhead shelter, and the nearby large shade bearing trees were too far away to filter the sun from our tennis court pen.

Exhausted, hungry and dazed, the surviving mob huddled together like frightened animals. No one seemed to know what to do or how to pick a spot to claim for his own. There was hardly more space available than there had been aboard ship. Considering that the sick and wounded had to have sufficient space to lie down, the rest of us were left with scarcely six square feet per man. Outside the fence a slow trickling water spigot stood. With Japanese permission, a long line to it formed.

Many began to suffer from a stage of nutritional diarrhea in which the stomach can hold nothing. Those who had scrounged food and water from the Jap galley aboard ship found that their bodies would not retain it. There was an unending procession through the court gate to and from the open pit latrine just beyond the wire.

Stout-hearted doctors, with no medicines or equipment, were constantly busy rendering what first aid they could. What was designated as a hospital area was nothing more than a few extra square feet of concrete sheltered from the sun by two sheets and a couple of donated raincoats. Those were attached to the fence on one edge and supported by bamboo poles along the other.

Commanders Bridget and Portz, hoarse from the constant shouting of orders and words of encouragement in hold #3, now grew weak. Both men had body wounds and Portz suffered an additional shrapnel gash to the head. Each had shown exceptional leadership and courage under conditions unimaginably dreadful. Had Bridget not hit the right note in his appeal to reason on the *Oryoku*, madness and murder would have overtaken us all. The leadership would now have to fall to someone else.

Lieutenant Colonel Curtis T. Beecher of the 4th Marine Regiment, a native of Chicago who looked like the movie version of a Marine officer, took charge. Rugged and graying, he had been active in trying to keep order in the forward hold. Major Reginald Rigley, also a Marine, assisted him. Rigley's thunderous voice gave him the nickname "Bull" and also empowered him with the volume necessary to be heard now.

Sitting atop a referee's platform which had been pulled to center court, they began taking the roll. It was an almost impossible task. The prisoners, in a state of shellshock, murmured and moved about, some in search of friends, some in the water line, and others going to and from the latrine. Getting few responses from their call of names, Beecher and Rigley realized that some semblance of basic order had to be established. Figuring the dimensions of the court and the number of men to be seated, they hit on the idea of rows of fifty-two. That meant that each man in the row would sit with his knees drawn up, or he could take a spread-eagle position with the haunches of the man in front pressed into the forks of his legs.

We had barely gotten settled in this seating arrangement when everyone jumped up, startled by the approach of a flight of three Navy planes. We crouched for a moment, in fear of the possibility of being strafed again. One bomb would get us all, I thought to myself. The planes swept directly overhead, but no doubt the pilots knew us from the day before for they continued west-wardly. It turned out that their target was an antiaircraft gun on a hill beyond our location.

The gun rattled off rapid shots. The lead plane roared down and silenced it. As they flew over again empty, hot 50-calibre shell casings fell among us; some hit sunburned bodies.

Next the planes headed for the abandoned *Oryoku Maru*. One's bomb missed; the other two scored direct hits. The ship, which had been smoldering since the previous attacks, burst into flames all over. There was no sign of life on deck. I won-dered if the Captain had ever come ashore. Angry flames leaped up through the dark black smoke. After two hours she settled a little deeper into the water as if nestling down to sleep, and there she rested. From a safe distance we witnessed the whole show and enjoyed every minute of it. Each of us harbored an intense hatred for the *Oryoku*, as if it were something beastly and alive which had to be destroyed.

The sun was dropping low behind the trees. It grew somewhat cooler. The voices of fatigued but patient roll callers droned on to a largely indifferent audience. There would be a spurt of twenty to thirty answering to their names, then a blank as no response was heard. Major Rigley would repeat the name sev-eral times and then ask "Does anyone know what happened to this man?"

"He suffocated last night," someone might answer. To an-other someone would say "He was killed by shrapnel," only to be contradicted by another who swore to having seen him swim ashore. In some instances the missing person, having been at the latrine, would report present at a subsequent roll call. It was vir-tually impossible to account for everyone with accuracy.

After they had gone through the roster several times that afternoon and again the following morning, it was estimated that we had lost three hundred in the forty-eight hours since leaving Manila; fifty each night from suffocation and two hun-dred from the air attacks by our own planes.

Among those answering present were: Captains William R.

English, Beverly N. Skardon and Albert M. George, Lieutenants
Tom H. Patrick and A. H. Bryant of South Carolina; Major
W. J. Latimer, Philadelphia, Lieutenant Charles Youngblood,
Milledgeville, Georgia. Also answering up were: Lieutenants
Francis Barker, Kenneth Wheeler, Douglas Fisher, Major George
Orr, and Captain Gary Anloff, all of California; Lieutenants
Tom C. Cox, Frank Forni, James W. Chaney, Pfcs. Jose S. Garcia
and Walter Goddard of New Mexico, and from New Jersey,
Captain Paul H. Krauss and Lieutenant Arthur O. Holmes.
Lieutenant Colonel Arnold D. Amoroso, who had been an in-
spiration to me at Davao, also answered to his name. All of
these men were personal friends of mine and would with me suffer many more days of hell before this horrible journey would
end. Major Karl Bauer, executive officer of my regiment in Bataan, died aboard ship. It was reported that the bomb got him.

The blazing sun, incapable, like the Japanese, of compassion,
bore down mercilessly. None of us had hats, so our heads, faces
and necks baked. Most wore no upper garments, leaving bare
backs to be blistered. Those with g-strings only soon looked like
boiled crabs. The cement on which we sat seemed to have its
own heating system; with sweat from our bodies added in, it appeared to give off steam. Not only was the cement hot, it was
also hard and rough against our unpadded bones.

The twilight hour after sundown brought welcomed relief
from the oppressive heat. Gentle sea breezes worked their way
among us and soothed our sweltering, aching bodies. In the distant barrio, smoke drifted up from family cooking fires. Water-
fowl, headed for their nesting places, flew swiftly overhead.
Monkeys in nearby trees chattered gleefully as if enjoying their
final climbing and jumping contest before darkness enveloped
the earth. Guards outside the fence enjoyed their evening meal.
There was no food for us, but around us all seemed cool and
peaceful.

The period of respite from physical torture was brief. Soon
the friendly breeze changed to a strong, almost angry wind. Our
concrete bed, which during the day had absorbed and magnified

the sun's rays, now seemed to distill the chill from the wind and wrap it around our defenseless bodies. Men with raw backs and limbs cooked red during the day now shivered in the darkness. They wrapped their arms about themselves and snuggled tightly together trying to keep warm. Though fully clothed, I too was cold.

Some men, drained of strength and energy, were simply too weak to sit up in the rows of fifty-two. They fell over and broke the seal of the closely packed bodies. Finally a plan was worked out in some of the rows for everyone to lie down on their right side, with bodies intertwined, for a while, then, on signal, shift to the left side. Cold, hurting and hungry, few slept.

Early morning of the second day brought a short moderate period when it was neither frigid night nor scorching day. Again the slow and tedious roll call began from atop the referee's platform. As before, some names had to be repeated several times before their bewildered owners answered up. And as on each roll call of the day before, the names of the missing were repeated several times for final verification. During the night six more had died. Permission was granted to bury them outside near the seawall.

Around midmorning of that second day on the tennis court we received our first meal: rice, raw, two tablespoons per man. As a farm boy I had sampled individual grains of raw cereal—corn, wheat, rice—just to see what they tasted like, but never had I dreamed of making a meal of uncooked rice. Now it was that or nothing. One canteen cup full was issued to the end man of each row and, with care and patience, he ladled it out by the spoonful to his fifty-two men. We chewed it eagerly, like the starving animals to which we had been reduced.

Colonel Beecher asked the Japanese why we could not have more food. Mr. Wada explained that while we were aboard ship we were under Navy control and it had been their responsibility to feed us. Now, back on land, we had reverted to Army control and the Army could not ask the Navy to furnish supplies. He and Toshino were housed and well fed. It was now December 16. We had left Manila three days earlier.

In the early morning hours, while it was still cool, Army and Navy doctors worked valiantly at trying to care for the sick and wounded. With no medicines or sanitation, it was a near hopeless task. I remembered the hideous early days at Camp O'Donnell where men suffering with malaria and dysentery died for lack of drugs. Here on the tennis court, in addition to total lack of medicines, there was no shelter, and no anesthesia for wounded patients who were in desperate need of surgery. Men with fingers blown off could only have them wrapped with a strip of dirty shirttail to stop the bleeding. Lacerated flesh was merely sponged off with tap water.

The first major surgery was done on Marine Corporal Specht. His arm, mangled by bomb fragments aboard ship, dangled by muscle and tendons. The broken bone stuck out to one side. It had grown gangrenous and threatened to poison his entire body. His fever was high. There were no surgical instruments nor antiseptics. Manpower had to be substituted for pain killing anesthesia. Lieutenant Colonel Schwartz, who had been rescued from the water by Wheeler, and Lieutenant Colonel James McG. Sullivan of San Francisco, cauterized a razor blade to serve as a scalpel. Two stronger men held the Marine down while the doctors cut the infected arm away. Specht screamed in agony but, knowing it had to be done, did not try to stop the operation. He lived for five days on the exposed tennis court with death constantly hovering over him. Finally, on the day we were moved from Olongapo, his weakened, feverish body succumbed.

Other doctors working with Schwartz and McG. Sullivan were: Lieutenant Commanders Thomas H. Hayes of Norfolk, Virginia, and Clyde Walsh of Chicago, Lieutenant Bruce Langdon of North Carolina and Lieutenant Arthur Barrett from Louisiana—all Navy officers. Their combined skills and years of experience held few answers for so desolate a situation.

As the sun slowly climbed above the treetops on the third day, it seemed to concentrate all its rays on the small tennis court packed with 1,300 debilitated, half-roasted prisoners. At midmorning we sweated. By noon we baked. It seemed slightly less sweltering to stand and mill around than to sit still on the hot cement. It was pathetic to watch fellow prisoners with exposed skins bake to blisters under the hot sun. Having saved my clothes, I was at least spared that torture. Being so protected, I felt a sense of guilt, and yet there was no solution. Sharing with them would weaken me and would not be enough to help anyone else appreciably. I hung onto my shoes and blue denim jacket and pants.

In milling around I saw and talked to several friends whom I had been anxious about. Captain Albert George seemed to be recovering from the cuts inflicted on his arms by the vampire in the hold of the ship. Lieutenant Francis H. Scarborough and Lieutenant Wilson Glover were sticking together and doing as well as the average. Captain George Brundrette looked weak, as did Lieutenant Jack Leonard. Sergeant "Mo" Gardner, my benefactor at Cabanatuan, seemed to be especially down in the dumps.

It seemed incredible that the Japanese would keep us so closely confined and so cruelly exposed to the sun for so long. Twenty-four hours of such treatment could be accepted, but forty-eight, ninety-six, and beyond were inexcusable. Even by Japanese standards it was sadistic.

Relief from the heat was all around us, but unreachable. Less than a hundred yards away the waves of Subic Bay splashed on a sandy beach. In small groups we could have refreshed our bodies in its cool waters. On every side large groves of giant shade trees could have sheltered us from the sun. In nearby Olongapo local Filipinos, I am sure, would have brought us food. And it seemed that the local Navy commander could have been persuaded to issue supplies. I wondered if the lack of action was due to insensitivity, inefficiency, or to a deliberate infliction of punishment on us by the Japanese for the damage done to them by American planes—perhaps all three, with an overdose of hatred thrown in. The result was agony for all of us and death for many.

The food ration was increased on December 17, the third day. In the morning and again in the afternoon we received two spoons of raw rice. Meals were maintained at that level, un-cooked, for the remaining three days on the tennis court. Even-tually a small supply of miscellaneous clothing was brought in. The quantity and sizes were so inadequate that there was no easy way to distribute them. The completely naked had to be taken care of first, yet no one could be completely outfitted. To one a shirt was issued. Another got a tight-fitting pair of pants. Some got only a pair of socks or a pair of straw sandals.

The scorching days and freezing nights continued for five days. On the sixth, December 20, a convoy of nineteen trucks pulled in and half of us were loaded. The following morning the trucks returned and hauled the balance of the prisoners away. Both groups were taken to San Fernando, Pampanga, a town through which many of us had wearily trudged nearly three years earlier on the infamous Death March. Half the prisoners were put in the provincial jail, the balance in an old theatre.

To reach San Fernando from Subic we had to cross the Zam-bales Mountains. There was only one road for miles, north or south. When it had been built fifty years earlier, there were no bulldozers; consequently the work was done with dynamite and picks and shovels. The resulting roadbed followed the con-tour of the hills, curving around the edges of cliffs, rather than through or over them. At its crookedest stretch the road was un-officially called the "zig zag," a name which has stuck.

As our convoy wound around the hairpin curves of the "zig zag" four miles east of Olongapo, I remembered the week I had spent there in January, 1941. At the time our main forces were fighting a delaying action to the northeast. It was vital that the enemy be denied use of this road to bring in a flanking thrust. With five hundred men of the First Battalion, Thirty-first Infan-try, Philippine Army, I was assigned the job of protecting it. "If the enemy comes in numbers too large to handle, you are to blow the zig zag off the face of the mountain," had been General Bluemel's orders to me.

While the troops were busy setting up defensive positions over-looking the sharpest and longest curves, an engineer company set about boring holes in the roadbed to be filled with explosives. Meantime, Lieutenant Alejo Santos, our aggressive and fearless supply officer, foraged around in Olongapo and Subic Navy Yard for supplies; the enemy had not yet taken the area. On the very first afternoon Santos returned with a truck loaded with items gleaned from abandoned Navy warehouses and several cases of whiskey from a burned out store in town. Among the items delivered to me for my personal kitchen were: one case each of Scotch and bourbon, three hams and one case (30 dozen) eggs. Recalling that I had grown rather tired of ham and eggs three times a day for nearly a week, I dreamed of what I could do with just one such meal now.

The enemy did not choose to land at Subic at that stage of the war. Instead, with reinforcements, they penetrated our main line with a frontal attack from the north. This pushed the front back several miles. Unknown to us, we were in danger of being isolated. A convoy of buses was sent in to pick us up in the middle of the night. Major Karl Bauer, who headed the evacuation, said, "There isn't much time. Forget about the road." We loaded our troops and equipment in the darkness and hastily departed, leaving the dynamite in place, unexploded. Nearly three years had passed since that night. Now, prisoners, we were crowded into Japanese trucks, being moved to a destination unknown to us.

The forty-mile trip from Subic to San Fernando was uneventful, except for frequent stops under the shelter of roadside trees when planes were heard approaching. Each such stop strengthened our hope that MacArthur's forces would rescue us before it was too late.

Riding into San Fernando, I thought of that dreadful day in April, 1942, when some of us now present had wearily trudged down that same main street on the atrocious Death March. I could see ghosts of exhausted, thirsty men with sunken eyes and empty bellies plodding along beyond physical endurance, too fatigued to march on and yet too fearful of the consequences of faltering.

Of the 10,000 Americans who had begun that nightmarish march, 1,000 fell by the way and were killed. Another 4,500 perished from illness and starvation within the next six months. The remainder, some 3,000, had lost their identities as a group, having been mixed in with prisoners from Corregidor and the southern islands. Perhaps 500 of the original marchers were in these trucks now riding into San Fernando. I could identify some of them by the haunted looks in their eyes and the silent movement of their lips; they, like I, were seeing and feeling it all over again and were saying a prayer for those who had fallen. Jose Garcia, Tom Patrick, Harold K. Johnson and Tom Cox looked like men in a trance; visualizing things not there and knowing things unknown to those around them.

The convoy stopped in front of the provincial jail. We were ordered to unload. Senior officers and the sick and wounded were placed indoors in unlocked cells, their first shelter in nearly a week. The rest of us were crowded into its sixty-by-eighty-foot fenced-in yard, on the ground.

The setting was familiar to many of us; we had been there before. As before, it was crowded, dirty and soon smelled of human waste. A shallow drainage ditch along the fence served as an open latrine. Blue flies swarmed in and out of it and all over us as if they had been trained to do so. A lemon tree stood in the center of the yard. Within minutes it looked as if a swarm of locusts had stripped it bare of foliage. The starving prisoners devoured the fruit and leaves like hungry animals.

In spite of our weakened, sunburned, half-naked condition and the filthy, crowded confinement, morale was good; we were confident of being rescued and we had food and water. Two meals of cooked rice were served that day, and from broken indoor toilet pipes we got all the water we could drink. The rice was brought in on sheets of corrugated tin roofing, but no matter, it was cooked and it was not cold. Considering that we had existed for six days on a daily handful of raw rice, this was luxury.

Though the majority of us felt much better and seemed to be regaining our strength, there were dozens of seriously ill among us, the wounded in particular. Our doctors pleaded with the Japanese to send the worst cases to a hospital. Reluctantly they finally agreed. Fifteen weak, badly wounded prisoners were loaded on a truck, believing that they would be taken to Bilibid for treatment. We never heard of them again until after the war; it was revealed in the 1946 war crimes trials that they were taken to a nearby cemetery, beheaded, and dumped into a mass grave. Toshino and Wada were said to have supervised.

We remained in San Fernando three days and nights. On December 24, joined by the five hundred others in the movie theatre, we marched down the tree-shaded main street. Grim faced Filipinos watched from the sidewalks. We knew they desperately wanted to help us but couldn't. I learned years later from Blair Robinette of Centerville, Maryland, that among the onlookers were some of his guerrilla fighters, male and female. Robinette had escaped from the Death March and later organized a band of freedom fighters based in the Zambales Mountains. He said he could have rescued us, but knew that he could not care for so many sick and weak men.

A short march brought us to the railroad station. There another shock awaited us. On the siding a battered steam engine with small boxcars stood waiting to receive us. Horrified, I recalled a hot, suffocating ride on it once before. That train ride and the following six weeks of hunger, untreated diseases and daily processions of fifty corpses being hauled to the graveyard flashed before me like a bad dream.

"Are we going to Camp O'Donnell?" asked Lieutenant Colonel Harold K. Johnson.

"No. You are going to Japan," the hunchback Wada informed him.

In disbelief and filled with dread, we began climbing into the freight cars. Not only was the destination distasteful, but also the likelihood of arrival there without mishap was doubtful. With American planes patrolling the island, chances of moving rail traffic undetected were slim. I could visualize 50-calibre bullets ripping through the thin steel tops of our cars and bombs smashing us to bits. Mr. Wada, however, was shrewd as well as sadistic.

"Wounded men wirr ride on top of cars. If American pranes come they wirr wave bandaged arms so we wirr not be attacked."

With one hundred men jammed into each car and fifteen to twenty clinging to the catwalk on top, our train moved out on Christmas Eve, protected by wounded prisoners of war. Destination: San Fernando, La Union, on Lingayen Gulf, landing place of the main Japanese invasion force three years earlier, and where American liberating armies would come ashore three weeks after our departure.

Leaving at eight in the morning, it required nearly seventeen hours for the slow moving, often stopping freight train to make the trip. We stood packed together, sweating and weary, for the entire journey. One stop was in a recently bombed rail yard where smouldering freight cars stood wrecked and useless. At several stations along the way groups of small Filipino boys chanted "Merry Chreess Mass, Joe."

It was after midnight when we arrived at San Fernando, La Union, where we were marched to a small one-storied schoolhouse. During the morning a light serving of poorly cooked rice was distributed. Drinking water came from an unsanitary open well. It was Christmas Eve. We remained on the school ground that day and night. Several died there. In the early morning hours we were marched over a coral shell road to a beach area near the docks. Merely to march was hard for most of us, but for those without shoes, tramping on shells was an added agony.

As night fell, it grew cold on the beach. To protect ourselves from the chilling wind we dug holes in the sand and huddled together. With our bony frames molded into the soft sand and the hastily constructed dunes breaking the wind, we were more comfortable than we had been on the cement of the tennis courts. Still, we shivered and shook from cold. Two men died that night, one of them Lieutenant Colonel H. J. Edmonds.

The rising sun next morning signaled a cessation of the strong breezes which had added to our misery during the night. Its rays soon absorbed the dew dampened coolness of our beds of sand. There were no shade trees or bushes within hundreds of yards. On the desertlike landscape behind us nothing stood up to the sun but a thin growth of stunted brown grass. Glare from the China Sea to our front hurt our eyes. The heat began to build up. By midmorning it was intense. Men with bare skins, already sunburned on the tennis court, parched and blistered. We grew thirsty and begged for water. A small rice ball per man was issued, but even distribution was impossible. Hungry, thirsty men often forget courtesy and fairness when survival is at stake. There was pushing and shoving. Some got two; others none. Japanese guards shook with laughter at the spectacle of once proud Americans fighting for food.

The blistering heat grew to be as serious a problem as the parching thirst and gnawing hunger. Lieutenant Colonel Beecher, with Major John Pyzig acting as interpreter, got permission for the prisoners to cool their burning bodies in the sea water. In small groups we were allowed five-minute swims; barely enough time to get wet. For a short while afterwards the evaporating water left a soothing coolness to our skins. One captain, crazed from thirst, dashed into the water out of turn and began frantically drinking the salt water. A guard raised his rifle. Someone snatched the man back in time.

Beecher renewed his plea for drinking water. The Japanese finally relented. An issue of one canteen cup for each twenty-man group was issued. It had to be measured by the spoonful; four for each parched mouth. The bizarre scene of thirsty men with open mouths awaiting a spoon of water like baby birds being fed by their mother must have delighted the Japanese. They brought more water and held it in plain view. After another hour and a half in the sun we got another issue; again four spoons full.

With nightfall on December 27, strong winds blew landward. The agitated China Sea hurled giant waves against the shore. It grew cold again. We burrowed in the sand. Thinking of home at Christmas with food and a warm bed we grew more depressed.

Thoughts of escape were futile; there was no place to go. We were at land's end and, for many, life's end. To the north were miles of angry ocean; to the south, acres of barren land. Added to that was the bitter realization that MacArthur's men would not rescue us now. Thirsty, hungry, cold and forlorn, we could neither sleep nor rest.

14. Hell Ship #2—The *Enoura Maru*

In the predawn hours we were routed out and marched to the nearby port. The docks were stacked with recently unloaded supplies. We looked for items of food which we could pilfer. With no time to loiter and search, we had no luck. Six large freighters lay at anchor in the harbor. The masts and stacks of twice that number of sunken ships thrust up through the water. The Japanese seemed more anxious and impatient than usual.

Lieutenant Toshino and Mr. Wada jabbered back and forth in Japanese. It appeared that a worried Toshino was scolding the subservient Wada and urged us to quicken our pace.

"You must get into the barge quickly," he impatiently shouted. "Hurry! Hurry! Ship must leave soon."

The barge deck was eight feet below the dock. Being weak and having many injured among us, we were reluctant to jump down. Guards nudged us with rifle butts. Some prisoners were literally pushed from the dock and were injured upon landing on the barge below. One missed the barge entirely and fell into the water, hitting his head against the side of the barge as he went down. When he was pulled from the water he was dead.

One of the freighters awaiting our loading had the name *Enoura Maru* lettered on its side and was numbered 1 on its stack. It was of about 10,000 ton displacement. The other, #2, was the *Brazil Maru*. The former already had steam up and its engines were turning. Perhaps because of an earlier air raid alarm, the skipper was nervous and anxious to get underway. The slow climbing of prisoners up the rope ladders seemed to tax his patience to the breaking point. Looking down from the bridge, he indicated "no more" when slightly over one thousand had been sent to his ship. Weighing anchor, he headed north into the China Sea with the balance of the barge load still climbing aboard.

Prisoners remaining on the dock, some 236, were loaded on the *Brazil Maru*, which was somewhat smaller. Two of my South Carolina friends, Lieutenant Otis F. Morgan from Laurens, and Lieutenant Tom Patrick of Chester, were in that group. The numbers 1 and 2 had no significance insofar as quality of accommodations were concerned; both were typically terrible. Henry and I, still sticking together, were among the 1,069 aboard the *Enoura Maru*.

The date was December 28, 1944. The sky was overcast. In the holds of the two ships there were 1,305 surviving prisoners. In spite of hunger, thirst, shipwreck, days and nights of torture on the tennis court and beach and an insufferable train ride, we still lived. Three hundred fourteen of our comrades had died. Many of the lingering, had they known the horrors which lay ahead, would have chosen death.

The *Enoura Maru* was an old, rusty-looking freighter. Having just unloaded her cargo, she rode high on the water. From the deck we looked thirty feet down into the midship hold which was to be our quarters. It was spacious and the floor was littered with wheat or oat straw. There were no bays or partitions. Enough of the hatch covers had been removed to allow sufficient light and air to drift in.

"It looks better than anything we have ridden in yet," observed Henry, with an air of optimism.

"Maybe we are finally getting a break," I answered.

We had climbed no more than halfway down the ladder when an ammonia-like odor penetrated our nostrils. Upon reaching bottom, we were greeted by swarms of flies. As we spread out to find space to bed down, we found piles of horse manure. Now the significance of open hatches and light and air dawned on

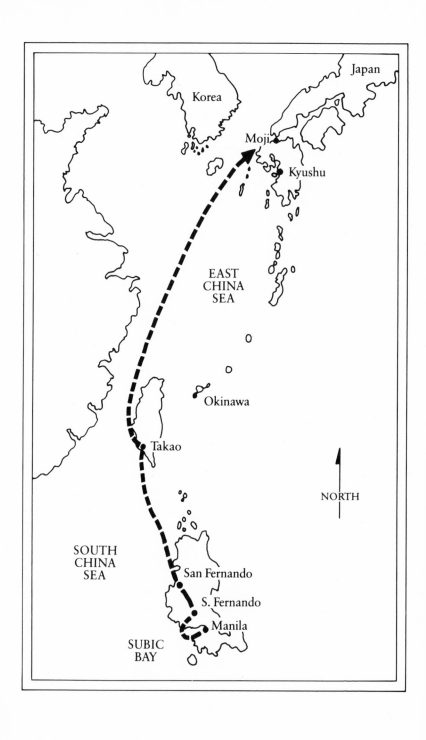

Korea

Japan

Moji

Kyushu

EAST
CHINA
SEA

Okinawa

Takao

NORTH

SOUTH
CHINA
SEA

San Fernando

S. Fernando

Manila

SUBIC
BAY

me. This was no troop ship. Horses had been the previous cargo; their health and comfort were important to the Japanese. They were an asset to the war; we were a liability.

Before the sun was two hours high, we were well on our way. It was noticeable that the voyage began hurriedly in early morning, whereas the *Oryoku Maru* had lingered at the Manila dock until nearly dark. Her short voyage had been an overnight one, clinging close to shore. Over the next week we were to see that tactic reversed. The *Enoura*, sailing the open seas, would move by day and anchor at night. Someone came up with a logical theory: American planes were too far away to reach the ships now, but submarines, prowling the waters almost up to Tokyo Bay, were deadly at night.

On the first day out we ran into a storm. The high riding ship pitched and tossed. It was drafty and cold in the hold. No food or water were served that day. We searched around in the horse troughs for grain. I found a few kernels of barley which had been slobbered over by animals and crawled on by flies. I threw them greedily into my mouth. They were more tasty and easier to chew than raw rice.

On the level above us were hundreds of wounded Japanese soldiers being taken back to Japan. They were fed three meals a day. Prisoners who had any valuables left began trying to trade them for food. Lieutenant Colonel Harold K. Johnson, in charge of the group, forbade trading with the Japs. The civilian gambler who had headed up the Cabanatuan black market ignored the order. He made a deal for rice and candy. Angry fellow prisoners scattered it in the litter.

One man died during the night. Captain Preston Taylor, an Air Corps chaplain, held a brief funeral service for him before he was lowered into the sea.

On the second day it rained again. Thirsty prisoners scuffled for positions to catch the dirty drippings of water in their mess kits. The lucky ones caught a few drops of water.

A small ration of cooked rice was issued that day. As it was lowered into the hold in wooden tubs attached to long ropes, swarms of flies followed it like bees swarming from a hive. When the tubs reached bottom they were so covered with black crawling flies that the white rice could not be seen. At the insistence of the Japs, the containers had to be emptied immediately and sent back up. The rice was dumped on raincoats and straw mats. In the process the flies were thoroughly mixed in. That dampened no one's appetite in the least; it was cooked, and we were starving.

The lineup for chow presented a pathetic picture. An outsider in better circumstances would have viewed it in shocked disbelief. Like beggars we stood, eagerly reaching for a share, barefooted, unshaven, dirty, many befouled with diarrhea. The majority, lacking utensils, ate from hats, pieces of cloth or from their filthy hands. Among them were senior grade officers who had commanded a thousand men in battle. These individuals, clutching a handful of rice against naked, dirty chests to hide it from the flies, were nearly all officers of the United States military services, with vanity and pride taken away from them. They were at a state of existence where only survival mattered.

At dusk on December 29, we heard loud blasts of guns on deck. This was followed by the rumble of depth charges being hurled over the side of the ship. Guns from other ships could be heard joining in the firing. We listened, silent and tense, expecting any minute to hear a torpedo tear through the side.

"The subs have found us," said Henry in a nervous stage whisper.

"If they hit us we may get back to Luzon yet," someone answered. "We're only one day out."

After thirty minutes the firing ended. On deck the Japanese laughed and clapped their hands. "Imperial Japanese Navy has sunk American submarines," we were told. A short while later the *Enoura* dropped anchor for the night. It was cold. We burrowed in the filthy straw trying to keep warm.

The storm was still with us the next day. The high riding, nearly empty ship pitched and rolled. One-half cup of rice and a few spoons of water were the only issue for the day. That night the *Enoura* did not stop. We assumed it had run out of nearby land and was forced to make a dash across open sea headed for Formosa. Around 8 p.m. there was more dropping of depth charges. With each underwater explosion the ship shuddered. Either the ship's navigator was expert at evasive maneuver or the alarm was false; no torpedoes struck the ship.

December 31 was no better than the several days before. We did get a half cup of water, but no rice. Colonel Johnson pleaded for food. The hateful hunchback answered, "No cooking can be done in this stormy weather."

"We will all die," said Johnson.

"Everybody must die. This is no time for sympathy," answered Wada. By nightfall we left the rough, stormy sea and sailed into a relatively calm landlocked harbor. It was New Year's Eve. The weather was still rainy and cold.

January 1, 1945, was the bleakest New Year's Day I had ever spent. Twelve months earlier, at Davao, there had at least been a modest amount of hot food and we were warm and had a bunk to sleep in. The year before that, at Davao, though crippled with beriberi and recovering from surgery, I was confident things would get better. On the first of January, 1942, in Bataan, we were fighting a war and expecting reinforcements to come in.

This day, in the filthy hold of a Japanese freighter, we were starving and shivering from cold, with absolutely nothing to look ahead to. The ship was headed for the enemy's homeland. Already we had been en route nineteen days. No one knew how much longer it would take to reach our destination. There was a constant danger from submarines. The farther north we went the colder it would get. Wounded and ill men lay all around, untreated. Each night brought more deaths. There was neither sympathy from the Japanese nor prospect for relief. Hope had worn thin.

We learned that the harbor where our ship lay at anchor was Takao, on the southwest coast of Formosa. The Japanese soldier patients were taken ashore by barge. After their departure some of our men volunteered to help clean up the area they had vacated in hopes of finding extra food and clothing. Colonel Johnson again requested food.

"American submarines sink Japanese supply ships. No food for you," said Wada, in his most spiteful tone.

In the afternoon we were fed two-thirds of a cup of rice and one teaspoon full of powdered, dried fish. No water. Though the storm had abated, the skies were still overcast and it remained chilly below deck. As night came on it grew cold and the built up stresses of discomfort and uncertainty began to surface. Some showed signs of cracking mentally. They roamed around talking strangely and trying to vandalize others. Having experienced two nights of marauding madmen aboard the *Oryoku Maru*, Henry, Bill English and I took positions with our backs against the bulkhead so that no one could get behind us. Captain Arthur Wermouth, referred to in Bataan as "the one-man army," still relatively strong, was stationed at the foot of the ladder to prevent anyone from trying to escape. No violence developed, but several more men died during the night.

The following morning slightly over half of us were transferred to the forward hold, from which the cargo had been removed. This gave much more room and it was cleaner—no horse manure and flies. We continued to ride at anchor for several days in Takao Harbor. There was very little activity on the part of the Japanese. We wondered if they were waiting to join a convoy or whether there had been a change in plans for us. Our apprehension grew stronger as our physical conditions deteriorated. The Japanese were completely indifferent to the starvation and dying going on below. At times guards dropped cigarette butts through the hatch for the amusement of watching the Americans scuffle for a smoke. The death rate of three or four nightly continued.

On the morning of January 6, the prisoners from the other ship were brought aboard the *Enoura Maru*. All were put with us in the forward hold. Among them were Otis Morgan and Tom Patrick. Their report of the voyage on board #2 was a bleak picture, equally as bad or worse than ours.

Morgan, a former neat, square-shouldered, aggressive lieutenant with the Philippine Scouts, was hardly recognizable now. His normal 180 pounds had shrunk to no more than 120. His hairline had receded another inch and his once sparkling brown eyes were deep and hollow; sunken cheeks added more emphasis to his high cheekbones and his bottom lip looked parched. An open tropical ulcer just below the shoulder on his bare back explained the care with which he moved his right arm.

Tom (Lieutenant Patrick), my private barber at Davao, was fifteen pounds lighter than when I last saw him. Dirt and grime and three weeks' growth of red beard hid his freckles. His once neat crew-cut hair was a matted tangle of unkempt red. Both men looked weak and worn. We sat together in a tight circle.

"We received neither food nor water during the first two days out of Lingayen," said Otis. "When we were finally fed on the third day it was only the leavings from the guards, and they don't leave much."

Both praised Lieutenant "Johnny" Johnson for the raw courage with which he tried to stand up to the Japs. On the fourth day, Tom said, he went up the ladder and held out a spoon for the Japanese commander to see. "This spoonful is all we have had to eat in three days," he told him. "If it continues like this we will all die."

"We want you to die," answered the Jap angrily. "American submarines are sinking our ships."

They reported having lost about a dozen men during the trip. Our losses had been twice that, though our total numbers were triple theirs. On both ships the burials at sea were the same. Corpses were not allowed to be brought up until five or six had accumulated. In all instances the bodies were stripped of their scanty clothing, wrapped in burlap or straw matting, weighted down and eased over the side. Chaplains said brief prayers for each. Brief, unemotional, it was all that could be done in the way of a Christian burial.

Two days after we had moved from the aft hold, a few more prisoners from there moved in with us. They said that a few days earlier a small shipment of bagged sugar had been loaded into the hold and separated from the prisoners only by cargo netting. Orders were issued by the Japanese that anyone caught stealing sugar would be severely punished. In spite of threats, the temptation was too great. Starving and cold, they felt the energy from the sweet nourishment would give them a boost. Most felt they would soon die anyway, so the predictable happened; someone ripped open a bag of sugar. Quietly, with eyes peeled toward the hatch, those around him pilfered a portion.

For all of the stealth and caution with which the distribution was made, someone clumsily spilled a cup full of the brown sugar in easy view of the guard staring down through the hatch. Within minutes Mr. Wada was angrily calling for Colonel Johnson.

"Someone has storen Japanese sugar. You wirr bring the thieves up for punishment immediatery," he demanded in a rage.

"I cannot determine who opened the bag, Mr. Wada. Everyone ate some. We are all starving," answered Johnson, attempting to emphasize the desperately hungry condition of the men.

"Untir you deriver the thieves there wirr be no food or water for any of you," warned the adamant Wada.

Johnson faced an impossible dilemma. To report someone to the Japanese would certainly mean torture for the individual; not to do so could result in starvation for all. He had seen men beaten mercilessly for less serious offenses. Remembering the incident of David Peace being knocked to the ground with rifle butts, kicked and stomped into unconsciousness, then tied up to a post for forty-eight hours in the sun, he resolved not to comply. Peace's crime had been to bring some bananas into camp—a fruit which the Japanese did not eat and which would rot on the tree. Sugar, scarce and valuable in Japan as both a food and a raw material for war, belonged to the Emperor. To steal it would be classed as a major crime.

Johnson and his staff held a whispered conference. In silent fear everyone else looked to them. With angry impatience, Wada sent a final warning.

"Coroner Johnson, you have onry ten minutes to deriver the rogues." His voice went high and cracked on the final word. Everyone fell silent.

Suddenly the hush was broken by a firm voice calmly saying, "I'll go." As all eyes turned to see who was so daring, a medical corpsman, Sergeant Arda M. "Max" Hanenkrat, stood up and moved toward the ladder. It was said that Max had been cited for bravery in Bataan for carrying a wounded man thirteen miles on his back. Before he had taken two steps a second voice with an accent spoke up:

"I'll join the sergeant." The solemn words came from a British Army sergeant named Trapp.

As everyone else sat still and quiet in shocked disbelief, the two nervy men climbed up the ladder. No doubt there must have been a spontaneous urge to applaud, but the shame of allowing someone else to suffer for an offense to which all had been parties suppressed the impulse.

There was no doubt in anyone's mind that execution would be the final fate of the two. What everyone shuddered to contemplate was the preliminary tortures to which they would be subjected. Visions of the hapless victims being battered back and forth with clubs in a circle of merciless guards tortured their guilt-ridden minds. It wasn't beyond the cruel nature of the Japanese to rip out the fingernails of the guilty slowly, one after another, or to dunk them, suspended by their heels at the end of ropes, up and down in the murky waters of the harbor. And finally, the thought of two bleeding, swollen bodies, with aching muscles and broken bones, tied to the cargo boom to die a slow death from exposure, brought tears to the eyes of their stunned comrades.

Acts of courage were frequent and almost commonplace among our prisoners of war. To volunteer to be tortured and executed, however, was pure valor.

The longer we remained in Japanese captivity the more inept we became at predicting their behavior. Offenses which we might consider minor quite often proved to be an insult to the Emperor.

Others, which we avoided committing for fear of summary execution, might result in only mild reprimand. If there was anything certain about the Japanese, it was their inconsistency.

After a brief period of tense waiting, the shocked prisoners rose as the two who had confessed returned virtually unscratched. To the amazement of all, they reported that there had been no severe beatings or threats of death. With only minor scuffings and stern warnings they were set free. Perhaps they were saved by the Japanese admiration for raw courage.

Tinko (roll call) on the evening of January 7 revealed our total number to be 1,262, which meant 357 had died prior to that hour—314 on and immediately after the *Oryoku Maru* and 43 from Lingayen to Formosa. Most of us were in extremely poor physical condition.

The following day 37 English and Dutch prisoners were taken ashore. It was learned that they were to be put in a camp on Formosa where others of their countrymen were already encamped. All of us longed to join them, knowing that conditions there could not be much worse than what lay ahead of us aboard ship.

Early on the morning of January 9 we heard a drone of aircraft and the rattle of antiaircraft guns in the distance. Remembering that our ship was tied up to another freighter in the middle of the harbor, I feared it would be a likely target. I was in the center of the hold. The planes' engines grew louder and nearer. I knew it was headed our way.

"Let's move to the bow of the ship, Henry. That being the narrowest area, it will be less likely to be hit," I said.

We jumped up, and scrambled to the very nose of the freighter and fell forward on our stomachs. Face down and with my left hand covering my head, I waited in terror as the American dive bomber roared downward, released its bomb and climbed up and away. The furious rattle of gunfire failed to drown out the menacing whistle of the falling bomb.

Suddenly there was a crunch of metal against metal and a deafening explosion as the bomb hit the deck near the port side rail. A blinding orange flash illuminated the semidarkness.

Hatch covers and timbers plunged into the hold along that side. Hunks of metal, large and small, ripped through the air and ricocheted off the steel walls. Agonized screams of the crushed and wounded rent the air.

Like a furious tornado, the bomb had struck, destroyed, and left misery and desolation in its wake. After it was over there was a brief moment of dead calm and silence as dazed, shocked men sat up and looked around them in disbelief. Then groans of pain and pleas for help could be heard from every direction. Stunned and trembling, Henry and I turned to each for comfort and reassurance.

"Are you all right?" he asked.

"I think so, but I did feel something hot hit my temple," I answered. "What about you?"

"I'm o.k.," he said, "but I see a trickle of blood on the side of your face." Turning my head toward the light he said, "I see it now. You have a small cut on the right temple. Press your finger against it. That should stop the bleeding."

Further examination revealed an injury to the middle finger of my left hand. Seeing that, I realized what had happened. As I had lain prostrate with my left hand covering the side of my face, the small piece of flying metal had hit the finger before glancing across my temple. Had the finger not broken the force of the blow, the hot steel probably would have penetrated my brain.

With nearly a third of the overhead decking having been ripped away by the explosion, it was no longer half dark in the hold. The sky was clear now and the sun sent bright shafts of light penetrating into our devastated pit of horrors. What met the eyes would have been better left unseen. Dust and the smell of explosives filled the air. Dead bodies were strewn across the length and breadth of the rubble-filled floor; some by themselves and others clustered in small groups. At first glance it looked as if nearly everyone had been killed, then wounded men began to cautiously pull themselves up from the floor as if surprised to be able to move. Most looked dazed and frightened.

Having no wounds of consequence, we began to move about

trying to help the more seriously injured. Hundreds of bodies lay in the tangled, grotesque positions of violent death; limbs had been ripped from bodies and heads and torsos wrested apart. Among the living, blood trickled from noses, ears and mouths of concussion victims or gushed from body wounds of others torn by shrapnel.

In the very area from where we had fled when the plane approached, a huge steel girder lay across the width of the hold with a dozen helpless men pinned beneath it; some had died instantly as the full weight of the girder crushed their chests, others still lived, trapped by arms or legs. Unable to move, their pitiful eyes and weak voices pleaded for help.

"Can you please help me?" a faint voice implored. You could tell his life was nearly spent.

"Get this monster off me," demanded another, half crazed with pain.

Some of the uninjured looked on unfeeling and unthinking, seeming powerless to move. With pleading and scolding, I rallied twenty of them. We tugged at the heavy beam but our efforts were futile. It weighed tons. Powerless to help, we moved on, leaving the trapped men to die.

Fifteen feet away on the port side, we found a mass of tangled dead bodies. Having been directly under the bomb blast, they had caught the full load of the falling timbers and planks. In that small area alone nearly a hundred lives had been snuffed out in an instant. They appeared to have huddled together, as if cringing from the impending blow. I saw no living wounded among them. Mercifully it had been sudden and final. All were dead.

On the edge of the group I saw, lying close together, Lieutenants Otis Morgan and Tom Patrick, the two good friends we had talked with at length only the day before. Neither showed any outward marks of injury. Their bodies were intact, but lifeless. Henry and Otis had been close friends through four years of college and had lived, worked and played in the same town over the following several years. For nearly a decade, both single, they had been carefree, fun loving and inseparable. Now, with a terrible suddennness, it had ended. Henry looked at me with tear-filled eyes. I knew the hurt ran deep.

My friendship with Tom was of a shorter duration and had developed under extremely austere and oppressive conditions. It began at Davao at a time when there was little room for frivolity, niceties and the extending of a helping hand. I was recovering from surgery, weak and pretty much alone. Tom had a small barber business going. His pay was a cigarette or some item of food. One day he offered to take care of me at no charge. With scissors, comb and a messkit knife made into a straight razor, he kept me neatly shaven and shorn. Quiet, steady and dependable, he had helped me through a tough period. We began to eat together and to share what little extras we could get and to depend on each other. I was deeply saddened to see him die so defenselessly.

There being nothing physical to be done for them, we bowed our heads, said a silent prayer, then moved quietly away. There were many injured who, with a little help, stood a chance to survive. The seriously wounded were doomed to die, as there were no drugs or disinfectants. Doctors and corpsmen were busy rendering what first aid they could. With pieces of wood gleaned from the debris, they applied makeshift splints to broken limbs. Tourniquets and bandages were made from dead men's clothing.

We moved back to where we had lain when the bomb hit. There, in the bow end of the ship, a fifteen-square-foot area looked unscarred and clear of debris. Remarkably, there were no dead or injured. It appeared to have been shielded from the destructive blast.

"You guessed that one right, Manny," said Henry with a half smile. "It was no doubt the only safe place in the entire hold."

"We were lucky that time," I said out loud. But secretly I pondered what had prompted me to move when the plane approached. Was it fate, fright, a natural instinct to flee from danger, or was it the hand of God protecting me? Whatever it may have been, I became more convinced that I would survive this hazardous journey.

For the next two days we remained in that terrible pit of wreckage and suffering, unnoticed and unattended by the Japanese. Neither food, water nor medicines were supplied. The wounded slowly died from shock, loss of blood or infection. Corpses bloated and smelled. Either the Japanese were afraid that we were all insane, or they were repulsed by the ghastly sight which met their eyes.

On the third day, January 12, a large cargo net was lowered into the hold for the removal of the dead. When fifteen to twenty bodies had been laid on it the ship's winches turned and the boom slowly lifted them the thirty feet up and gently lowered them to a barge tied up alongside. Chaplains said prayers. This sad ritual was repeated over and over until one hundred fifty bomb victims had been taken out. A burial detail which went along reported that forty-five were taken from the aft hold, where damage was relatively light. They were brought ashore and buried in a common grave on the sandy beach. The following morning the remaining one hundred bodies were taken ashore and buried.

Our ranks had now dwindled to 930 weak, debilitated prisoners, many of them ill and wounded. Thirty-one days and nights of hazardous stop and go travel had cost the lives of forty percent of our men—652 in total. This latest bombing had taken 295; the prior one and the journey in between, 357. It was doubtful that many of the remainder would ever see Japan.

When the pallbearers and grave diggers returned, Mr. Wada informed us that we would be transferred to another ship. Our first food in three days was issued—one-half canteen cup of cooked rice and a small portion of water. It proved to be the last meal for some; for others it represented a short extension of life on a cruel road to death.

Dirty, starved, many wounded, the weak survivors were about to embark on the last leg of a nightmarish journey which would grow increasingly horrible the longer it lasted. In spite of almost insurmountable obstacles, the Japanese perseverance and determination remained constant, while their stupidity, hatred and inhumanity increased. Thwarted by shipwreck at the very outset, they switched to truck and rail and then to ship again. Threatened by prowling submarines during night movement, they sailed by day and lay at anchor during darkness. Advised that their prisoners were dying from hunger and thirst, they admitted cold-bloodedly that they wanted them to die. Their second ship bombed into uselessness, they were now recklessly exchanging it for a third. With nearly half of their prisoners already dead and many of the others critically wounded, they appeared relieved rather than concerned.

It was obvious that Lieutenant Toshino and Mr. Wada faced neither the obligation to keep us alive nor accountability for letting us die. To reach Japan with a mere handful of surviving prisoners apparently would fulfill their covenant. Their chief concern seemed to be that none escape and that the sugar cargo not be disturbed; either would cause them reprimand.

Though getting out of the wreckage and stench was desirable, transferring from one ship to the other was not easy for us. The only exit was by way of a ladder running thirty feet up the partition wall. Even the ambulatory were almost too weak to climb; the seriously wounded could not. To move them at all was to condemn them to death. But the order had been given.

Men absolutely unable to scale the steep ladder included shock victims, those with broken limbs and crushed pelvises, and many so weakened from dysentery they could not even stand up. They could not be left behind and yet no one was physically capable of carrying someone up so steep a climb on his back.

15. Hell Ship #3—The *Brazil Maru*

With the help of Navy men, the medics figured a way. They tied a rope around the patient's thighs and secured it around his waist with a square knot. This made a sort of bos'n's chair in which the groaning man was hauled to the deck by a half-dozen of the more sturdy prisoners at the other end of the rope.

To move those unable to sit up, a litter was made from a hatch cover secured at the corners by rope. Lying immobile on the crude stretcher, the helpless injured were pulled up. It was pathetic to see the doomed prisoners clinging to life in agony. It was revolting to see Mr. Wada watching with a smile on his face, as if he were enjoying the sad spectacle.

From the deck, in groups of twenty, sick and well were loaded onto a small wooden platform which was raised by the ship's boom high over the water and lowered at dizzying speed onto a tugboat which waited below.

A short trip across the harbor brought us to the *Brazil Maru*, the smaller transport which, upon reaching Takao, had discharged its prisoners to our ship and taken on a cargo of sugar. Upon reaching it the wounded faced another obstacle; two barges were tied up to the ship. Reaching the rusty freighter's accommodation ladder would mean crossing their decks. Those unable to walk would have to be carried.

Many of the wounded displayed a strong will to live and a

desire not to be a burden to others. Some with splinted legs started hobbling across the rocking barges unassisted, only to fall from weakness and pain. It was reported that Captain Walter Donaldson of Deming, New Mexico, a 200th Coast Artillery officer, put on a display of courage and independence of spirit which those present would never forget. With both wrists sprained and both ankles fractured, he tenaciously worked his way, on elbows and knees, across both barges, up the thirty-degree ladder, and onto the ship's deck, where he fell over exhausted. Even the Japanese admired his determination.

Six men died during the transfer. Thirty more succumbed during the night. The bodies were stacked in a pile for later burial at sea.

The *Brazil Maru*, like the other two ships we had traveled on, had no markings to indicate that it carried prisoners of war. Like the *Oryoku*, its cargo space had been divided into bays for the transportation of troops. We were all crowded into the midship hold. Though our numbers had decreased by nearly half, there was, as always, insufficient room. The bays measured approximately ten feet by fifteen feet, with four feet of head room. Twenty men were assigned to each such space. We could either sit with our legs extended, or lie down with knees drawn up. Standing or lying down full length in the bays was impossible. Out in the open center space there was more room, but that area was assigned to the sick.

Our ship sailed out of Takao just before sundown on January 13. In a convoy of six or seven ships she moved through the Formosa Straits toward the China coast. By morning we had traveled perhaps one hundred miles north and into the East China Sea. The water had a dirty yellowish color and the hilly coastline looked rugged and barren. By afternoon of the second day it had grown much colder. We huddled together and shivered. Men with only underwear for clothing suffered hard chills.

Still threatened by submarines, the convoy moved cautiously. Avoiding the open sea, it zigzagged between coastal islands during daylight hours and lay at anchor during the night—a procedure which was to stretch a forty-eight-hour journey into more than two weeks. Though our progress northward was slow, the increase in bone chilling coldness was rapid. The hatch was covered with a tarpaulin which, though tied down, was frequently lifted by gusts of strong wind. Each blast of the rain-filled gale sent a bitter draft into our prison pit. A constant cloud cover shielded off any warmth which sunlight might bring. From morning until evening we milled about in a chill twilight. In the black darkness of night the cold built up to a benumbing agony.

The coldest spot was in the center directly below the tarp covered hatch. It was there that the dead were laid. In the area adjacent to the corpses the dying were placed. They were too far gone to try to eat, so their food was retained in the bucket for distribution to those who might live.

So critical was the need for clothing that the garments of dead men were stripped away for the use of the living. In some instances men still living, but unconscious, were unclothed prematurely. A committee was appointed to handle the unpleasant task of disrobing the deceased and redistributing their tattered garments to the covetous shivering survivors. Such callous insensitivity to the dignity of the dead would be normally unthinkable. Now it was imperative. To choose between the observance of the niceties of a social code and freezing to death was simple. Survival was the only thing that had any meaning.

Latrine facilities for prisoners were on deck, a doghouse-like box extending over the side of the ship. Only two men at a time could use it. There was a constant lineup of prisoners awaiting their turns; two on deck, two returning and two standing at the top of the stairway peering through the tarp. Though the chill wind penetrated to the marrow of our bones, it was worth the discomfort just to inhale fresh air and to exhale the stench of death and human waste from our lungs. A five-gallon bucket was provided for those too weak to make the climb.

Hunger, cold and thirst stalked among us like marauding giants; frightening and incontestable. Starvation, freezing and dehydration each took its daily toll in multiple numbers. To quench their maddening thirst, men reached for scattered flakes of snow drifting down through the lone opening, or jostled each other to capture dirty drippings of rain leaking from the filthy, greasy deck above. To dull their gnawing hunger, they stole and ate forbidden sugar, itself an agent of death through diarrhea. Trying to keep warm, they huddled together under pieces of straw matting to hide from the constant flow of chilling drafts. These desperate efforts to live served only to hasten death for many. Having witnessed the price of panic on the *Oryoku Maru*, I decided to keep still, conserve energy and to try to control my anxieties.

With the increasing cold, now well below 20 degrees, pneumonia added its crushing weight to the already overburdened strugglers. Coughs, labored breathing, high fever and delirium soon became quite common. Of the many lonely, horrible ways to die on that terrible trip, death by pneumonia was perhaps the most merciful.

I saw my good friend Captain William R. "Bill" English succumb to that illness. Lying on his back with his knees drawn up, he had a fixed smile on his face. I felt his forehead. It was hot. He did not shiver and he said he felt no pain. While some around him shook with chills, he was still. During his last day he was restful with a fever-induced warmth. It was on January 21 that Bill English died. The following day Lieutenant Charles "Charlie" Youngblood, another good friend from Milledgeville, Georgia, died of the same ailment.

Our food, never more than a half canteen cup measure twice daily, varied between boiled barley and steamed rice. Water continued to be doled out by the spoonful. I was convinced that the Japanese deliberately planned for us to perish from thirst. On the first ship, in spite of ample supply facilities at Manila, we had very little water. On the *Enoura* it had been equally as scarce. Having sat in the harbor at Takao for more than a week, the *Brazil Maru* could certainly have had its water tanks filled. Nothing was done. Requests for more water were answered with, "The supply is very limited."

One morning when I went up to the latrine I found the deck covered with thick ice and a crust of snow; the rain had turned to sleet and snow during the night. On my second trip up in the afternoon I noticed it had begun to melt. Returning from the latrine and naïvely thinking that the guard would not mind, I quickly scooped up a two-foot square sheet of it. Rushing over and yelling angrily in Japanese, he began flogging me across the back with his rifle butt. The ice dropped to the deck as I snapped to attention, bracing myself against being knocked down. Several hard blows and a stern scolding seemed to satisfy his urge to punish. Dismissed with no serious injuries, I rushed down the steps and spread the word, "Don't try to get ice from the deck."

As the days dragged by, conditions grew progressively worse for the victims of two shipwrecks. The high death rate continued. It was no surprise that the critically injured died, for there was no way to care for them. In the absence of infection-preventing drugs and pain-relieving narcotics, living for them was no more than a tortured lingering. In such cases, dying was a yearned for relief. Lieutenant Wilson Glover of Greenville, South Carolina, lasted until January 27, and Major W. J. Latimer of Philadelphia followed on the 28th. Each had a relaxed passing, free of struggle.

The area in the center of the hold set aside for the dead and dying soon became shocking and repulsive to behold. Half naked men, who had recklessly gorged themselves on stolen sugar and developed severe diarrhea, lay in their own body waste. Too weak to move and too far gone to care, they were indifferent to their surroundings. Of once healthy muscular bodies, only skin and bones remained. Their bones protruded as if trying to burst through the skin. As if focused on something beyond the present hell, their eyes, blank and glassy, stared upward. Their whole frames trembled as if resting on a hidden vibrator. In that final condition they were beyond feeling and anxiety.

The bodies of the dead were tallied and hauled up each morning. Only twice in sixteen days was the count less than thirty—twenty-three on January 24 and fifteen on the 26th. Most days they numbered thirty. The average was twenty-seven.

There was no way to remove the corpses by manpower. The living were so weak it would have required at least six to carry one. To solve the problem, a boom was lowered over the open hatch and a rope dropped down to be tied around the ankles of the deceased. On signal the ship's winch would turn, rewinding the rope and lifting the body skyward. Once all the wasted skeletons were laid out on deck, a chaplain was allowed to go up and hold a burial service; then they were lowered into the lonely China Sea.

For the most part the atmosphere of desolation and hopelessness ruled out civility and charity. Each man, in his personal agony and struggle to survive, seemed to grow numb to the misery of others. Yet occasional acts of decency and tenderness surfaced. Over the dead body of a dear friend a man would stand in an attitude of prayer with tears dripping down his cheeks. Another would share with a fever-ridden buddy a cup of precious water, purchased from a guard at the price of a treasured wedding band. More than once I saw a weak, starving prisoner, with nothing but hope left in his own heart, cradle the head of a comrade in his arms and plead with the dying man to hang on.

Medical corpsmen on duty showed a nobleness of character and a resoluteness of purpose which was uncommon, considering that they themselves were weak and hungry. It was their duty to nurse the sick, comfort the wounded and gather the dead. Never did I see them act with impatience or callousness in ministering to their charges. Among those who worked diligently were Frank L. Marwell of Birmingham; Dean A. Coburn, Charleston; Estes Meyers, Louisville; John T. Istock, Pittsburgh; and Oscar Otero of Los Lunas, New Mexico.

When we boarded the *Oryoku Maru* in Manila there were sixteen chaplains among us. Before we reached Japan they had dwindled to a number which could be counted on one hand. From the beginning in prison camp, chaplains, like doctors, far exceeded the normal complement of officers of their professions. It turned out that way because most of them had served with the Philippine Army and, upon being captured, had been separated from the Filipinos and put in camps set up exclusively for Americans. There being official duty for only a few, most of them worked in the rice fields like everyone else.

Aboard the hell ships there was really no official chain of command or table of organization. The senior field grade officer was considered to be in charge, and in each hold one of the seniors either volunteered for or had the distasteful job of dealing with the Japs thrust upon him. Chaplains, too, planned to fill their normal role only as need arose. That need hit them with overpowering force on the second day out, and never let up.

To console the distressed, to convince the unbelievers and to make the acceptance of death easier for those who could struggle no longer became a never ending task for those capable of spiritual leadership. In battle, one accommodates himself to death, for there is a cause and a reason. But here, even though living was terrible and unreal, dying was monstrous and frightening. Perhaps it was the great distance from home and loved ones which made the contemplation of it so much more lonesome and forbidding; perhaps it was the degraded, abandoned and ignominious condition we found ourselves trapped in, a state of filth and horror in which it was hard to imagine God's presence.

Having been brought up in the Christian tradition, I believed that in dying a man should have the chance to do so with dignity. Whether his time comes in the prime of life or during the waning years, his passing is an occasion for the gathering of loved ones and friends who mourn and pray. Such a loving custom, though incapable of altering the inevitable, helps the dying to feel that his life has counted for something. On the hell ships, a man had none of that. Most had to face death alone, feeling forsaken. If he had faith it was easier. Lacking that, it was frightening and desolate. In such instances, and they were innumerable, even the most courageous need reassurance.

Time after time that final, special bravery was supplemented by our chaplains. In spite of their own harsh conditions—starved into weakness, trembling from cold, uncertain of life for themselves—they continued to speak softly of hope and salvation. Like runners in a relay race, each, when his strength was spent, passed the torch to another.

I am not in position to vouch for the performance of all the chaplains, for I did not know them all. Perhaps some performed mechanically with little conviction, merely because it was requested of them. Others, no doubt, contributed nothing at all of a spiritual nature, having themselves, like so many others, been dragged down to an uncaring, subhuman condition. That was understandable. I believe that most of the wearers of the cross of the Chaplain Corps who were physically able helped many to face death with hope.

Two who were especially noteworthy for their steadfastness came from different sections of the United States and had dissimilar religious backgrounds. Chaplain Robert Preston Taylor, a Southern Baptist, claimed Texas as his home. Father William "Bill" Cummings hailed from San Francisco, California. No matter that Taylor's creed required immersion as a prerequisite for salvation and Father Bill's Catholicism held that sprinkling would cleanse one of sin, both earnestly believed that confession and faith would save men's souls. The important thing to them on the hell ships was to see that no man died alone and uninformed of the chance for salvation.

Taylor, a tall, slim, soft-spoken redhead, was ever on the job holding burial services and encouraging the living. Being a victim of brutality was nothing new to him. At Cabanatuan he had spent nine successive weeks in the "sweat box," a small wooden cage four feet long and four feet high. Having a six foot frame, he could neither stand up or lie down full length during the entire period of confinement. The box, into which two prisoners were crowded, was so located that the relentless tropical sun bore down on them all day; at night swarms of malaria-carrying mosquitos stung their sunburned flesh. Blue bottle flies buzzed around their faces and crawled over their unwashed bodies constantly. There were no latrine facilities. Food and water were withheld for days at a time. Most prisoners subjected to such torture gave up and died. Taylor, reciting scripture and psalms to exercise his mind and renew his faith, maintained his sanity and lived.

At the time of Taylor's arrest and placement in solitary confinement, he was serving as hospital chaplain. Due to the lack of quinine and other drugs, the death rate had been extremely high. Learning that he could have medicines purchased on the outside and smuggled in, he collected money from fellow prisoners and got a flow of the badly needed supplies moving in. The risk was great, but the clandestine operation saved many lives. Unfortunately for Taylor, in a raid on a secret guerrilla headquarters, the Japanese found his name on a list. Though threatened with execution, Taylor admitted no knowledge of outside activities; neither would he reveal the names of anyone inside camp working with him. Though the sweat box ordeal drained his physical strength, his faith and courage never wavered. Such a man was respected and looked up to by the tormented souls on the unbearable voyage to Japan.

Father "Bill" Cummings possessed an absolute faith in prayer and salvation. So constant and sincere were his daily petitions to Heaven that even unbelievers stood in reverence as he spoke. In Bataan, Father Bill was credited with the line "There are no atheists in fox holes." Each evening in the hold there was stillness and quiet as he began "Our Father, who art in Heaven. . . ." Many joined the chant, having been convinced by him that God would listen.

As long as his strength lasted, Father Cummings moved among the dying administering last rites and prayers for redemption. Their particular creeds were unimportant to him then; their salvation was. When the Padre became too weak to move about, his voice could still be heard praying for his fellow prisoners. Standing in place, with the support of a friend on each side, he offered up his morning and evening prayers for us all. Finally, unable to rise at all, with his back braced against a fellow prisoner, he died with Our Lord's Prayer on his lips. As if he planned it that way, Father Bill's last words in this world were "Give us this day. . . ." Years later a book with that phrase for a title was written by Sidney Stewart, a witness to the scene.

The last week of January, 1945, was the coldest, most desolate and miserable period I have ever spent in my life. The topside deck was constantly coated with ice, the wind blew continuously, and the sun never shone. Below deck each night seemed
colder than the previous one. There was no relief from hunger,
thirst and the presence of death. The *Brazil Maru* moved at a
snail's pace. Twice she stopped to take in tow another freighter
which had been damaged by torpedoes. The convoy speed at
best was slow; with the added drag our forward movement was
barely four knots. In order to evade submarines, we moved in a
zigzag course, thus doubling the distance traveled. One night
the many sharp turns in direction were especially noticeable, a
sure indication of imminent danger. For a while everyone sat
tense, contemplating the frigid water beneath us and the horror
of a torpedo exploding in our midst. To survive the latter would
only be a temporary reprieve, for certainly no one could live
long in the dark, freezing China Sea.

The engines groaned and steel plates made a growling sound
as they rubbed together with each change of direction. The ship
listed heavily to port on one turn and just as steeply to starboard on the next. Strong gusts of wind from the outside seemed
to find their way through the tarp covering the hatch opening,
no matter what our direction. Cold, hungry and tormented, I
measured the immediate danger against the likelihood of survival, even if there were no shipwreck. Already we had lost
1,000 of the 1,619 who left Manila on the *Oryoku Maru*. Of
the 600 still alive, many were near death. The daily sea burials
hung at around twenty-five. Pneumonia and diarrhea were rampant. Should the voyage last another two weeks, even the
strongest could not endure.

Faced with such tenuous prospects for survival, I came to the
conclusion that a sudden massive explosion which would end it
all in a split second would be the merciful ending for us all. Such
morbid thoughts must have been rather general among the helpless lingering survivors, for I soon began to hear comments like:
"I wish a torpedo would blow this filthy tub to bits," and "Come
on, Yanks, you can do better than that," as the ship made an-

other sudden turn. It was obvious we were in dangerous waters.

No one seemed frightened anymore. As the erratic movements of the ship grew more pronounced, more voices joined in: "Come on, Navy. Send Mr. Wada to hell." It got to be a game of betting on how soon one would hit; an odd sort of diversion it was, like betting against yourself. A bull's-eye hit and its deadly consequences didn't seem to bother anybody, for hit or miss, death was near at hand anyway. So there was a bright side. A well-planted torpedo would mean a victory for our side, a loss to the enemy, and an end of our tormented lingering.

Soon after leaving Takao my injured finger had become infected. Knowing that the doctors had nothing to work with, I saw no need to bother them with my problems. As the swelling increased, it throbbed and pained more each day. Finally Henry convinced me that I should let a doctor look at it.

Lieutenant Colonel Jack Schwartz and several corpsmen were holding sick call the morning I reported. Their station was near the forward end of the hold. I waited in line behind ten others whose ailments ranged from shrapnel wounds to pneumonia. There was so very little the doctor could do, but he went through the motions anyway. Adjusting a splint or draining an infection could bring temporary relief, but drugs and disinfectants were needed to cure infections, and food and warmth to cure respiratory ailments. None of those luxuries was available. However, it seemed to help the patient just to have a kind word from a doctor.

"What is your main problem, Lawton?" asked Doctor Schwartz. He sat on an upper bay four feet from the floor. I extended my feverish left hand as I stood in front of him.

"This finger, Doctor. I caught a hot piece of metal in it when the bomb hit."

"It needs to be drained," said Schwartz as he pressed the swollen appendage between his thumb and forefinger. An acute pain shot up my arm. My knees weakened and I felt dizzy. As quick as a flash his knife slashed into the wound. Pale blood and

pus oozed out. I crumbled to the floor in a faint. When I came
to, sick call was over.

"Are you feeling better now?"

"Yes. Much better, Doc. Thanks."

That was the way sick call was handled on the Hell Ship: no
pampering, petting or catering to. That was how it had to be;
just the basics. There were no frills to hand out. Survival was an
individual's private struggle.

Doctors, like everyone else, had no immunity to the ravages
of starvation, dehydration, cold, dysentery and madness which
tormented the beleaguered prisoners. More than a dozen of
them started the hazardous journey from Manila; less than half
would reach Japan. Of those few, Lieutenant Colonel Jack
Schwartz, Lieutenant Colonel James McG. Sullivan, and Major
"Mac" Williams somehow remained physically able to attempt
to care for the ill.

I remember Schwartz especially, for he took care of me after
we reached Japan, and later in Korea. Always serious and professional in attitude, even under the most bizarre conditions, he
never seemed to recoil or to consider quitting. His common
sense and untiring efforts brought relief to many.

During the week of January 20 each night seemed to get much
colder and every day grew more dreary. By then food was down
to a quarter cup measure, some days twice and others only
once. Water continued to be measured by the teaspoon. Dehydration became a problem even more acute than hunger. Other
than for the resulting weakness and malnutrition diseases, man
can adjust his mind to the lack of food; the gnawing hunger
pains eventually go away. But unquenched thirst builds up into
a maddening obsession. It soon makes thieves out of normally
decent human beings. Men with willpower enough to have
saved back a little water had to try to stay awake at night to
guard it. Some rogues became so cunning in their quest for
water that they could ease down beside an unsuspecting comrade in the darkness, quickly uncap the victim's canteen and
noiselessly suck it dry undetected.

The high death rate continued night after miserable night. Before it was over, four out of nine in each group in the hold had passed away. Pneumonia became the main killer as we slowly moved farther and farther north. Commander Frank Bridget, who had started the journey with outstanding energy, courage and leadership, finally ran out of time and resistance during the last week of January.

16. Japan at Last

On January 30, 1945, the *Brazil Maru* docked in Moji, Japan, in northern Kyushu. This freighter/troop carrier, which had transported thousands of young Japanese warriors to battle staging areas and returned with food and raw materials for the homeland, had this time been a dealer of misery and death. In its wake, from Lingayen to Moji, were strewn the corpses of nearly one thousand of its prisoner of war cargo.

At dockside neatly dressed Japanese officers came aboard and asked for the American senior officer. Some of them were dressed in white uniforms, all were wearing shiny leather boots. You could tell they were trying hard to not show any emotion, but it was obvious they were shocked at what met their eyes and nostrils.

Lieutenant Colonel Beecher, with a month's growth of matted beard and hair, dressed in filthy pants and shirt and with a dirty towel wrapped around his head to protect a wound, climbed out and gave a feeble salute. That done, he leaned back against the bulkhead, as if exhausted from the effort.

It was the end of January, the dead of winter. The temperature was just above freezing and a chill wind blew. The sky was overcast and a damp fog hung over the port area. We were ordered to come up and stand in formation on deck.

"We've reached Japan," said Henry. "Come on. Let's climb out of this filthy crate."

I got up and began crawling out of the bay. It was one of my bad days. From dehydration and lack of oxygen, my thinking was unclear. I was crawling toward the bulkhead instead of out toward the center. Henry caught me by the arm and led me out. Upon reaching the cold fresh air on deck, my mind cleared.

We were ordered to disrobe for delousing. In most cases it was simple; a pair of thin shorts. Everyone was sprayed: our heads, beards and then our entire shivering bodies.

Sniffing the foul odor from below, the Japanese doctor said "dysentery," and ordered a test to be made. Anywhere else in the world that procedure is accomplished by a simple stool examination: not so now. The hard way must have seemed better. With the exception of the prisoners lying helpless below, whose illnesses were obvious, everyone was subjected to the added indignity of having a glass rod inserted rectally. This included corpses lying on deck. One man collapsed and died under the eyes of the Japanese after the so-called "physical examination."

One last roll call aboard ship was held. Some say the number answering to their names was 425; others put the number at 435. In either case we had lost about half of the men who had survived the Formosa bombing and now only about one-fourth of those who had left Bilibid on December 13 were still alive; some merely lingering, close to death.

From beginning to end Lieutenant Toshino and Mr. Wada exercised their authority with baseness and callous indifference to our suffering. By their own admission, they wanted us to die. Mr. Wada, the hateful little hunchbacked interpreter, seemed to derive a certain pleasure from the daily body count.

From the dock we marched two or three blocks to a large warehouse building. The dingy-looking city, with shop fronts boarded up, showed no evidence of commerce. Japanese women, dressed in quilted-looking, heavily padded olive drab pants and jackets, stared at us as we hobbled past. They wore thick woolen scarfs draped over their heads and tied under their chins. Their breaths steamed against the frosty morning air. Their brown eyes mirrored only curiosity, but as our creeping crippled column drew directly opposite the short, shapeless women, they clasped handkerchiefs over their noses and appeared to be retching. Our stinking odors and ghostly, filthy appearance was nauseating even to peasants like these, accustomed to hauling human waste to their gardens.

The warehouse into which we were marched, with its cement block walls and concrete floors, was far from inviting, but at least it sheltered us from the cold wind. To everyone's surprise, however, we learned that there was a community bath with hot water, which we would be allowed to use. It was made of cement and was four feet deep and twelve feet square. Beside it glowed a small coal-burning furnace.

In organized groups of twelve, we eased into the enticing warm pool. It was my first experience at group bathing of that kind. I am told that Japanese men and women share such facilities with no pretense of modesty or embarrassment. It would have mattered little to me if females had been present at the time. Soaking in the steaming hot water was pure ecstasy. It warmed and relaxed my aching muscles, as if someone with soft, gentle hands were rubbing on tepid oil.

I could feel the grime of nearly two months' buildup slowly sluffing away. My pores seemed to open up to allow the poisons to ooze out. This was instant spring and summer, warm sunshine and velvety softness, a gentle purging of evil and suffering. To be warm, clean and relaxed all at the same time was a luxury I had come to believe Wada and Toshino incapable of sanctioning. Brief though it was, for that fleeting ten minutes I felt like a dignified human being once again. After the bath we were issued wool uniforms.

We spent that night in the warehouse. Though the cement floor was hard and cold, our new woolen uniforms kept us much warmer than we had been aboard ship. Another advantage was the absence of body lice, which the spraying had eliminated.

At sunup the following morning, January 31, a Japanese chow detail returned with food. In addition to a full canteen cup of rice, each prisoner got a steaming cup of seaweed soup and all the hot tea he could drink. I began to believe that someone more humane was in charge.

While we ate, military buses and ambulances pulled up in front of the building. Those of us who had sufficient strength helped the sick and injured into them for movement to the hospital. One hundred eighty-five were in that group. The remaining 240, able to walk though by no means strong and healthy, boarded a train for distribution to various camps.

The train, a passenger type, had upholstered seats and ample room for all to be seated. The steam engine pulled us at high speed. The engineer seemed fond of blowing his whistle with the universal mournful musical sound. There was no heat in the passenger cars, yet all round it was the most comfortable transportation we had experienced in over three years.

A group of one hundred was put off at Camp #1. Henry and I were in a group of one hundred assigned to Camp #3. The remaining forty or so went on to Camp #17 some distance away.

Within thirty days 161 of the 425 who reached Japan were to die—85 at the so-called hospital, 30 at #1, 31 at #3 and 15 at #17—leaving only 264 of the original 1,619 with a chance of getting back home. Eighty-four percent had perished. Sixteen percent survived for a while longer.

It was still bitterly cold when we reached Camp 3. The ground was covered with eight inches of snow and a raw wind whistled through the leafless trees surrounding the unpainted buildings. The austere bleakness seemed to warn, "go away. You should not have come here." Our new home was similar in design to Philippine Army barracks; long, low and narrow, though built of wood instead of bamboo. The aisle down the middle was covered with hard red clay. Wide boards floored the raised platforms, or bays, down each side of the aisle. There was no heat. The lone charcoal brazier midway of the building was for heating water for tea, not for warmth.

Upon arrival, each prisoner was issued three woolen blankets. We soon figured out how to interlace the edges so that they formed an airtight sleeping bag with two blankets on top and one folded doubled to lie on. Upon getting mine put together, I crawled in the open top end and seldom came out.

In spite of having been lanced twice aboard ship, my finger

soon became infected again. When Dr. Schwartz worked on it for the third time he had proper tools, sanitation and light. Slicing the finger open with a surgical scalpel, he mopped it out with an alcohol swab. "Here is the trouble," he said, with the pleased tone of one who knows he has solved a problem. Holding a small sliver of bone in his forceps, he explained, "When that piece of metal hit it chipped the bone in the joint. With this in there it never would have healed."

Though we were protected from the cold, warmth alone could not cure respiratory diseases and malnutrition. Antibiotics were unknown at the time and sulfa drugs were not made available. Several men died each day from pneumonia.

Across the aisle from me was a civilian mining engineer with whom I had struck up a friendship. He was more than fifty years old and greying. He sat up one afternoon and talked of his many interesting experiences. "Lawton," he said, "for the most part I have had a good and interesting life. There isn't much I would change except the past three years. But it's about over now. I won't live much longer."

"Don't talk that way," I said. "We've been through the worst part of it. The war is about over now."

"No. My days are numbered. But you are young. Hang in there. You will make it."

The next morning he did not wake up; another victim of cruelty and inhumanity. With him went a storehouse of knowledge and experience which would be so badly needed after the war.

Shortly after arrival at Camp 3, I, along with Henry and several others, was given an intravenous infusion of saline solution to replace lost body salts and liquids. It seemed to help. I felt better and gained some strength. Henry, however, complained of chest pains and general discomfort. On the night of January 10 he was given a pint of blood plasma. Privately I asked the doctor what his problem was.

"Pneumonia," he whispered. "Captain Leitner is a very ill man. I hope this will help."

Early the next morning I awoke to find him, dressed only in

cotton underwear, headed for the door with a canteen cup in his hand. His face was flushed, an indication of fever.

"Where are you going, Henry?" I yelled to him.

"To get some of that cool, wet snow," he answered. "I'm burning up."

"Come back," I pleaded. "You'll freeze out there."

"I'm hot and dehydrated. I must have something cool to drink," he answered as he staggered through the doorway on bare feet, oblivious to the freezing temperature.

That night Captain Henry D. Leitner, my closest friend, passed away. His death was more than another sadness for me. It shocked and stunned and left me feeling alone and abandoned. I had become so accustomed to seeing men die—by bullet and bomb, by disease, starvation and exposure, thousands of them in every cruel way—that I thought I was hardened against sentiment, emotion and tears. But now I buried my face in my blanket and wept.

Something went out of me that day with Henry's death; something of the poetic beauty of thought and feeling, of kindness and consideration and understanding which comes with true friendship. But he left me with memories of occasional laughter and of helping each other through tough times, of sharing what was scarce and of looking ahead to the future with hope. Most important, his death broke away the defensive shell which I had built around my mind and heart to steel me against the hurt of tragedy. In the midst of my sorrow I felt solace in the rediscovered ability to shed tears and to mourn the loss of a friend. Whatever else might happen, I was surviving as a human being.

It was mid-February when Henry died. The weather was still bitter cold, and stayed that way throughout that month and well into March. Snow remained nearly a foot deep on the ground. By drinking several quarts of hot tea daily and remaining under my blankets most of the time, I gradually thawed out, and in general began to feel somewhat better, but gradually I became lame in my left leg. Soon it was sore and tender and feverish. Finally I couldn't put any weight on it when I tried to get to the tea bucket.

After several days of pain, I decided to go to sick call. With the swelling and redness and extreme tenderness from hip to ankle, I feared that it might be blood poisoning or something of a serious nature.

The doctor on duty was a very nice gentleman from Java. After careful examination, he pronounced it a severe case of malnutrition.

"You have an acute case of beriberi," he said. "I saw some liquid B-1 in the Jap dispensary this morning. If I can steal some I will give you a shot. Come back tomorrow."

The following morning I hobbled back to sick call again. The doctor proudly held up a bottle of liquid thiamine, which he had found among American Red Cross supplies which the Japanese would not turn over to us.

"This will have to be a spinal injection," he said. "I must warn you that there is some danger in spinal injections."

"I'm willing to take that risk," I quickly answered. "I must have relief from this pain."

That injection was one of the good luck things which happened to me during those dreary years. Within three days the pain and inflamation had disappeared and I could walk normally once again. It seemed miraculous.

Though the temperature still hovered around freezing, March 1, by decree of the Emperor, was the first day of spring. From that date on there would be no more fires for heating, which meant that we would no longer have our charcoal burner to heat water for hot tea. Tea would be available only at mealtime.

By mid-March the snow began to melt and the weather moderated considerably. Men who were well and strong enough were assigned duties within the camp. My doctor continued to carry me on the sick list, so I avoided such duty. I stayed under the blankets and slept a great deal.

17. The Last Move

In early April we were informed that all prisoners in our camp
would be moved. As usual, there was no hint of destination. I
dreaded the thought of being transferred, for such journeys were
always tough and debilitating. Our number of survivors was
getting smaller. Of the 100 who had ended up in our camp after
the nightmarish trip from Manila on the *Oryoku Maru* 31 had
since died. Another such ordeal would certainly finish us all off
quickly.

On the appointed day we were loaded into trucks in the early
morning and driven away. In spite of the fact that the 60-
day rest had rehabilitated me considerably, I was uneasy over
what lay ahead. Though much weaker than I had been upon
leaving Manila on December 13, I could walk under my own
power and had high hopes of lasting until the war would come
to an end.

A two-hour ride brought us to an area of the port different
from where we had landed at the end of January. It appeared to
be more of a passenger terminal than a cluttered up cargo area.
After being unloaded from the trucks we marched through a
warehouse building and out to a wooden dock. Here we sat under a bright, warm sun. For once, things seemed to be perfectly
timed, for we had hardly settled down when a seagoing ferry
tied up directly in front of us and began discharging several
hundred Japanese civilians. They had serious, tense expressions,
and moved with haste and purpose. None spoke to us or even

218

acknowledged our presence. Their frequent skyward glances suggested they had experienced recent air raids.

An equal number of Japanese approached and began boarding the same boat. Several family groups were among them. It was eye-catching to us that the girls and mothers of the families were heavily laden with belongings in carriers on their backs, while the male children walked empty handed. The head of the household strolled along with only a valise, suggesting superiority. It occurred to me that if there were pedestals for women in Japan, they were to be carried by them, not sat upon.

Once the civilians were loaded, we were marched aboard into a segregated compartment. The boat, with tiled floors and walls, was neat and clean-looking. It sturdy structure suggested it to be amply seaworthy. There was no doubt it was designed for short people, as the ceilings and doorways had scarcely more than five feet of head clearance. Fortunately there was ample room for everyone to sit on the floor.

Our party numbered 139 Americans, the survivors of the 100 who had been assigned to Camps 1 and 3, and 11 British and Dutch. The 232 who had ended up in the hospital and Camp 17 had dwindled to 132 and were now being sent to Manchuria. The combined remnant added up to 271, all that were left of 1,619 passengers of the hell ship.

On a warm, bright spring afternoon our ferryboat headed into the Tsushima Straits. The water was calm except for small waves churned up by the busy harbor traffic. A northerly course took us past Tsushima and other small islands. Darkness fell after we reached the open sea. By morning we had completed the hundred-mile trip to Pusan, a port city on the southeastern coast of Korea.

Awaiting us at Pusan was a guard detail and kitchen crew. They served us a full meal of rice, fish and soup. The guards were civil and did not harass or hurry us. The combination of good food, friendly guards, and the absence of Mr. Wada made me feel that things were getter better. Our morale was higher than it had been for six months. After breakfast we marched a short distance to the railroad station.

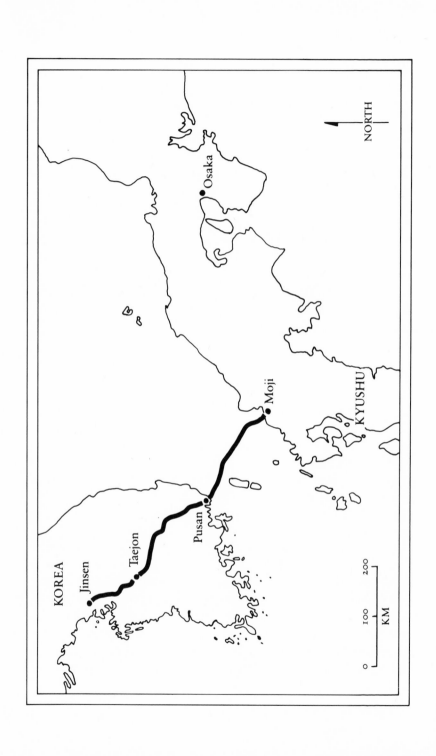

While awaiting the train's arrival, I thought back over the dozen times I had been involved in moves from one camp to another. Five were by train, four aboard ships, two in trucks and one a long march. All but two, the just completed ferry ride and the short train trip to Camp 3, had been terrible even by Japanese standards. The truck rides were substandard even for cattle. Sea transport by freighter was always crowded, airless and filthy. The sixty-five-mile journey by foot, later called the "Death March," was not misnamed. By far, the worst of all was the recent journey from Manila to Japan on the Hell Ships. Beginning in the sweltering tropics and dragging out for days on end in the freezing north, it had cost the lives of over eighty percent of our number. What lay ahead for us now, I wondered anxiously. Would it be another crowded freight car, or an overloaded open truck bouncing over dusty roads, or a combination of all the inadequate, inhumane ways of transporting prisoners of war?

The rail yard was busy with noisy switch engines shuttling freight cars back and forth. Pusan being the terminus of the main Korean north-south rail line, it was the receiving point for raw materials destined for Japanese war production. Seeing nothing but boxcars, I feared the worst—a repeat of the suffocating, murderous trip from San Fernando to Capas in the Philippines.

A passenger train pulled up and stopped in front of the platform. We looked at each other with cautious smiles, daring to hope this would be our conveyance. As hurrying Korean stevedores and factory workers boiled out, we were alerted to prepare to board. Once inside we were amazed to find ourselves in a clean, modern, standard sized passenger coach. Not only were the seats cushioned, they were upholstered with a red velvet material. Equally surprising, there was ample room. Only two prisoners were assigned to a seat. Lieutenant Arthur O. Holmes of Brooklyn and Hoboken and I sat together. Captain Paul H. Krauss of Newark, New Jersey, and Captain Lee G. Miles of Eminence, Kentucky, took seats behind ours. In front of us were

Pfc. Jose (Joe) Garcia of Los Lunas, New Mexico, and Private Charles Towne from Salem, Oregon, both medical corpsmen. Across the aisle were Captain Gary J. Anloff, Jr., Los Angeles, California, Lieutenant Kenneth Wheeler, Fullerton, California, Lieutenant Colonel Curtis Beecher, so outstanding in his leadership aboard the *Oryoku*, and Lieutenant Colonel Jack W. Schwartz, the tireless surgeon who had performed his skills without proper instruments. All were comfortably seated, uncrowded and free to move about. None of us had ever expected to be treated like human beings again for as long as we remained in Japanese hands. There was almost a holiday mood among us.

The train headed north upon leaving the station and continued in that general direction, though it was hard to tell with any degree of accuracy. With the shades drawn, estimating speed by noting the frequency with which telephone poles or objects on the landscape were passed was not possible. At times our rate of movement seemed rapid; at others, slow and labored. We surmised that ascending and descending some of Korea's rugged mountains accounted for the variation.

After several hours of riding, relaxed and cheerful, we began to wonder about food. No one dared ask, of course, but we doubted that a kitchen car had been brought along for our convenience.

As if reading our minds, a chow crew of two civilians came through at noon pushing a food cart. From it they passed out individual hot box lunches to each prisoner. The lunches, packaged in thin veneer wood of the size and appearance of cigar boxes, were all alike. Each contained a full helping of rice, a generous chunk of fried fish, and several pickles. Mine contained two beautiful, large red cherries. With saliva flowing, I popped one of the cherries in my mouth, expecting a delicious sweetness. A mouthful of raw salt and vinegar could not have been more sickening. Then I remembered: the Japanese do not cook with salt, choosing instead to serve it as a side dish to be used along with the meal, usually in the form of briney pickles. I gave my cherries away and enjoyed the fish and rice saltless.

We wondered where they were taking us and what conditions we were heading into. There was no way of knowing what lay ahead, but since leaving Camp #3, our treatment, food and traveling conditions were superior to anything we had experienced in three years. It was the week of April 10, 1945, the third anniversary of the Death March from Bataan. Though we were about as far out of reach of American rescue forces as we could get, we were warm, comfortable and not so hungry now. There was reason to hope our luck had changed.

The train trip continued throughout the day and night. Box lunches were served in the evening and again the following morning. It was like a continuous picnic. Morale was high. At noon of the second day we arrived at Jinsen (now Inchon), about fifty miles below the 38th parallel.

From what we could see of it, Jinsen appeared to be a fairly large city. Everywhere there was the look of poverty. Buildings were dingy and people poorly clad and lean-looking. We marched to a camp on the edge of the city, perhaps no more than a mile from the main street. The compound was enclosed by a ten-foot-high board fence, the boards standing vertically and close together so that there were no cracks. Approaching, we could not see in, and once inside were unable to see out. A guardhouse, manned by a platoon of armed soldiers, stood at the entrance gate. With the exception of our short stay in Bilibid Prison in Manila with its tall brick wall, this would be the first camp in which we were completely blocked off from any view of outside life or sound.

Despite the better treatment we now seemed to be receiving, the realization that we were totally isolated brought a feeling of loneliness and frustration. So walled in, there would be no way to communicate with local Koreans, even if they were inclined to be friendly. Our situation also foreclosed any possibility of barter and black market dealings. It was generally known that Koreans hated their Japanese masters, but the wall blocked out any prospect of that ill feeling working to our benefit.

Though on the afternoon of our arrival in Jinsen the sun shone brightly, the air was crisp and chill. The warmth of spring comes late in that part of Korea, which is situated as far north as Chicago. Sitting on the unthawed ground awaiting arrival of the Japanese camp commander, I was glad to be dressed in winter clothing.

The compound, obviously a small troop garrison, contained several small buildings and one much larger than the rest. All were single-storied and made of wood. Two were assigned to us: one housed a small hospital, and another, at the entrance, served as Japanese headquarters. Most of the buildings were used for warehousing and work projects.

Before leaving Japan many of us began having problems with swollen feet and legs. The long trip aggravated the condition. Once getting back to normal exercise and activity, most threw it off; others got worse. I was among several who were hospitalized. The swelling progressed from my legs to my body and then on up to my head. At any point on my body, pressure with a finger would leave a sink or indentation which required several minutes to level out. Dr. Schwartz diagnosed the ailment as wet beriberi and offered no solution. "You, like the rest of us, need protein and vitamins. I wish there was something I could do," he said with great sympathy.

Once my head became soft, my thinking was affected. It grew progressively harder to carry on a conversation. Often in the middle of a sentence I would lose my trend of thought. It was a helpless and disturbing feeling. Getting up and down became difficult. When I walked my legs felt as if fifty-pound weights were attached to them. My sense of balance was poor.

One day when my state of confusion was at its worst, I was ordered to Japanese headquarters. Though I could think of nothing I had done wrong, I was frightened. Hobbling in, I stood at attention and saluted. The Japanese lieutenant berated me for a full minute before stopping. He looked dead serious and angry. The interpreter then informed me that I had more money than I was entitled to possess.

"You have been gambring. This is serrious. You wirr be severry punished," he said emphatically.

I tried to explain that I had been ill in the hospital. "No gambling goes on there," I pleaded.

"Then why do you have too much money?" he demanded.

"I don't know, sir. I didn't even realize I had too much."

"You wirr be punished," he continued, ignoring my feeble excuse. "Who did you gambre with? Tell us or you wirr all be punished."

Visualizing being knocked down and kicked and stomped, I was desperate. Suddenly I recalled that Japanese in previous camps seemed to fear insane prisoners, so I decided to put on an act. Raising a finger to each side of my head and staring wide-eyed at the lieutenant, I made the circular movement indicating lunacy. It worked. The Japanese looked at each other, shook their heads, and dismissed me with no further comment.

The hospital accommodated twenty patients—approximately ten percent of the camp population. It was usually full. Such ailments as multiple raw skin ulcers, eye infections and slow healing wounds inflicted in the ship's bombings were common. The most serious problems were the cases of wet beriberi. Captain George Brundrette, a Texas A&M graduate from Dallas, and I were the most severely afflicted.

George was short, hardly more than five feet six inches, and brunette. He wore his black hair in a crew cut and sported a neatly trimmed mustache. His normal weight should have been 150 pounds. In his swollen condition, with face so puffed that his eyes were nearly closed, and his thirty-inch waist stretched to forty-five or more inches, he appeared to be carrying twice that poundage. His kneecaps were indistinguishable from the legs and his fingers and toes stood apart, inflated and stubby.

This bizarre, swollen condition was due to the inability of his body organs to eliminate liquids normally. The fluids, trapped, worked their way out into the tissues. My appearance was similar, but I was at least mobile. George was bedridden.

Malnutrition was the cause of our problem. Its cure was high protein and vitamin foods. Lacking those, we could only hope to outlast the war and survive until relief came. Quite naturally the intake of water aggravated the condition. In spite of my confused mental condition (my ability to think clearly grew weaker), I realized that I must drink sparingly. George seemed to swell more each day, as he consumed large quantities of tea and water.

"George, you must stop drinking so much," I warned.

"I'm dehydrated," he answered. "I don't seem to be able to satisfy that terrible thirst."

"You can't possibly be dehydrated. Look at us. We are both waterlogged now."

"I'm thirsty," he said almost defiantly, "and I intend to keep on drinking until I get enough."

It was strange to see a person whose body was ballooned to elephantine proportions from excessive fluids craving water. He seemed to have an insatiable thirst. Perhaps the harsh memory of forty-seven days aboard ship during which water was rationed by the spoonful still haunted him.

The doctors, with limited equipment, did all they could for Brundrette. They even tried tapping his tissues with needles to drain him, but that was unsuccessful. Finally the skin on the inside of his thighs, stretched beyond capacity, split open and rivers of water drained out. Within minutes the blanket and matting beneath him and a space for several feet around were saturated. His body rapidly shrank from a giant circumference to a mere shadow. Having lived for weeks with too much fluid, his system seemed unable to cope with its absence. Captain George Brundrette became our first prisoner to die in the Jinsen camp. Not only was his death saddening to me, it was shocking as well. It made me realize that edema could be fatal if not kept under control.

On the day that George was buried I devised a simple plan to keep tabs on my body fluid level. Finding two empty salmon cans, I labeled one DRINKING and the other BENJO. The former I kept with my eating gear and the other in the latrine. With marks at different levels on each, I kept an accurate measure of intake and output, never consuming more liquid in a day than was eliminated. While this was no cure, it at least prevented further swelling.

At about the same time the Japanese unintentionally helped my problem. Due to the scarcity of rice, they began substituting soybeans as a part of the ration. Though the soybeans were tasteless and we were never able to cook them to a palatable softness, they contained a high level of protein, our greatest dietary need.

Within ten days the soybean diet worked wonders. Suddenly one morning a small trickle turned into a seemingly endless flow. As if a drain plug had been removed, I lost at least a gallon of liquid and an hour later an equal amount. It was as if all the little creeks and tributaries in my body had merged into one main stream and caused a flood. Within twelve hours my body was so reduced in size that many could not recognize me. For once I was happy to be a bag of bones.

With my skin ailment under control, I moved back to barracks and got into prison camp routine once more. It was good to have regained a sense of balance and to be able to walk easily without fear of falling. My assigned space on the straw-matted floor was between Arthur Holmes and Paul Krauss, both of whom were close friends at Davao. Nearby were Major Houston Parks Houser, Captain Gary J. Anloff, Jr., Navy Lieutenant Ken Wheeler, and Captain Douglas R. Fisher. Fisher had been employed by a candy manufacturing company before the war and could always hold a sweet starved audience spellbound with a description of the delectable delicacies it had been his job to distribute.

There were several light duty details within the compound. I was assigned to the matchbox project. It was an indoor operation and required very little effort and no skill. The tools of the trade were a block of wood approximately four inches square and ten inches long, a pot of glue, one small brush, and a stack of precut paper. With these supplies we made paper containers which were designed to hold a dozen boxes of wooden matches.

Seated around a long, narrow table, unguarded, we worked individually and at our own pace. The procedure was to place the block of wood, or form, on the center of the paper, fold the left edge over, dab it with glue, fold the right edge over on top of it and slide the thumb along the seam to make it stick, fold one end, and glue, leaving the opposite end open. The final step was to glue on preprinted labels which indicated the contents of the package once filled. That done, the form was then dumped out and the package placed on the floor, open end up, to dry.

An ambitious laborer, being paid for piecework, could have turned out a finished product every two minutes. We took ten minutes or more, and exercised no care to make them uniform in size or neat-looking. In fact, as in all things made by us for the Japanese, we took pains to make them as nearly unusable as we could get by with. No two packages had the same dimensions.

Lieutenant Ken Wheeler worked in the sewing room with another group of light duty, or disabled prisoners. They soon began calling the project "sew-sew" or "so-so," an expression which the Japanese soon used themselves. A Korean factory near the compound manufactured flimsy cotton uniforms for the Japanese Army. The garments were turned out without buttons or buttonholes. The job of the prisoners was to cut and stitch the holes and attach buttons opposite. Production quotas were assigned.

The inherent awkwardness of the American male with scissors, needle and thread soon became evident. "Each day," Wheeler said with glee, "we ruined many garments by cutting buttonholes in places where buttons could never serve a useful purpose. The boys rather enjoyed appearing stupid and really worked hard at it."

They finally learned to sew on buttons to a passable degree, but the Japs abandoned any hope of teaching them the buttonhole skill. The project was ultimately shut down for three days while a solution was worked out. Meanwhile, a cut in rations was ordered for the "stupid" Americans. When work was resumed they found that another supply of garments had been brought in with buttonholes already cut and stitched, leaving them only the buttons to do. Now the "dumb" Americans would have to figure out a way to mess up a task so simple and not be caught at it. It didn't take long.

The buttons had four holes and the prisoners were carefully instructed to pass the thread through each hole four times. The finished products were inspected each day under threat of punishment if they were not done correctly. It was soon noticed that the inspector merely counted the number of threads, rather than checking to see how securely the buttons were attached to the jackets.

"There was the answer," explained Wheeler. "From that point on we merely threaded the buttons first and then attached them with only one thread. 'Sew-sew' became fun then, as we pictured Japanese soldiers dashing out to formation with buttons popping off, or one of them standing at attention undergoing severe slapping for not having his blouse buttoned." The conspiracy was never discovered.

By mid-June I was well enough for regular duty. The only physical labor job was farm work. About 100 yards southeast of headquarters, separated by a cross board fence within the compound, was a three-acre vegetable garden. I was assigned to duty there along with fifty other prisoners. We grew spring onions, white potatoes, a turnip-like root vegetable which was too fibrous and pulpy but had a peppery, spicy flavor somewhat like radishes, cabbage and sweet potatoes.

We were forbidden to eat the produce on the job, but of course did so when the guard's back was turned. Onions, with their pungent odor and savory taste, were particularly tempting. They were just the right size to be taken into the mouth with one bite, but unfortunately we had to eat the tops too, in order to destroy the evidence. We should have restrained ourselves for not only was there danger of being punished, there was also a health hazard: the garden was fertilized with human waste. There comes a time, though, in man's struggle for life when he will eat anything that passes for food, so long as it is not known to be instantly deadly. We had long since passed that point. Further, we felt we had built up certain immunities to stomach parasites and dysentery. Even spoiled fish failed to upset our stomachs.

In addition to planting, hoeing and harvesting, our duties included fertilizing the garden. The main material for plant nutrition in a great part of the orient at that time was "night soil," collected from the latrine. Each morning, by rotation, two of our number were assigned to the "honey bucket" detail. Their job was to dip the waste from the pit with long-handled scoops, pour it into a wooden bucket and transport it to the garden. The bucket was three feet deep and fifteen inches in diameter. A grass rope served as its handle. My day for the detail came during the second week on the job.

After filling the bucket, we slipped a bamboo pole through the handle, as was the custom, placed the ends of the pole on our shoulder and straightened up, thus lifting the smelly load clear of the ground. My partner took the forward end of the bamboo and I brought up the rear. We had learned from observation and experience that when carrying a sloshing liquid load, it is more efficient to move in a slow trot, with a springy motion of the knees; that way the load, being in suspension, is lighter and spillage is avoided.

With our bodies and steps perfectly synchronized, we had moved along smoothly for about fifty yards when, glancing up, I noticed the rope beginning to separate.

"Drop it!" I yelled. "The rope's coming apart!"

Simultaneously we slipped the pole from our shoulders. I jumped back clear of danger. My partner, with the cargo behind him, froze in his tracks. The bucket dropped flat on its bottom but tilted forward. The full load splashed him from head to foot. That was my third and last experience with "honey buckets," and was the only one in which I came out a winner.

Though walled in and completely cut off from the outside world, we soon developed a source of news, or rumors. The guard detail was made up mostly of Koreans who, like most of their countrymen, had no love for the Japanese. One of them was rather friendly and often came into the compound to visit during off-duty hours. He seemed to take great pleasure in informing us that the Japanese were losing the war. To support his claims, he cited specific battles in which the enemy had suffered heavy losses in manpower and territory. "Okinawa has been taken by the Americans," he said. "The Japanese have lost most of their fleet. Soon their homeland will be invaded."

We had no way to verify his reports, but they sounded good to us. Our morale picked up considerably and we thought we detected a different attitude on the part of the Japanese as well. It seemed significant that the lieutenant who was second in command and who each evening at roll call could always find an excuse to slap or kick a prisoner, was suddenly transferred out. It was fortunate for him that he found duty elsewhere, for I am sure he would have been murdered by the prisoners when the war ended.

Having heard so many good-sounding rumors over the more than three years, I restrained my enthusiasm for fear of having another letdown in case the war continued for another six months or more. A comparison of America's industrial potential against Japan's limited natural resources dictated ultimate defeat for Nippon. Yet caution reminded me that the Japanese were a proud and tenacious people, who would not give up easily.

It was around the tenth of August that we knew that victory and freedom would soon be ours. The revelation came not from the Korean's assurances or the more civil attitude of the Japanese, but from one of our own men.

From the beginning of imprisonment I had made it a policy to surround myself with optimistic, humorous men. The one exception to that rule was Captain Paul Krauss. Paul, a fine gentlemen and sincere friend, was perhaps the most pessimistic man I knew during those years. He always looked on the gloomy side of things. "We will never make it," he often said. "Our side will win, but we can't possibly hold out that long." It got to be a joke and an actual source of laughter for me.

Suddenly that morning of August 10, Krauss came out from under his blanket, sat upright and said to me in all sincerity, "Manny, I have the strangest feeling this morning. Something tells me the war is about over. I can't explain it, but it's as real to me as if the Emperor had announced it. I am convinced we will soon be free."

I felt his forehead to see if he were feverish. He wasn't. "Paul, if you believe that, I am convinced the war must have ended last week."

He was steadfast in his conviction. "I don't know if it was a dream or a premonition, or the voice of God," he continued convincingly, "but it is real to me and I believe it."

A few days later Colonel Jack Schwartz noticed that the Japanese doctor, a young lieutenant who assisted him at the infirmary, seemed extremely nervous and worried.

"Something is bothering you, Lieutenant," said Schwartz. "What is it? Can I help?"

The lieutenant broke down and unburdened himself. With tears in his eyes and almost pleading, he began, "I fear for my safety. We have lost the war. Now the Americans will come in and kill me. I have done nothing wrong. I was only serving my country. Now I must die for that."

Despite all the horrors he had endured at the hands of the lieutenant's countrymen Schwartz was deeply touched. "You need not fear for your life. Americans don't act like that. I will speak up for you. You have been kind and helpful to me and to all the prisoners."

The lieutenant seemed reassured. "The Americans have a new bomb," he explained. "It is called an atomic bomb. It has enough power to destroy a whole city at once. One explosion wiped out Hiroshima with its 250,000 people."

"How do you know this?"

"The Emperor has announced it. He has ordered all forces to surrender."

That conversation took place on the morning of August 16, 1945. Schwartz spread the good news, though he advised that it should not be taken as official. There was subdued and quiet delight. It was like smelling the savory odors of a roasting pig, knowing it would be yours to feast on but not quite yet done.

At lunchtime it was announced that there would be a formation at 2 P.M., at which time the Japanese camp commander would like to speak to us. It was significant that we were being asked, not ordered, to attend. The excitement and tension built higher, but after years of strict and severe discipline we had learned to control our emotions.

At the appointed hour all hands assembled at the designated place and eagerly waited. Shortly the Japanese guard detail marched in and stood at attention with rifles at present arms. A small portable platform was rolled out to serve as a center stage. An old Japanese colonel, the camp commander, slowly mounted the steps and took a position directly in front of us. The tension mounted. The colonel looked serious and troubled. Calmly and in a subdued voice he read in Japanese a short prepared statement. The interpreter followed with an English pronouncement of the same message while the colonel stood aside, distressed, humbled and yet dignified.

"The war has ended. His Imperial Majesty, the Emperor, has ordered that all hostilities cease. I am to surrender this garrison to the senior American officer present. My duty now is to protect you from outside harm; not to guard you. All arms and supplies will be turned over to you. It is suggested that, for your own safety, you do not leave the compound until American forces come in. However, if you do desire to go into the city, I request that you stop by headquarters and allow me to send a soldier with you for your protection." At the completion of the announcement the colonel bowed to our senior officer Lieutenant Colonel Curtis T. Beecher, of the Fourth Marine Regiment, and handed over his sword.

It was high drama, the moment we had dreamed of for so long, a time to shout and to be merry. And yet there was only stillness and quiet. Our long captivity was over.

Epilogue: Coming Home

In October, 1941, I had left San Francisco en route to a military assignment in the Philippines. Four interminable years later I returned to American soil in this same memorable city. Coming home, however, was a matter of degree.

Anywhere under the American flag had seemed somewhat like home after being in enemy hands for so long. I began to savor the feeling even in faraway Manila, where I met my brother Paul. I sensed the warmth of it progressively increase in San Francisco and Albuquerque and Savannah, as the place of my origin grew nearer. Any bed with a mattress felt comfortable after years of bamboo bruises to hip, knee and ankle bones sustained from fitful nights on unpadded wooden floors. But none gave that dreamed-of feeling of security until I snuggled between clean sheets on the engulfing feather bed in the same blue-walled room in which I had slept as a child. The rambling farmhouse had been the dwelling place of my father and his father before him.

Outside, under moonlit skies, familiar sounds made it more convincing. I could hear the distantly spaced all-night vigil of whippoorwills calling down curses on evil spirits of the forest. Hoot owls seemed to be warning off intruders. The predawn, authoritative blast of a backyard rooster sounded reveille to man and fowl. In the distant barnyard came a plea for breakfast from a newborn calf, answered by its mother's reassuring moo.

Daytime love calls of mourning doves in nearby tall pines could be heard—all these familiar sounds of my boyhood served to reassure me that the threat of bayonet-carrying enemy guards and the invisible chains of bondage were gone forever. I knew now that my roots were finally reestablished in the land of my forebears. Secure in this setting I looked back on the events following surrender.

When the old colonel concluded his message of capitulation the mood of the prisoners was not what any of us had foreseen. Even before the commander of our captors finished speaking I could sense in all of us an unexpected calm. We were stunned and relieved. To our complete surprise we had already begun to feel fragments of pity for this humiliated old man. Though the years of degradation and abuse heaped on us by his countrymen were fresh on our minds, and the starvation and clubbings still ached in our bones and muscles, we felt inclined to reach out and help him rather than to increase his humiliation.

The guards, though armed with rifles, looked frightened. All of the hateful, inhumane treatment we had suffered flashed through my mind: the Japanese soldiers who had abused and robbed us at the surrender in Bataan; the exhausting, murderous Death March; the caustic major at O'Donnell who vowed eternal hatred for all Americans; Mr. Wada, the merciless hunchback who appeared to enjoy seeing our men die from thirst, suffocation, starvation and freezing on the Hell Ships.

I am sure that the mind of each of my comrades was crowded with its own reasons to hate. Among us were sufficient fresh scars, both mental and physical, to have incited us to rush forward, seize their weapons, club them to the dirt and stand astride their helpless, prostrate bodies. But nothing so bizarre happened. Indeed, nothing akin to hateful, revengeful, derisive conduct on our part occurred at all. We merely stood and stared across the twenty-five feet of bare dirt separating us, the newly freed, from them, the soon to be prisoners of war.

Perhaps our restraint was the result of our own experience of the bitterness and the agony of defeat. I prefer to believe it was the natural product of generations of American civilization and its spontaneous compassion for the underdog. Christianity, no doubt, played its role.

Once the dejected soldiers were marched away to be posted to guard the camp's entrance, we broke into victory yells which must have been heard miles away. There were shouts of Victory! Freedom! Food! Home! America! Come on Yanks!

Paul Krauss could not help saying "I told you so!" Houston Houser, with a normally husky voice, was soon too hoarse to speak. Art Holmes lit up a big handmade cigar which he had been saving for some special occasion. There was dancing and embraces and tears of joy. When the revelry eventually settled down, the British chaplain gave an emotional prayer of thanksgiving for our deliverance. This was followed by a passionate group singing of "God Bless America."

Meanwhile the cooks, always serious about their responsibilities, had raided the storehouse and come out with bountiful supplies of rice, beans, dried fish, pickles and various condiments. From the garden they brought in fresh onions, cabbages and turnips. It was obvious that the quantities of each being prepared were sufficient for twice our number. "For once," explained the mess officer, "I want you to have all you can eat and still have some left over to throw away."

At midmorning the following day we heard the drone of approaching aircraft. It turned out to be only one, a B-29. Its powerful four engines made it sound like a flight of several planes. We had never seen the beautiful monster before. It flew low, directly over the camp, circled, and reversed its course. The pilot cut his speed to minimum and approached as if in a glide. We could see the stars on its wings. The bomb bay opened. As the giant bomber reached the edge of the drill field, fifty-gallon barrels began cascading from its belly. Beautiful red, white and blue parachutes attached to the barrels blossomed open. The barrels slowed and drifted to the ground. To our great joy they contained food—hams, turkeys, corned beef, canned fish, vegetables, fruits, candies, puddings—medical supplies and clothing. It was food that would be tasty and nourishing and filling, and in quantities far greater than our immediate needs.

Bathed, shaved and dressed in neatly tailored uniforms which had been dropped with the food, we sat down to a noonday banquet. Our taste buds worked overtime identifying delectable flavors we had long forgotten. After an hour's siesta we snacked on sandwiches, sweets and coffee. By evening our appetites were as keen as if we had not eaten at noon and in between. On and on it went, night and day, three huge meals and bountiful snacks to tide us over from one sitting to the next. It was an eating orgy. The members of the rescue team which came in to make plans for our evacuation shook their heads in disbelief as they watched each of us consume as much as three of them and then go back for more.

For two months after liberation that pace of ravenous eating continued without letup. I am sure there was something more involved than merely the enjoyment of the good taste of food. No doubt it was psychological, too. To have talked of favorite dishes during all waking hours for three and a half years, and dreamed of gourmet dishes at night, left us with gluttonous cravings which were almost insatiable.

After several days of feasting and doing absolutely nothing in the way of physical exertion, Art Holmes and I decided to go down into the city and see the U.S. army of occupation come ashore. We went by the guardhouse and asked for a Japanese guard to go along with us. Neither he nor we spoke the other's tongue, but we let our wishes be known by sign language.

The city of Jinsen seemed to be at a standstill, though shops and stores were open for business. By the appearance of the business district, we judged the population to be around 150,000 at the time. The people on the streets were anxious and nervous, as well they might be with one occupying army being driven out and another, of unknown behavior, moving in. They paid no attention to us as we strolled along.

As we approached the main street we heard the chanting of

slogans from a large group of voices. Police, armed with shot-guns and clubs, occupied the intersection immediately ahead of us. They motioned us to move back.

Arriving at the corner, we saw several hundred students two blocks to our right marching in our direction. It was they who were doing the chanting. The police yelled to them through bullhorns. We assumed they were ordering them to turn back. The marchers continued to move forward. Our guard motioned to us to step into a store entrance. We had no sooner done so than the police began firing. The marchers halted and then dispersed at a run.

Several blocks before reaching the waterfront we met the incoming American troops. With the war over and they the victors, I expected to see joking, laughing, happy-go-lucky young conquerors proudly marching in on an unopposed landing to relax and enjoy the fruits of their final invasion.

Young they were and strong-looking. With full field packs on their backs and rifles at the ready however, they gave the impression of men capable and ready to go into battle immediately. No doubt the memory of places like New Guinea, Saipan and Okinawa, islands where the enemy, though defeated and surrounded, refused to give up and had to be killed to the last man, was still on their minds. Also probably fresh in their memories were the instances in which Japanese had faked surrender and then begun fighting all over again. Now they were taking no chances. Until the last enemy soldier laid down his arms, these troops would remain constantly on alert.

From the uneasy streets of Jinsen to the welcome streets of San Francisco involved a number of starts and stops. Some of the stops, as in Manila, threatened to prolong themselves beyond reason. Although the official word was that ex-POWs would have top priority on air and sea transport, the facts did not reflect the policy. Day after day C-54 passenger planes left without us. We were stuck.

It was at this point that one of our homeward-bound group

emerged as leader. This was George Faulkner, a handsome, dashing, confident Air Corps type. Perhaps he could be labeled an accomplished actor. At one moment he could be the smiling, bowing affable gentleman, and the next a belligerent, argumentative, forceful challenger. However, his encounters were usually won verbally rather than through physical force. In Manila George, a first lieutenant, took on the commanding general. He was not overmatched.

At first he got the brush-off from staff people. Undaunted, he insisted that his business was important and would be brief. The general happened to come into the outer office as George was pressing his case with the chief of staff. Overhearing, he was impressed. "Come in, Lieutenant," he gently invited.

"Thank you, sir," responded George, with the air of a winner and a disdainful glance at the colonel.

"Now what is your problem?"

"General, we have been in Japanese prisoner-of-war camps for the past three and one-half years. The Army daily bulletin of three weeks ago stated that we would have top priority on transportation home. I happen to know that other people are getting that space. We just sit and wait. Sir, we want to go home."

The general picked up his telephone and barked an order. The transportation officer rushed in and saluted.

"Colonel," ordered the general, "I understand that this man has been waiting for three weeks to get home. I further understand that other people are getting out. I don't want excuses. I want action! Immediate action!"

Air Force headquarters was approximately ten miles from our hospital area. Before George returned, we had orders to pack up and prepare to fly to the States. Within four hours we were airborne.

Because of George's demonstrated ability to get things done, as well as knowing his way around in San Francisco (he was a native son and a product of Stanford Law School), we automatically looked to him to unlock the mystery, gaiety and excitement of the Golden Gate city. That George did, with the deftness and savor of an off-duty tour guide who knew all the places and people but had always lacked the time to enjoy them leisurely. He took us to Fisherman's Wharf by day, where we indulged insatiable appetites on the delicacies of the sea; to Chinatown by night to delight in, to our full satisfaction, exotic Chinese dishes.

The glass-enclosed Top of the Mark, with its unparalleled view of the city, was San Francisco's most popular bar. The Mark Hopkins Hotel also boasted a popular nightclub where big name bands played. At the time, Carmen Cavallaro and his orchestra were featured. Those were perhaps the two night places most frequented by returning servicemen. We took them in, but didn't let others go neglected. With George in the lead, we covered them all—from the reputable to joints where a slip of the tongue or an unapproving look could ignite a brawl.

The four of us enjoyed San Francisco immensely. It was there that we reoriented ourselves to luxury, plenty and freedom. It was there, in that exciting two weeks, that our minds and bodies came alive once more, and we were able to get back in step with the everyday reality. It was that reality which we had inhabited and taken for granted before we came to know what horrors could be endured by ordinary human beings.

During those unforgettable days and nights, George Faulkner always seemed to know just the time and place for any mood. However, there was one area in which he let us down. Flying across the Pacific, he had boasted of how he would fix us up with all the beautiful girls he knew. It wasn't until he had gone halfway through his little black book of numbers and gotten such answers as: "Sara! Sara who? Nobody by that name lives here"; and "Jean got married three years ago," that he finally realized that girls of marriageable age just don't sit around for four years waiting for George to come home.

From San Francisco I headed home to Garnett, South Carolina. My cousin, Air Force Major Tom Lawton, and his co-pilot Captain Pettigrew gave me a lift in a B-24 bomber to Savannah, Georgia. There to greet us were his parents, Uncle Tom and Aunt

Nannine, and my mother. My dad had died just before the war and my brothers were still in the Pacific—Paul, an Army captain, and Walter, in the Merchant Marine. My sisters, Adelaide and Ella, had married and were living in Forsyth, Georgia.

As we met that day, I could see the joy in Mama's smile and hear the glee and excitement in her voice. I sensed the intensity of love and exploding emotion which must have been hers. Those were the visible, outward marks of gladness. Beyond those, what went on in her heart and mind, only she could know. Since that time, having reared two sons and a daughter of my own, I know, from a father's point of view, what it feels like to welcome a son, Russell, safely back home from the war in Viet Nam.

For Mama, who at the peak of the war endured the lonely burden of having her three sons in the danger zone at once, welcoming her last-born back to safety must have been an ecstatic experience. The other two she had word from periodically during the course of the war. In my case there was no information during the first year after the fall of Bataan, except a listing as being missing in action. Following official notification that I was a prisoner of war, she had endured for two and one-half years more the torment of reading belated news accounts of the Death March and the subsequent atrocious treatment of prisoners by the Japanese. Now, with the taxiing of the B-24 up the runway, the unbearable burden of doubt and fear had been lifted from her frail shoulders; the tortured years of clinging to faint hope and the prayers of a strong faith had been rewarded. I felt inclined to apologize for all the grief my unchosen ill-fate had caused, but then I realized that this was a time for celebration, not for looking back. It was then that I resolved to erase the ugliness and hate of the previous four years from my thoughts and look to the future, which held the promise of so much beauty and adventure.

As was to be expected, with a four-year lapse of time during which our nation had fought and won a worldwide war, things were different at home. None of the immediate family now lived in the old farm home where I had grown up. My uncle and aunt were spending the winters there. Mama and I moved in with them for the few days' leave I had while en route to Valley Forge Hospital in Pennsylvania.

Relatives and neighbors in the farm community and nearby towns showered me with kindness and attention. There were dinner parties and visitors. Pretty girls who weren't even cousins kissed me on the street. Of the calls of well-wishers one, my first grade teacher, long-retired Miss Helen Fletcher, still burns pleasantly in my memory. Miss Helen had administered my only spanking in school twenty years earlier. With a hug and a kiss on the cheek she said, "I prayed for you, son. I'm so happy that those prayers were answered."

Mr. Eddie McKenzie, operator of the nearby country store and cotton gin, a close lifetime friend of my father, seemed especially happy to see me. Sitting in his rocking chair in front of the open fire in his store office, he commented between puffs on a well-worn pipe, "Boy, you caused us a lot of worry. Glad you made it back." I could tell by the emotional pitch of his unsteady voice that he was deeply touched. No doubt he, like I, was wishing that my father could have been there.

Perhaps the most demonstrative welcome came from the assembled Negro families on the farm. There was hand-clapping, dancing and rejoicing. Frank Holmes, seventy-five years old and somewhat crippled, hobbled up late, pushed through the crowd, grabbed me up in his arms and yelled with an emotion-packed, trembling voice, "thank Gawd! thank Gawd! you got back home again." Such displays of good will left a mark that I hope time will never erase.

That festive week of homecoming was an emotion-packed experience for me. It kindled love and affection so long absent in those recent lonesome, dreary years. It gave a new birth to a bruised self-respect which had been ground into the mud of Asiatic rice paddies. Not for a moment, however, had those experiences dulled my taste for food or shrunk my capacity to consume it. Every meal was an event, and every morsel an epicurean delight. For the first thirty days of freedom and easy access to plentiful food, I had gained weight at the rate of a pound per day. While the weight gain had leveled off when I reached 185 pounds, my appetite remained insatiable. At each sitting I consumed as much food as any three working men. In between there was always room for ice cream, milk shakes and candy bars. While it got to be somewhat embarrassing to my mother, the numerous good cooks around Garnett and Estill seemed delighted. I couldn't say that all the years of denial of family, friends and food was worth the pleasure now being reaped in catching up on each, but this rapturous festival served rapidly to blot out unpleasant memories, and convince me that, really and truly, it was all over, and that, more fortunate than many brave men, I had survived.

Appendix I

The following documents are informational summaries prepared by the Supreme Commander for the Allied Powers at the war crimes trials of the Japanese personnel involved in the "Hell Ships" episode.

They are included in a photocopy publication, *The Oryoku Maru Story*, prepared by Lt. Col. Charles M. Brown, 13680 Andover Drive, Magalia, California, 95954, in August, 1982, copies of which were placed on sale to help raise funds for a memorial to be placed near the site of the sinking of the *Oryoku Maru* at Subic Bay.

GENERAL HEADQUARTERS
SUPREME COMMANDER FOR THE ALLIED POWERS
LEGAL SECTION

APO 500
25 Feb. 1947

File No. 014.13

Public Relations Informational Summary No. 510

SUBJECT: U.S. vs Junsaburo TOSHINO, Shusuke WADA, Kazutane AIHARA Shin KAJIYAMA,
Suketoshi TANOUE, Jiro UEDA, Hisao YOSHIDA.

Charges and specifications for the trial of seven war criminals alleged to
have been responsible for the deaths of more than 1300 American prisoners of
War, have been signed by Colonel Alva C. Carpenter, Chief of the Allied Powers.
These charges and specifications have been forwarded to the Commanding General
of the EIGHTH ARMY who will appoint the military commission to hear the case.
The court is expected to convene on 27 February 1947.

Junsaburo TOSHINO, heads the list of accused. He was born in Nishinakajima-
mura, Onsen-gun, Ehime-ken, on 27 December 1903. He took his early schooling
in Ehime-ken. He graduated from the Physical Education School of Japan, at
Tokyo, in 1925. In March 1925 was drafted into the Army as a Private and
served with the Matsuyama 22nd Infantry Regiment in Ehime-ken. He was released
from the Army in August 1926 as a probationary officer in the infantry.

In May 1941 he was again drafted into the Army, and stayed in Japan until
November 1941, when he was sent to Fagi, Formosa. In December 1941 his unit
left Formosa for Luzon. On 1 January 1942 the unit landed at Lingayen, Luzon.
The unit was stationed in the northwest portion of Luzon Island. He became the
Adjutant of the 2nd Battalion, Maysuyama 122nd Infantry Regiment, and remained
with the unit until August 1943. In September 1943 he was assigned to the
Philippine Prisoner of War camp at Cabanatuan, Luzon. He worked in the office
and took care of the Adjutant's duties, as no one had been assigned to this
position. In December 1944 TOSHINO was ordered to escort some prisoners of War
from Luzon to Japan, landing at Moji, Kyushu, on 30 January 1945. During February
1945 he rested at Kamonso Hotel in Moji. In March 1945 he came to Tokyo and
went to the Prisoner of War Information Bureau where he reported the details
of the voyage from Luzon to Japan to a Lieutenant Colonel, whose name is unknown.
On 27 March he left Fukoka, Kyushu, by plane for Formosa. On arrival at Formosa,
he joined the Taiwan 112th, mixed Infantry Brigade.

TOSHINO was badly injured in a truck accident at Giran, Formosa, on 6 June
1945 and was put in the Giran Hospital. In October 1945 he was moved to the
Taihoku Hospital. On 23 February 1946 he left Kirun, Flormosa, aboard a hospital
ship, and landed at Otake, Honshu Island, 6 March 1946. He went to the Otake
Hospital and then to the Iwakuni Hospital. On 28 March 1946 he went to the
Zentsuji, Shikoka Island. He stayed there until he was apprehended on 26 July
1946.

Shunusuke WADA was the offical interpreter for the prisoner of war Guard
Commander Lieutenant TOSHINO. He is charged with failing and refusing on his
own responsibility and by neglecting to transmit to his superior requests for
adequate quarters, food, drinking water, clothing, sanitary and hygienic facilities,
and medical attention so badly needed by the prisoners. In case of Lieutenant

-5-

TOSHINO's absence WADA took command of any and all situations. He was merciless in his dealings with the prisoners, they received absolutely no consideration at all.

Kazutano AIHARA was a lance corporal in the Japanese Army. He performed the duties of a guard on the prisoner shipment. He is said to have been very vicious, the prisoners nicknamed him "Air Raid". When he came around, the prisoners would look for an excuse to get away from him. They did not even want to be within calling distance. He was in charge of the gardening details and other details that the prisoners were working on during their stay in Cabanatuan. He was one of the guards that accompanied the prisoners to San Fernando, La Union. He was the most hated guard at Cabanatuan.

Shin KAJIYAMA was the master of the ship, Oryoku Maru. When the Oryoku Maru was sunk he took charge of the Brazil Maru and completed the voyage to Moji, Japan, via Takao, Formosa.

Suketsohi TANOUE was a Sergeant Major and was supposed to have performed the duties of a medical non-commissioned officer. He was at the Davao Penal colony.

Jiro UEDA was a private in the Japanese Army. He was a prisoner guard and is concerned in the mass execution that occured at San Fernando, La Union.

Hisao YOSHIDA was also a guard and a private in the Japanese Army. He is also concerned with the mass execution at San Fernando, La Union.

In the latter part of October 1944, the American forces began to push back to the Philippines. The air Offensives began to make themselves felt by the Japanese. American carrier based planes were making daily raids into the heart of the Japanese strongholds in the Philippines. On or about October 1944, word came thru that all able bodied prisoners of war being held in Cabanatuan and Davao Prisoner of War Camps would be transferred to Bilibid prison, Manila for eventual shipment to Japan. This group of prisoners gathered and stayed at Bilibid until 13 December 1944. On that date at 1000 hours a total of 1619 American and Allied Prisoners of War were assembled. This group was divided up into groups of about 500 men each. Of the 1619 about 1100 were officers, a majority being field grade. All of the group were American except 30 who were Allied Nationals. At 1000 hours the entire group marched in a column of fours through the main streets of Manila to Pier #7. Pier #7 was known as the Million Dollar Pier because it is reputed to be the longest in the world. Lieutenant TOSHINO, the Prisoner of War Guard Commander, was standing at the gate checking the number of prisoners as they left the camp. TOSHINO was not seen again until the prisoners arrived at the pier.

The group arrived at the pier at about 1100 hrs and waited several hours before they were loaded onto their ship. At 1500 hrs a combat laden ship moved out in convoy from the pier and Japanese civilians, some sailor and a group of soldiers to man anti-aircraft guns, total numbering about 1500 persons embarked. The prisoners were then loaded aboard.

The ship was the Oryoku Maru, a new cabin type vessel which appeared to be designed for luxury travel in the Orient. It's capacity was about 15,000 tons, it was the best Japanese vessel the Americans had seen until that time. The ship carried absolutely no markings of any sort. It was heavily armed fore and aft with 3" anti-aircraft guns, dual purpose, and pom-pom guns. The prisoners were about 20 feet below the main deck.

-6-

When the prisoners started to embark Mr. WADA, the Japanese interpreter, was supervising the loading. While waiting at the pier somehow the groups got mixed up so that when Commander Portz led his group aboard the ship he had about 700 men in his group and they were placed in the after hold. It took about one and one-half hours to lead group #1. Group #2 in charge of Lt. Colonel Curtis T. Beecher, started loading about 1530 in the forward hold. In this group there were over 600 prisoners. The hold was 60 by 100 feet. There were temporary troop accommodations built about four feet from the floor and extending out 12 feet from the bulkhead, and running around the entire hold area in a square, with no partition, and all wood. The Prisoners went down into this hold via wooden steps from the hatch to the hold. Light and air could only come through the hatch opening, which was about 20 feet by 20 feet. There were no ventilators, no port holes. Group three went aboard and were loaded in the hatch amid-ships with approximately 300 men.

In group #2 the conditions in the hold were so crowded that the men, a few minutes after entering the hold began fainting. The Japanese were asked to move some of the men out, the request was refused and they were told that there would be about 200 men put into the forward hold. There wasn't enough air and men were fainting due to the lack of air and intense heat. The Japanese were hurring men into the hold, in some cases these men were being pushed down the stairs and beaten with rifle butts and shovels. Men were knocked down and off the ladder falling on the men already below. AIHARA, one of the guards is alleged to have been one of the men standing at the hatch entrance beating the prisoners as they entered. All during this time WADA was present during the loading and without a doubt observed the treatment being given the prisoners, although he did nothing to stop it.

At about 1800 hrs all the men were loaded. The weather in the Philippines is tropical and extremely hot. In the lower bays when all men were in they had to assume a crouched position because they couldn't stand upright. No men were permitted in the center under the hatch by order of the Japanese Guards. In the upper bays one could stand or crouch but could not lie down.

Prior to embarking, the last meal that the prisoners were given was on the night of December 12th, at about 1900 hrs in Bilibid. For this meal they were fed a ½ canteen cup of steamed rice and ½ canteen cup of soup. There was also an issue of a ½ canteen cup of rice to be eaten the morning of the 13th. The men were allowed all the water they wanted, the majority of them had canteens and canteen cups. The next meal the prisoners received was the night of the 13th at 1900 hrs. The meal amounted to nearly a full canteen cup of steamed rice and a teaspoon of salt and seaweed for each man, and one canteen cup of water for one whole bay of approximately 45 men. Each man received the equivalent of three teaspoons full of water. The distribution of the food and water was left entirely up to the Americans, the Japanese had nothing to do with it. Never were the Japanese ever physically present in the holds. Other than this meger ration no food was received while the prisoners were aboard the Oryoku Maru, except on 14 December men in the center hold received morning chow.

When the prisoners first boarded the ship there were a few cases of active diarrhea and dysentery. No provisions had been made for any latrine facilities in the holds. After repeated requests, four five gallon buckets were lowered into the holds. They were placed in the corners. Although repeated requests were made to the Japanese for more buckets no action resulted. The four buckets that they

-7-

received were overflowing within 1½ hours, and requests to empty them were refused. By 2400 hrs the lower floor in the vicinity of the latrine was a sea of human waste. The stench in the hold at about 2400 hrs due to the lack of air and human waste was overpowering.

When the men first entered the ship the temperature was between 85 and 90 degrees. About 0200 hrs on the 14th due to the noise and excitement, the hatch, which was the only opening for air, was completely battened down, cutting off all air except that which seeped through the hatch cover. The temperature then rose to about 120 degrees. Men against the bulkheads, in the bays, were passing out for lack of air. These men were removed to the front of the bay where they were revived. For the remaining time on the Oryoku Maru the air situation became worse, because of the dehydration, weakness, thirst, and stench.

No sick bay had been designated. There was no room for it. Repeated requests were made for permission to bring the most aggravated cases of heat prostration and dehydration on deck where they would at least be able to get some air. All these requests were denied by WADA.

During the nights of the 13th and 14th men became deranged and would wander about the hold stepping on other prisoners, screaming for water and air. Some became violent to the extent that they lashed out with canteens or striking with their fists or feets at anyone with whom they came in contact. It was pitch black in the hold. In this chaos there was no possibility for much needed sleep. On this first night about 40 to 50 men went out of their minds.

About 0300 hrs on the morning of the 14th the Oryoku Maru weighed anchor and headed out towards the China Sea. At dawn of the 14th the forward hatch was opened and in the forward hold there were 8-10 men who had died during the night. At about 0800 hrs an air raid alarm sounded. The ship was strafed, riccochets began flying into the holds. The ship had been damaged, and was moving now with difficulty. Several men had been wounded during the raid by the riccochets. During the air raid, it was learned, that at least 30 men had died in the aft hold the night of the 13th, mostly due to suffocation. After the raid medical groups were called on deck to treat the Japanese wounded. These groups were severely beaten because "American planes were sinking the Japanese shipping". When requests were made for medical aid for men in the holds, and food and water, they were beaten up and told that the Japanese would do nothing for the prisoners.

On the night of the 14th, and the morning of the 15th conditions grew worse. Men were suffering from thirst so acutely that many went out of their minds. Much screaming was audible. There was almost a complete lack of discipline, no matter how hard the hold leaders tried to restore order. The need for water was so acute that the men were drinking their own urine and sewage running in the open drains along the side of the ship. These hideous actions were revealed to the Japanese but there was no action taken. The hold was a bedlam with screaming, swearing, fighting. Men went beserk and the conditions were like some fantastic nightmare.

On the nights of the 14th and 15th the ship was bombed. The Japanese beached it making minor repairs, and discharged all Japanese passengers, moving back to Subic Bay. The prisoners were still aboard. It was felt that the Japanese knew the ship would be bombed again and for that reason they took the Japanese passengers off and left the prisoners on.

-8-

On the morning of the 15th while the ship was anchored in Subic Bay about 300 yards off shore from Olongapo Naval Reservation, about 0830 hrs WADA came around and told the men that the prisoners would be evacuated from the ship shortly; that they would not be able to take their shoes or any other gear as they would have to swim. He said that the Japanese were instructed to "shoot to kill" so they, the prisoners, had better be very careful. Several of the guards fired into the holds prior to evacuation. About 0930 hrs the order for the evacuation came through. Prior to this order there had been an air raid in which a direct hit on the aft hold had been made, and about 100 men were killed. There were no life preservers or lifeboats in evidence. Men were forced over the side of the ship with no reguard given as to whether or not they could swim. While the men were leaving the ship six U.S. planes dived on the ship but just prior to the bomb release point the lead plane zoomed up and wagged its wings in recognition. No bombs were released. During the swim for shore some of the men got aboard the debris from the ship and attempted to float ashore. In one case a raft with five men on it headed for shore, was fired upon by a machine gun set up on shore. Two of the men on the raft leaped off into the water, the remaining three were killed.

During the disorder of the evacuation some of the half-starved men attempted to salvage whatever food and medical supplied available on the ship. While going in the compartments in search of food they observed American cigarettes, candy usually in Red Cross parcels.

Whatever food and medical supplies the men managed to salvage were con-fiscated by the Japanese. During this salvage operation some Japanese came upon the prisoners in the compartments and began firing on them. Lt. TOSHINO came upon Lt. Wm. H. Brewster in one of the compartments and shot him, killing him instantly.

Once on shore the prisoners were assembled in the area adjacent to a tennis court. During the period of assembling, the men were permitted to fill their canteens at a water tap outside the tennis court, but to do this they had to stand in line four to six hours. Fifty percent of the prisoners received their first water since the night of the 13th, the rest didn't get any because the Japanese as a result of the confusion chased them back into their assembly area. About 30 minutes later WADA came around and had the prisoners marched to the tennis court so that a count of men could be made against the rosters. Placing such a large group of men in the area of a tennis court was almost impossible. The court was surrounded by a checken wire fence. A small area had been set aside for the sick and wounded. There was not enough space for a person to stretch out and lie down. Rosters were called off several times. All personnal were told to give any information available to them on persons not present so as to be able to determine how many men were dead or missing and how many present.

In the gathering at the tennis court it was learned that the conditions in the aft hold had been worse then the conditions in the forward hold. Many of the deaths in this hold were caused by suffocation. At roll call there were less than 1300 prisoners still alive out of the 1619 that had left Manila. At 1430 hrs American planes came back and bombed the Oryoku Maru, all the prisoners by this time having been evacuated. No food was issued on the 15th or the 16th, and the water situation was still very bad. On the evening of the 17th one sack of uncooked rice was issued for 1300 men. This amounted to about two tablespoons full for each man. The same amount of rice was issued on the 18th

-9-

and 19th. On the 20th the ration increased to four tablespoons full, all of
this was eaten raw, although facilities for cooking were stored close by and
within sight.

   While the prisoners were kept at the tennis court, there was no provision
made for protection against the sun. On the third day the men were allowed
to leave the court and go into the shade for a few hours. Most of the men
had on only a pair of shorts, some, more fortunate, had shirts and some trousers;
there were no shoes or hats. At night it was very cold and since there were
no blanckets, the prisoners were forced to lie on the hard concrete and suffer
from the cold. While waiting at the tennis court, six or seven men died from
wounds and exhaustion and were buried nearby.

   About the 18th, after repeated requests made to the Japanese to hospitalize
a prisoner, Cpl. Eugene L. Specht, USMC who was suffering from a gangrenous
arm, and having no action taken, it became necessary to amputate his arm at
the tennis court. There was a mess kit knife for use as a surgical instrument,
no anesthetic and no medical supplies of any kind were provided by the Japanese.
Specht had been shot in the arm by a guard aboard the Oryoku Maru. It had
swollen to incredible size, and the odor from it was overpowering. There was
no outcry from the patient, only a few groans and "Oh Doctor". Specht survived
a few days and subsequently died. It is alleged that Specht would have had
an excellent chance to live if he would have been given normal hospitalization.

   On the morning of 20 December 1944, 500 of the men were taken to San Fernando,
Pampanga and the second group left on the 21st. The first group were placed
in the provincial jail, and second group in the movie house. While there the
prisoners were finally issued a canteen of rice. There was a spigot at the
theatre with running water and by keeping order everybody received enough water.
Ample water was also available at the jail.

   About 1800 hrs on the 23 December WADA came to the two group commanders
and wanted the 15 sickest men to be selected for return to Manila for hospitalization.
Among the group selected were Lieutenant Dwight D. Edison, Lieutenant John
W. Elliot, Lieutenant Colonel Ulysses J. L. Peoples Jr., Lieutenant Colonel
Samuel W. Freeny, Pharmacists Mate 2/c Deenah R. McCurry, Second Lieutenant
Herman V. Sherman, Major Wendell F. Swanson and eight other unidentified American
Prisoners of War.

   About 1900 hrs a truck was brought to where the group was waiting and
the sick were driven in the truck to a small cemetery on the outskirts of San
Fernando, Pampanga. When they arrived at the cemetery there were a group of
soldiers who had dug a hole about 15 feet square. When the guards on the truck
and dismounted, they took up positions about the hole. Two of the guards brought
one of the prisoners to the hole. He was told to kneel at the edge of the
hole and to take a position as though in prayer. The prisoner was brought
to the hole and he was bayonetted and decapitated. This procedure was followed
until all fifteen of the prisoners had either been bayonetted or decapitated.
It is alleged that at this execution both WADA and TOSHINO were present, that
they supervised and took part in it.

   From San Fernando, Pampanga the prisoners were moved by train to San Fernando,
La Union, on the 24 December. The prisoners were marched to the railroad
station. At the station the men were loaded into box cars. WADA and TOSHINO,
by this time having returned from the scene of the execution. WADA again
apparently in command, instructed the group commanders that 170 to 180 men

-10-

would be put in each box car, which was actually physically impossible. However, 40 men who were the sickest were allowed to be placed on top of the cars. During the trips, in the train, the conditions were very bad. The heat was terrific, and due to crowding and lack of air many men passed out. When a man became unconscious he was passed from hand to hand to the door of the box car to revive.

The train arrived at San Fernando, La Union about 0500 hrs Christmas morning of 25 December 1944. The weather was bitterly cold. The men were Marched from the train to a school house about a half a mile to a mile from the railway station. When the group arrived at the schoolhouse, WADA announced that water was available. A detail of men were ordered to dig for water. After digging five feet below the surface water was found, and iodine was used for purification.

At nine A.M. on 25 December, orders were received that the men were to line up and prepare for a march to the beach. After remaining on the beach for two days and two nights; on the morning of 27 December, the first group of 236 men were loaded aboard the Brazil Maru, the remainder of the men on the beach were loaded aboard the Enoura Maru. The men were marched to the piers where landing barges were waiting to carry the men out to the transports. While loading into the barges men were compelled to jump from the pier into the barges, some 20 feet below. If a man hesitated before jumping to the barge the guard would push him off the pier. In several instances men broke their legs. In one case, one man missed the barge completely hitting his head on the side of the barge and falling into the water. When this man was finally dragged into the barge he was dead. All during the time the loading proceeded, it is alleged that TOSHINO and WADA were present on the pier and witnessed all the incidents which occured during the loading operations.

The Brazil Maru was an old freighter of about 2,500 tons. It was armed and was loaded with sick and healthy Japanese soldiers. During the six day trip from the Philippines to Takao, Formosa, no food was received during the first two days except the food leavings of the five Formosan guards. This amounted to about one teaspoon of rice per man. On the third day an issue was made which was three men per mess kit of food. On the fourth day there was no food at all. On the fifth day prisoners were issued five Japanese rolls per man. These rolls were a type of hard tack infested with maggots and mold.

All of the prisoners on the Enoura Maru (about 10,000 tons), were confined to one hold with two levels, forward of amid-ships. The condition was very crowded but not as bad as on the Oryoku Maru. A man could lie down here by doubling up his legs. The food was scarce and there was a little water and soup available once a day. The amounts received were small but were much greater than those received by the prioners aboard the Brazil Maru. During the period of the trip between San Fernando and Takao, Formosa, there were 16 deaths. These 16 deceased were buried at sea. 236 men were moved from the Brazil Maru to the Enoura Maru in Takao Harbor, on or about 6 January 1945.

During the 7th, 8th and 9th of January the men received one mess kit of rice for each four men with one-half cup of soup for each four men. On the 8th of January in the afternoon, the Japanese ordered all men in the lower level of the hold to be moved into the forward hold so that sugar could be stored in the lower level. Approximately two-thirds of the men had been moved from the hold when the Japanese guards on the deck indicated that the other one-third would be absorbed into the upper level which created an overcrowded condition more than originally, since it was overcrowded initially.

-11-

Men were so hungry that they stole sugar despite the threat by WADA
that drastic punishment would be meted out. WADA stated "anyone who stole
sugar would be severely punished individually and the balance of the group
would be punished collectively for an unspecified period".

On 9 January in mid-morning, during the completion of the morning meal,
anti-aircraft fire was heard on the Enoura Maru and all ships in the harbor.
Soon the drone of planes was heard and almost simultaneously the whistle of
bombs was heard. The Enoura Maru rocked violently from a near miss, causing
a flail of bomb fragments and steel fragments from the sides of the ship which
killed about 300 outright and injured a considerable number. After the bombing
such first aid as could be rendered to men was made available by the Prisoner
of War doctors and corpsmen aboard. This aid consisted of collecting dirty
towels, undershirts, or anything that could be used for bandages that the other
prisoners would contribute. Outside of a few first aid kits which the doctors
and corpsmen may have had there were no medicines made available by the Japanese.
In fact, no aid was rendered until 11 January when two Japanese enlisted hospital
corpsmen announced they would treat those with minor injuries or wounds only.
Treatment consisted of dabbing injuries with mercurochrome. They further stated
that they were not interested in treating the more seriously injured.

The dead bodies in the holds were stacked in the center of the hatch area
like stacks of cord wood. They remained there until the 12th of January. During
this time, a majority of the men who were wounded and who soon thereafter died
from those wounds could have been saved with proper medical attention, but
with lack of bandages and medicines it was impossible for the doctors to do
much for them.

Finally in mid-morning of 12 January, permission was granted to remove
the dead bodies from the ship. The bodies were removed by placing them into
cargo slings and lowering over the side of the ship into barges. Some of the
dead were removed individually by tying ropes around the legs or arms and hauling
them upon the deck, then lowering them into the barges. The scene in the holds
was like a page from Dante's Inferno---dark, but one could see the wraithlike
figures wandering dazedly through a maze of stacked corpses. It was not uncommon
prior to the removal of the dead to sit on the dead and eat meals due to the
overcrowded conditions. Items of salvageable clothing that could be removed
from the dead were removed. Many of the bodies were in various stages of decom-
position when they were finally removed.

On 13 January, during the afternoon, orders came through from WADA that
all the prisoners aboard the Enoura Maru would be transferred to the Brazil
Maru. Reaons for this change were that the Enoura Maru had been badly damaged
during the bombing. Transfer to the Brazil Maru was affected by landing barges.
The move was completed in late afternoon. The wounded men, fracture cases,
etc., suffered great pain in transfer as in some cases they were lowered into
boats by ropes and hoisted aboard ship in the same manner. At this time, there
were approximately 900 men remaining alive out of the original group of 1619.
The ship sailed from Takao on the 13th of January for Japan.

The trip from Takao to Moji, Japan lasted from 13 January until 29 January.
During the trip there were two issues of cooked rice a day. There were two
or three men to a lightly packed canteen cup of rice. No soup was issued at
all. This diet was augmented by whatever sugar the men could steal. Numerous

-12-

protests to the prisoner commanders brought no results. A diagnosis for the cause
of the high death rate aboard the Brazil Maru was due to a combination of malnutrition, dehydration and exposure.

During the journey there was active trading for rings, watches, and fountain
pens between the prisoners and the Japanese guards and the ship's crew for food,
water and cigarettes. A lot of West Point and other graduation rings were
traded for a cup of water or ten cigarettes. Anyone who had anything to
trade did so.

The water situation was very acute for the first two days out of Takao
harbor, no liquids of any kind were issued. On the 15th approximately twice
a day until the 29th, water was spooned out. It was black, salty and unpalatable.
At no time even when the death rate was at its highest was the amount of water
increased.

Medical facilities aboard the ship were nil. Only the more seriously
sick were placed under the hatch which was considered as the hospital area.
It was the coldest spot on the ship. Whenever a man was placed in sick bay
it was almost a certainty that he would die. Only the men in the last stages
were sent there. The doctor and medical corpsmen had nothing whatever to
work with--no medicines, no bandages. It is said that one large bottle of
sulfathiazol pills aboard the Brazil Maru probably would have saved at least
100 men whose diarrhea was a contributing cause to their death.

When the ship first left Takao on the night of 13 January, about 15 men
died. Bodies were stacked in the hospital area after first being stripped
of all cothing by the hospital corpsmen under orders. Available clothing
was then distributed to the men who most needed it. Bodies were collected
over a two or three day period before permission was obtained from WADA to
get a burial detail to throw them overboard. The first group of dead was
about fifty. Generally, bodies would be taken up on deck and buried daily.
In the beginning the death rate was between ten and fifteen men per day and
it got progressively worse, finally reaching a maximum of about forty dead
per day a few days prior to arrival in Japan. The men outside of the hospital
area who had previously shown no evidence of suffering more than the rest
would be found dead in the morning. This became so commmonplace that a hospital
corpsman would make a circuit of all bays each morning and shout "Roll out
your dead". Bay leaders would then check their bays.

A Chaplin prisoner lead the men in prayer every night until he died
five days out of Takao. Another Chaplin gave all of his food and water to
the sick until he too died. Another Chaplin who overtaxed his strength by
helping the sick died.

Two or three times a day the roll would be called and if a man's name
was called without an answer, someone would say "dead" or give the circumstances
regarding his death, such as suffocation aboard the Oryoku Maru. Even though
the list had been called many times previously, this was done by order of
the Japanese.

The ship finally arrived in Moji, Japan, 29 January 1945. It was met
by a large boarding party of officers, enlisted men and civilians. It was
announced in mid-morning that clothing would be issued topside. There were
about 450 men alive then. It was bitterly cold. The prisoners were issued

-13-

a pair of wool trousers, a blouse, a suite of cotton underwear, but no socks.
Shoes were captured British shoes and were issued without regard to size.

This was the first time since 13 December that there was enough water
available for each man to have as much as he wanted, however, the men were
cautioned that the water might be contaiminated and that they had better take
it easy. Later on food was issued but many of the men were so sick they were
unable to eat.

When the men disembarked from the ship they were walking skeletons. The
Japanese corpsmen seemed to have a look of astonishment on their faces and
there were shocked expressions on the faces of the people at Moji as the prisoners
were marched through the streets. Men shuffled, some walked with the support
of others. The men were infested with lice and had not shaved since 13 December.

When the prisoners died aboard the Brazil Maru they were stacked like
cord wood and all of them presented a uniform appearance; lips were drawn
back exposing teeth in a half snarl due to skin contraction, ribs seemed to
be bursting out of the bodies and where the stomach would be was a hollow,
legs and arms were pipe stems. A combination of cold and rigor mortis
gave them a rigid unreal appearance. The eyes were sunken. Most of them were
stripped nude and all of them gave a definite appearance of starvation.

Lt. Col. Austin J. Montgomery is at present in Tokyo. Col. Montgomery
is one of the survivors of the infamous Oryoku Maru. He will be a witness
in the case against the accused. He will give eye witness accounts as to what
occured during the voyage. Col. Montgomery's home address is 1475 Greenleaf
Street, Sherman Oaks, California.

At the outbreak of war Col. Montgomery was a member of the Philippine
Division. He was a motor transport officer for the 2 Corps and commanding
officer of the 1st Battalion, 12th Quartermaster Regiment, Philippine Scouts.

After participating in the defense of Bataan and the eventual fall of
Bataan, Montgomery moved to Corregidor where he was taken prisoner by the
Japanese forces on 6 May 1942.

From Corregidor he was moved to the mainland and held prisoner at the
Cabanatuan POW Camp until October 1942. In November 1942 he was moved with
a group of prisoners to the Davao Penal Colony where he remained until June
of 1944. While at the Davao Camp Col. Montgomery was the prisoner of war
Adjutant. During June 1944 Col. Montgomery was moved back to Cabanatuan camp
where he remained until word was received that all able bodied prisoners would
be sent to Bilibid Prisoner of War Camp for eventual shipment to Japan. After
suffering the horrors of the trip on ship from Manila to Moji, Japan, Montgomery
moved to the Fukuoka Prisoner of War Camp #1, arriving there 30 January 1945.
In April 1945 he was transferred from the Fukuoka Camp #1 to Jinsen, Korea
remaining there until the surrender of the Japanese forces to Gen. MacArthur.
During the time he was incarcerated at the Jinsen Camp Col. Montgomery was
Liaison officer between the prisoners of war and the Japanese captors.

-14-

GENERAL HEADQUARTERS
SUPREME COMMANDER FOR THE ALLIED POWERS
LEGAL SECTION

Tokyo, Japan
9 May 1947
APO 500

File No. 014.13

Public Relations Informational Summary No. 574

SUBJECT: Result of the Trial of Junsaburo TOSHINO, et al.

    Death by hanging for two; 25, 20 and 10 year imprisonments at hard labor
were for four, and the remaining two of the eight defendants were aquitted.
These were the verdicts handed down by the Military Commission hearing in the
case against the eight Japanese charged with being concerned in the deaths
of more than 1300 prisoners of war being transported from Manila to Moji,
Japan, where they were destined to be disposed throughout Japan for use
in labor battalions.

    Junsaburo TOSHINO, former Lieutenant and Guard Commandant aboard the
"Hell Ship" was found guilty of murdering and supervising the murder of at
least 16 men. In other specifications the accused was found guilty of causing the
deaths of numerous other prisoners of war. TOSHINO was the first to receive the
death sentence, the other was Kazutane AIHARA, Lance Corporal. The prisoners
nicknamed him "Air Raid" because every time he came near the prisoners someone
would yell "air raid" and all of them would take cover to escape being beaten
by AIHARA. He was in charge of the gardening details and other details the
prisoners were working on during their stay in Cabanatuan. He was sentenced
to hang for killing numerous American Prisoners of War and participating in
the decapitation and stabbing of 15 others.

    Shusuke WADA, whose charges paralleled those of TOSHINO, was the official
interpreter for the guard group. He was found guilty of causing the deaths of
numberous American and Allied Prisoners of War by neglecting to transmit to his
superiors requests for adequate quarters, food, drinking water and medical
attention. WADA was sentenced to Life Imprisonment at hard labor.

    Suketoshi TANOUE, Sergeant Major, was found guilty and sentenced to 25
years at hard labor. He was found guilty of the charge and specification charging
him with the killing of 15 prisoners of war at the San Fernando Cemetery by
decapitation and stabbing.

    Jiro UEDA, Private, was found guilty of the charge and specifications and
was sentenced to twenty years imprisonment at hard labor. He was also connected
with the killing of the 15 prisoners of war at the San Fernando Cemetery.

    Sho HATTORI, Sergeant of the Guard, was found guilty of the charge and
specificiations four. As Sergeant of the guard he deprived the prisoners of
drinking water and failed to restain Japanese Military personnnel subject to
his supervision from beating the prisoners. He was sentenced to 10 years
imprisonment at hard labor.

    Hisao YOSHIDA, guard, and Risaku KOBAYASHI, medical corpsman, were
aquitted. They were charged with being connected in the murder of the 15
sick prisoners of war at San Fernando Cemetery.

-2-

The charges against TOSHINO and WADA are almost parallel. Both are charged with being responsible with the deaths and inhuman treatment received by the prisoners. TOSHINO is charged with failing to provide adequate quarters, food, drinking water and medical attention, and by refusing to provide reasonable measurers for the protection of the prisoners from the hazards of war. It was charged that TOSHINO did willfully kill an American Prisoner of War by shooting him. Another charge against the accused was the fact that he ordered and permitted his military subordinates to kill 15 American Prisoners of War by stabbing and shooting at San Fernando, Pampanga, Philippine Islands.

WADA was charged with refusing to transmit to his superiors requests made by the prisoner commanders and failing to provide adequate quarters, food, drinking water and medical attention.

The other members in the group of defendants are charged variously with taking part in the decapation of the 15 Prisoners at San Fernando, Pampanga, and with numerous beatings and other brutalities which occured during the voyage from Manila to Moji.

The Oryoku Maru sailed from Manila 13 December 1944. It was bombed by American planes at Subic Bay. The ship was damaged so badly that the prisoners and all other occupants were moved from the ship and interened at Olongapo Naval Base. While there, the prisoners were afforded no sanitary conditions whatsoever. Numerous deaths occured and prisoners were treated as animals. The group of prisoners were then moved to San Fernando, La Union, from whence they boarded the Enoura Maru and Brazil Maru, both Japanese transport ships which were to take them to Takao, Formosa. The ships arrived at Formosa and while laying in the harbor they were bombed. The Enoura Maru was damaged so badly that all the prisoners were moved onto the Brazil Maru. After several days at Takao, the Brazil Maru sailed for Moji, Japan, arriving on or about 30 January 1945.

Of the 1619 prisoners who boarded the Oryoku Maru at Manila, approximately 450 survived to disembark at Moji.

In making a statement on the case, Mr. Alva C. Carpenter, Chief of the Legal Section, General Headquarters, Supreme Commander for the Allied Powers, says, "Of all the cases of brutality and mistreatment acccorded prisoners of war that have come out of World War II, none can compare with the torment and torture suffered by our soldiers, who were prisoners of war of the Japanese, aboard the ships, Oryoku Maru, Brazil Maru and Endora Maru on the voyage from Manila to Japan during the months of December 1944 and January 1945. It is a saga of men driven to madness by sadistic and senual captors. Today, of the 1619 men who set sail on the voyage, less than 200 are alive. I have read diaries, written at the time, tomes of recorded testimony, have talked to survivors, and no place in recorded history can one find anything so gruesome and horrible. No mitigating circumstances can explain or condone such cruelty. The callous and vile conduct of the captors will live in infamy!"

The prosecutors for this case were Mr. Allan. R. Morrison of 4496 Aukai Street, Honolulu, Hawaii; Mr. Thomas D. Aitken of 540 Stockton Street, San Francisco, California and Mr. Leonard Rand of 537 Summer Avenue, Newark, New Jersey.

-3-

There were originally nine defendants in this case. When the Prosecution
rested its case, the defense made a motion for the dismissal of the case against
Shin KAJIYAMA, the Captain of the Oryoku Maru. The motion was sustained by the
Commission on the grounds that it was developed in the course of the trial that there
was nothing which KAJIYAMA could have done to have prevented the atrocities. It
was brought out during the trial that KAJIYAMA had protested taking the prisioners
aboard the ship at the start and continued to protest and was threatened with
court-martial if he did not take the prisoners aboard the ship without further
arguement. The evidence further indicates that he had made several attempts to
alleviate the condition of the prisoners but, inasmuch as he was a civilian
merchantman in command of a ship chartered by the Army, the group commander refused
to let him do anything on behalf of the prisoners. The Court, therefore saw nothing
for which he could be held.

In the fall and winter of 1944, the Japnese High Command had decided to
transport all able-bodied prisoners of war captured in the Philippines to Japan
for use as slave labor. The case against the eight defendants concerned a specific
case in which 1619 prisoners of war were herded aboard the Oryoku Maru, a Japanese
ship which was later christened the "Hell Ship". Christened with blood and sweat
of hundreds of prisoners of war. The story of the trip of the 1619 prisoners
of war was a shocking, gruesome, repulsive and hideous tale. The story that unfolds
for the court and world by the Prosecution was a story of large scale suffering,
torture, agony, horror, bloodshed, murder and death. It was an Odyssey which
began on 13 December 1944 when a group of prisoners variously estimated at between
1619 and 1630 shuffled through the gates of old Bilibid prison in Manila and
truged wearily to the harbor for embarkation on the Oryoku Maru. These prisoners
had been rounded up in compliance with a directive to send all able-bodied prisoners
to Japan for labor, and it appeared that the test as to whether or not a man was
able-bodied as "can-he-walk". Of course, some of these prisoners had to be helped
along by their comrades and some of them collapsed beyond the help of their
comrades and had to be picked up by trucks - but that did not affect their status
of "able-bodies". The Japanese were scraping pretty hard at the bottom of the
barrel when they rounded up this gang of "able-bodied" laborers. There were 92
Lieutenant Colonels, 5 Commanders, 170 Majors, 14 Lieutenant Commanders, 261
Army and Marine Corps Catains, 36 Naval Lieutenant, 400 Army Lieutenants, 12
JG Naval Lieutenants, 31 Ensigns, 14 Warrant Officers, 357 Army, Navy and Marine
Non-Coms, 181 Army, Navy and Marine enlisted personal below the rank of Non-Com,
and 47 civilians. Most of the enlisted mem were medical personal, and the largest
class of commissioned officers consisted of Chaplins, Medical and Dental Personnel.

The prisoners were hustled up the gangplank and jammed into three holds
with all the pandemonium of a herd of cattle being stampeeded over the ramps
and into the slaughter pens of the Chicago abattoirs. The Odyssey ended on or
about 30 Jan. 1945 when about 450 half-naked emaciated corpses shivered down the
gangplank of the Brazil Maru in Moji, Japan. Of those who disembarked in Moji,
not one was able to walk normally and more than one-half being carried ashore.
Many died within a few weeks as a result of the trip. Today it is estimated
there are about 200 to 300 of the original 1619 men who boarded the Oryoku Maru
in Manila still alive.

Those men who did not reach Moji died of suffocation, starvation, dehydration,
disease, bombing, shooting, and beheading, and every single death that occured
was caused by, or at least contributed to, by the defendants TASHINO and WADA.
The other defendants were involved in only a part of this mass murder.

-4-

Appendix II

This is a list of the 1,607 American prisoners aboard the three "Hell Ships," of whom less than 400 survived the forty-seven-day journey from the Philippines to Japan. Note that the listing for Manny Lawton gives an incorrect address. The names were compiled by four survivors of the ordeal for inclusion in *The Oryoku Maru Story* in 1982.

A

Reid S. Aaron - *UKN*

Wynard Aalbersbery - *UKN*

Cary M. Abney, Jr. - *508 West Crockett Street, Marshall, Texas*

Aaron A. Abston - *Coker, Alabama*

John P. Adams - *New Bloomfield, Perry County, Pennsylvania*

David C. Affleck - *4235 Floral Avenue, Norwood, Ohio*

George W. Agne - *1226 East Main Street, Alhambra, California*

Lorenzao Aguilar, Jr. - *115 Texas Avenue, Weslaco, Texas*

Frank G. Aigrisse - *Darlington & Middlesex Streets, Toledo, Ohio*

William T. Akins - *2311 9th Street, Lubbock, Texas*

Dwayne W. Alder - *53 Third Avenue, Midvale, Utah*

Irvin Alexander - *403 East Evergreen Street, San Antonio, Texas*

Robert P. Alkam - *Forsyth, Missouri*

Charles D. Allen - *Cameron, Texas*

Joseph H. Allen - *Spangle, Washington*

Lloyd C. Allen - *Stuart, Iowa*

James E. Alsobrook - *904 E. Main Street, Mayrilin, Arkansas*

Ralph Amate Jr. - *5309 S.E. Francis Street, Portland, Oregon*

Arnold Amorosa - *31 Mildred Street, Charles Town, West Virginia*

Godfrey R. Ames - *143 Beach 87th Street, Rockaway Beach, New York*

Jak Amos - *208 East Liberty St., Savannah, Georgia*

Don R. Anderson - *UKN*

Harold Anderson - *Kroningens Gate 8, Bodo, Norway*

Herman R. Anderson - *315 North "D" Street, Madera, California*

William C. Anderson Jr. - *Waynesville, Missouri*

Egil Andreassen - *Haque Gresswik, PR-Fredrichsted, Norway*

Graham H. Andrews - *1447 Station Medical, Ft. Benning, Georgia*

Garry J. Angoff Jr. - *244 N. Manhattan Place, Los Angeles, California*

Charles Arnao - *1437 So. 8th Street, Philadelphia, Pennsylvania*

Charles W. Armour - *501 Hollt Street, Little Rock, Arkansas*

Fab. Arsenault - *95 Hancock Street, Orange, Massachusetts*

Reinholdt Aschenbrenner - *304 "E" Street, Lincoln, Nebraska*

J. W. Ashcraft - *Dimmitt, Texas*

Bjarne Asheim - *Revheim, Madle, Stavanger, Norway*

Hulbert Asmussen - *UKN*

Willen F. Asmussen - *UKN*

John J. Atkinson - *Goliad, Texas*

Rex Aton - *304 1st Street, S.W., Minot, North Dakota*

Charles S. Atteberry - *Wilder, Idaho*

John E. Austin - *UKN*

Paul J. Austin - *UKN*

Thomas U. Austin - *1706 Park Avenue, Marshall, Texas*

Andrew J. Ayers - *2035 Averill Street, San Pedro, California*

B

David S. Babock - *Lynn, Indiana*

Elliott C. Babock - *P.O. Box 665, St. Augustine, Florida*

Jack F. Bachelor - *Sheridan, Arkansas*

Fred H. Backaus - *UKN*

Carl Baehr, Jr. - *214 E. 24th Place, Tulsa, Oklahoma*

Jack O. Baldwin - *407 E. Second Street, Pana, Illinois*

Lawrence C. Baldwin - *UKN*

Lee Baldwin - *415 Menick Street, Shreveport, Louisiana*

William P. Baldwin - *Hotel Garteret, New York City, New York*

A. W. Balfanz Jr. - *Box 687, Brownfield, Texas*

Herbert H. Ball - *58920 Enright Street, St. Louis, Missouri*

Samuel L. Barbour Jr. - *160 N. Bowling Greenway, Brentwood Heights, W. Los Angeles, California*

Donald E. Bansley - *Star Route, Claverack, New York*

Robert A. Barker - *UKN*

Louis D. Barnes - *Lanesboro, Massachusetts*

William S. Barnes - *1156 Garden Boulevard, Gardena, California*

Elvin L. Barr - *Eagle Nest Road, Waynesville, North Carolina*

Francis M. Bania - *5058 Hurlbut Avenue, Detroit, Michigan*

Harry L. Barr - *1301 30th Street, Madison, Iowa*

Arthur M. Barrett - *326 W. 3rd Street, Chanute, Kansas*

Francis J. Barker - *2534 W. 3rd Street, Los Angeles, California*

Daniel J. Barry - *229 E. 79th Street, New York, New York*

Percy R. Barry - *Lucas, Kansas*

Louis P. Batholomess - *258 South Monroe St., Denver, Colorado*

Howard M. Batson - *UKN*

John Bauer - *UKN*

Karol A. Bayer - *UKN*

Edward W. Bayer - *Crete, Nebraska*

Kenneth O. Beach - *Chelsea, Michigan*

Arthur C. Beale - *Bunnell St., Bridgeport, Connecticut*

John F. Beall - *3332 Tularosa St., El Paso, Texas*

Lynn P. Beaumont - *Mountain Side Ranch, Uvalde, Texas*

Charles D. Beck - *Oklaunion, Texas*

Darwin C. Becker - *Brenham, Texas*

Robert F. Becker - *UKN*

Louis C. Beck - *UKN*

Adolph Bede - *UKN*

Curtis T. Beecher - *UKN*

Melvin B. Beeching - *UKN*

Louis E. Beelen - *UKN*

Jack Beereeds - *UKN*

Joseph J. Beisler - *UKN*

Joseph S. Bell - *UKN*

William R. Bell - *704 NW 31st Street, Oklahoma City, Oklahoma*

John F. Bennell - *UKN*

Charles H. Bennett - *UKN*

John H. Bennett - *1705 Green Street, Columbia, South Carolina*

Gordon S. Benson - *UKN*

Charles C. Benthien - *538 Marion Street, Denver, Colorado*

Louis I. Bentz, Jr. - *UKN*

Harold Benvie - *Napavine, Washington*

Frederick L. Berry - *345 Kellogg Street, Palo Alto, California*

Gleneth B. Berry - *RR #4, Okemah, Oklahoma*

Donald R. Bertrand - *1931 South 2nd Ave., Maywood, Illinois*

Wesley W. Bertz - *1116 Larmie Street, Manhattan, Kansas*

Joseph A. Berg - *UKN*

Alvin J. Bethard - *Good Pine, Louisiana*

Richard C. Beven - *Leroy, Pennsylvania*

William D. Beus - *UKN*

Willibald C. Bianchi - *New Ulm, Minnesota*

Raymond E. Bibee - *R# 3, Lexington, Kentucky*

James E. Bickerton - *5445 N. Normandy, Chicago, Illinois*

Floyd A. Biddy - *UKN*

Elden W. Bjurling - *UKN*

Cecil Black - *Heavener, Oklahoma*

Clyde I. Bkooc - *UKN*

Harold F. Bishop - *1507 West 4th Street, Davenport, Iowa*

Harry B. Black - *Roseburg, Oregon*

James Elijan Black - *1711 South 3rd St., Waco, Texas*

Kenneth C. Black - *General Delivery, Heavener, Oklahoma*

William C. Blackledge - *1135 D. Dakota St., Manila, P.I.*

Howard L. Blizzard - *112 South 51st Ave., Omaha, Nebraska*

Ralph M. Blythe - *15 Andrew Road, Milton, Massachusetts*

Jesse C. Beck - *47 Brady Street, San Francisco, California*

Carl R. Bode - *UKN*

Thomas M. Bodie - *2454 Walnut Avenue, Venice, California*

Roy L. Bodine Jr. - *UKN*

Arden R. Boellner - *508 N. Missouri Ave., Roswell, New Mexico*

William O. Boger - *3046 Stone Avenue, Omaha, Nebraska*

Augustine E. Bolger - *UKN*

Stanley B. Bonner - *6153 Kimbark Avenue, Chicago, Illinois*

Frank Boon - *UKN*

James D. Boone - *321 B North Palm Street, Alhambra, California*

Maynard B. Booth - *c/o C.Q.M., Fort Huacucz, Arizona*

Lawrence A. Bosworth - *30 Miraloma Drive, San Francisco, California*

Marcus B. Boulware - *c/o Central Drug Co., Rock Hill, South Carolina*

Robert H. Bourn - *UKN*

Frank W. Bovee - *519 E. Oakwood Drive, East Lansing, Michigan*

Seloen C. Bowlin - *UKN*

Nicholes R. Bowden - *852 South West Temple, Salt Lake City, Utah*

Edward H. Bowes - *c/o W. H. McKee, Chestertown, Maryland*

James V. Bradley - *212 4th Avenue, Quantico, Virginia*

Vance A. Bradshaw - *2191 Pennsylvania Avenue, Ontario, California*

Jasper E. Brady Jr. - *618 West Highland Dr., Seattle, Washington*

Harvey E. Bragdon - *133 Magnolia Street, San Francisco, California*

Adam Branning Jr. - *UKN*

James C. Brannind - *UKN*

Homer P. Braswell - *UKN*

John B. Brettell - *302 N. Cedar St., New Castle, Pennsylvania*

George T. Breitling - *3333 Broderick St., San Francisco, California*

Norman A. Brewer - *423 N. Rosemead Blvd., Temple City, California*

Robert Brewster - *UKN*

William H. Brewster - *West 632 20th Street, Spokane, Washington*

Francis J. Bridget - *c/o Navy Dept., Washington, D.C.*

Harry L. Briggs - *UKN*

Joseph A. Brime - *UKN*

Lawrence L. Briscoe - *UKN*

Chester K. Britt - *1053 Wood Street, La Crosse, Wisconsin*

George M. Brooke - *1281 Essex Street, San Diego, California*

Charles M. Brown - *133 Homestead Ave., Salinas, California*

Ernest L. Brown - *871 Burr Road, San Antonio, Texas*

E. Sherrill Brown - *Boone, Iowa*

Ralph W. D. Brown - *4033 Wallingford Avenue, Seattle, Washington*

Hugh Brown - *Santo Tomas University, Manila, P.I.*

Robert M. Brown - *4017 Country Club Drive, Los Angeles, California*

Charles J. Brown - *101 King William St., San Antonio, Texas*

Frederick B. Browne - *3581 Mynders Ave., Memphis, Tennessee*

Theodore R. Brownell - *501 So. 17th St., Fort Smith, Arkansas*

Robert W. Brownlee - *General Delivery, Manila, P.I.*

George C. Brundrett - *UKN*

Jerry C. Brunette - *1352 Davern Street, St. Paul, Minnesota*

William E. Brunton - *Douglas Flat, Calaveras County, California*

Othello C. Bruun - *UKN*

Arthur M. Bryan - *3237 Asbury Ave., Ocean City, New Jersey*

Karl F. Bryan - *UKN*

Thomas S. Bryan - *Box 3, Greensboro, Georgia*

William C. Bryan - *320 E. Adama Ave, McAlister, Oklahoma*

Alton H. Bryant - *Orangeburg, South Carolina*

Walter J. Buboltz - *3134 N. 12th St., Milwaukee, Wisconsin*

Ralph H. Buchanan - *UKN*

Arthur H. Buckman - *3030 Jenkins Arcade, Pittsburgh, Pennsylvania*

Coy C. Hall - *2522 Gould Ave., Fort Worth, Texas*

Orlinza A. Bullock - *201 Blythe, Bartlesville, Oklahoma*

Wilber J. Bunch - *UKN*

John N. Bundy - *UKN*

Kenneth I. Bunn - *916 North 47th St., Seattle, Washington*

Arthur V. Burhold - *Port Clinton, Ohio*

Robert C. Burlando - *45 Stoughton St., Dorchester, Massachusetts*

Joseph L. Burke - *376 Third Avenue, Troy, New York*

Jack W. Burkhalter - *UKN*

Robert T. Burns - *UKN*

Virgil P. Burns - *UKN*

Richard H. Burr - *702 Sheridan Avenue, Des Moines, Iowa*

Charles W. Burris - *1224 West Admiral Avenue, Tulsa, Oklahoma*

Henry A. Burton - *UKN*

George F. Burwell - *UKN*

Edwin J. Butler - *UKN*

Isam J. Butler - *UKN*

Stephen M. Byars Jr. - *UKN*

Ernest W. Bye - *Overland Park, Kansas*

Damon B. Byfield - *212 W. Rio Grande Ave., El Paso, Texas*

Cornelious Z. Byrd - *UKN*

Jack R. Byrd - *UKN*

Patrick J. Byrne - *Yonkers City Court, Yonkers, New York*

Jan V. Bzoth - *UKN*

Paul A. Brown - *UKN*

Earl R. Brown - *UKN*

C

Richard E. Cabberry - *1127 Second St., Ames, Iowa*

Mathew E. Cahill - *UKN*

John J. Caikins - *UKN*

Leonard S. Cairns - *2929 Connecticut Ave., NW, Washington, D.C.*

Ray R. Caldwell - *UKN*

Robert W. Callacay - *1842 Oxley St., So. Pasadena, California*

Wilbert A. Calvert - *Archer City, Texas*

Johannes J. Cammzega - *UKN*

Harry R. Campbell - *130 Legarda St., Manila, P.I.*

Roy L. Campbell - *UKN*

Francis A. Campbell - *UKN*

Monroe O. Carison - *Gunnison, Colorado*

James B. Cambell - *UKN*

Samuel D. Carwell - *1492 Larkin St., San Francisco, California*

Arthur B. Carlton - *5436 Leland Ave., Chicago, Illinois*

Otis A. Carmichael - *2725 Wightman St., San Diego, California*

Harvey H. Carper - *46 Albion St., Lawrence, Massachusetts*

George D. Carpenter - *UKN*

Sam E. Carothers - *152 Clark Court, Lafayette, Louisiana*

David T. Carter - *2107 Carterdale Road, Baltimore, Maryland*

Raymond G. Carrizales - *R #1, Box 23, Richland, Texas*

Robert L. Carusso - *1129 S. Elm Drive, Los Angeles, California*

Coleman T. Caruthers - *470 Spencer St., Monterey, California*

Andrew B. Casey - *2349 Kemper Lane, Cincinnati, Ohio*

Howard M. Cavender - *512 30th Avenue, Seattle, Washington*

William D. Chalek - *7318 S. Oakley Ave., Chicago, Illinois*

Robert Chambers Jr. - *10 Pleasant St., Whitinsville, Massachusetts*

William E. Chandler - *New Eng. Mut. Life, 25 W. 43rd St., New York, New York*

Yancey B. Chancy - *American Iron & Machine Works, Corpus Christi, Texas*

James W. Chaney - *408 N. Lea Ave., Roswell, New Mexico*

Robert G. Charles - *313 Jackson St., Minerva, Ohio*

Cecil B. Chernour - *Nallen, West Virginia*

Thomas F. Chilcote - *3733 North 15th Ave., Portland, Oregon*

Oswald Chipchase - *UKN*

Robert P. Chrisman - *Tracy, California*

Merle L. Christenson - *Marshfield, Oregon*

Calvin E. Chunn - *711 W. Washington Ave., Jonesboro, Arkansas*

R. D. Churchwell - *Madill, Oklahoma*

John R. Cicha - *Pisek, North Dakota*

Colland L. Clark Jr. - *329 San Fernando St., San Diego, California*

Thomas I. Clanton - *Fairfax, Missouri*

John W. Clark - *1414 W. 6th St., Aberdeen, Washington*

Lincoln R. Clark Jr. - *UKN*

Robert A. Clarke - *UKN*

Vincent E. Clarke - *139 S. Lakewood Ave., Downey, California*

Arthur V. Cleveland - *1513 12th St., Des Moines, Iowa*

David L. Coale III - *South California Tele. Co., Los Angeles, California*

Deas A. Coburn - *533 Rutledge Ave., Charleston, South Carolina*

Julian T. Cochran - *RFD #3, Sandersville, Georgia*

Wade R. Cochran - *Greenwood, South Carolina*

William L. Cochrum - *Little Rock, Arkansas*

Sheldon S. Coe - *824 5th Street, Brookings, South Dakota*

Harold Cogswell - *UKN*

Maurice H. Cohen - *UKN*

Lloyd A. Coleman - *Doddsville, Mississippi*

Claude M. Coles - *UKN*

Doyle F. Collins - *P.O. Box 662, RR #9, Houston, Texas*

Harold W. Collins - *La Carne, Ohio*

Luther C. Compton - *UKN*

Irving Compton - *Route #2, Mineral Wells, Texas*

Francis S. Conaty - *UKN*

Clifford K. Condon - *UKN*

Robert E. Conn Jr. - *4870 W. Lake Harriet Blvd., Minneapolis, Minnesota*

James A. Connell - *93 Woodward St., Wilkes-Barre, Pennsylvania*

William L. Conover - *77 Adelaide St., New London, Connecticut*

Clair M. Conzelman - *Box 404, Barre, Vermont*

Collins W. Cook - *4261 9th Avenue, Los Angeles, California*

Terry M. Cook Jr. - *Rt. #1, Cloud Chief, Oklahoma*

John G. Cook - *266 Sherman St., Denver, Colorado*

Witney M. Cook - *12 Garland Road, Concord, Massachusetts*

Thomas J. Coolidge - *125 Hervin St., Lancaster, Pennsylvania*

Willard B. Coombe - *Geyersville, California*

Henry C. Cooper - *UKN*

Joseph W. Cooper - *UKN*

Robert G. Cooper - *Fort Totten, New York*

Frank L. Corbi - *523 North Liberty, Alliance, Ohio*

Lewil O. Corbitt - *No. 8 Urbano St., Baguio Mountain Province, P.I.*

Paul R. Cornwall - *8821 Prince Ave., Los Angeles, California*

Duane L. Cosper - *Seil Building, Walla Walla, California*

Richard J. Costello - *Fifield, Wisconsin*

Lionel J. Couchon - *UKN*

George D. Cough - *4222 No. Ashland Ave., Chicago, Illinois*

Harley W. Coulter - *Box 45, St. Mary's Road, Columbus, Georgia*

Alva R. Cowan - *48 Evarts Street, Newport, Rhode Island*

James W. Cowan - *UKN*

Leroy Cowart Jr. - *1169 Virginia Ave., Atlanta, Georgia*

Tom O. Cox - *Sepan, New Mexico*

Thomas D. Crabtree - *77 Church St., Audenried, Pennsylvania*

Dean H. Craft - *Box 899, El Paso, Texas*

Howard G. Craig - *701 South Diamond, Deming, New Mexico*

William R. Craig - *1181 N.E. Cleveland St., Clearwater, Florida*

Ralph E. Crandell - *UKN*

Daniel W. Cranford - *621 E. Main, Albermarle, North Carolina*

Leland W. Cramer - *UKN*

George H. Crawford - *Bowling Green, Virginia*

Jeremiah V. Crews - *1012 Johnston Ave., San Diego, California*

Stephen H. Crosey Jr. - *RFD #3, Greenwood, Mississippi*

Arthur B. Cross - *Eatontown Blvd., Oceanport, New Jersey*

George W. Crowell - *Berry, Alabama*

Royal E. Crowell - *UKN*

Charles G. Crupper - *Tyro, Kansas*

Augustus J. Cullen - *UKN*

George Curtis - *38 Ocean St., New Bedford, Massachusetts*

John Curtiss Jr. - *197 Puritan Ave., Forest Hills, New York*

William T. Cummings - *34 Atala Terrace, San Francisco, California*

William M. Cummings - *Patagonia, Arizona*

James R. Curran - *467 Harrison Ave., Redwood City, California*

Edwin D. Curry - *UKN*

D

Maurice F. Daly - *40 Stelling St., Hartford, Connecticut*

Albert C. Daroy Jr. - *73 Washington St., Stoneham, Massachusetts*

Gerald L. Darling - *1100 8th St., Deming, New Mexico*

James H. Darling - *R #1, Butlersville, Indiana*

Robert G. Davey - *1190 S. 8th West, Salt Lake City, Utah*

Frank A. Davis - *3730 31st St., San Diego, California*

George S. Davis - *UKN*

Harry H. Davis - *113 21st St., Homestead, Pennsylvania*

Howard L. Davis - *Box 367, Canton, Ohio*

James R. Davis - *413 10th St., Ames, Iowa*

John A. Davis - *9329 Yellowstone Ave., Detroit, Michigan*

John H. Davis Jr. - *250 Norfolk Ave., Lynchburg, Virginia*

Lee Davis - *General Delivery, Kirkland, Arizona*

Thomas A. Davis - *UKN*

Harry J. Dawe - *195 Church St., Oakland, Maine*

William Dawson - *Bellevue, Clay County, Texas*

Murray M. Day - *Temple, New Hampshire*

Harvey L. Deatherage - *UKN*

Henrick C. Deboer - *UKN*

Sidney L. Debriero - *604 N. Central St., Parsons, Kansas*

James R. Decker - *527 W. 39th St., San Pedro, California*

Paul E. Decker - *501 N. 4th Street, Sapulpa, Oklahoma*

Anton A. C. DeHann - *UKN*

Thomas H. Delamore - *121 N. Russell Ave., Ames, Iowa*

John Delaney - *San Isidro, Donsol, Sorsogon, P.I.*

Cyrus W. Delong - *Hotel Whitney, Savannah, Georgia*

Charles M. Dempwolf - *512 S. Walnut Street, Cleburne, Texas*

Walter L. Dencker - *267 Mallorac Way, San Francisco, California*

Henry H. Denning - *Box 59, Mitchel Field, New York*

Arthur L. Derby - *415 E. 51st St., New York, New York*

Hugh A. Derrick - *335 Vine St., San Antonio, Texas*

Ralph R. Derrick - *UKN*

William T. Derrick - *45 Antipolo St., Pasay, Rizal, P.I.*

Johnny A. DeRusso - *UKN*

Wiley J. Dessauer - *Tucson, Arizona*

Claude A. Dewberry - *Hurt, Virginia*

Nathaniel M. Dial - *325 Claremont Ave., Long Beach, California*

John Henry Dieckman - *UKN*

Gordon L. Dickinson - *Petersburg, Texas*

Charles Di Maio - *UKN*

August A. Dipaolo - *80 Rickert Ave., Buffalo, New York*

Ernest H. Dixon - *UKN*

Frank L. Dixon - *503 20th St., Corpus Christi, Texas*

Barney G. Doak - *1019 Water St., Corpus Christi, Texas*

Merrill F. Dodson - *UKN*

Evert Doegborw - *UKN*

Myronn E. Dolk - *230 Eucalyptus Dr., Salinas, California*

James W. Donaldson - *701 S. Zinc Ave., Deming, New Mexico*

John P. Donati - *750 Foraker Ave., Albuquerque, New Mexico*

Otto H. Donner - *515 N. Main St., Ann Arbor, Michigan*

John T. Donohue - *UKN*

Roy E. Doran - *754 Fulton Ave., San Antonio, Texas*

Walter W. Dorman - *R #2, Maryville, Missouri*

George E. Dorran - *240 Grand Ave., Brooklyn, New York*

Louis N. Dosh - *147 High St., Rockland, Massachusetts*

Francis M. Douglass - *215 W. Fairview, Tulsa, Oklahoma*

George M. Dowd - *R #2, Stroud, Oklahoma*

Courtney R. Draper - *1122 Continental Bk. Bldg., Salt Lake City, Utah*

Richard L. Duckwall - *Tuttle, Oklahoma*

Willis H. Drummond - *1665 N. Sycamore Ave., Los Angeles, California*

William A. Dudley - *UKN*

Richard B. Donnewald - *7313 Elm Ave., Maplewood, Missouri*

James H. Duff Jr. - *409 Naples St., Corpus Christi, Texas*

John E. Duffy - *2544 Parkwood Ave., Toledo, Ohio*

I. W. Duko - *Delight, Arkansas*

Patrick H. Duncan - *Laurel Ford, Virginia*

Robert C. Duncan - *Searcy, Arkansas*

William D. Dunn - *1112 Prairie Ave., Mattoon, Illinois*

Floyd A. Dunning - *UKN*

Albert E. Durie - *47 E. Main St., Freehold, New Jersey*

William J. Dummyer - *Wilmington, Delaware*

E

Joe C. East - *104 E. 10th St., Rolla, Missouri*

Earl J. Eberly - *509 E. Adoue Ave., Goose Creek, Texas*

Dwight D. Edison - *3847 W. Side, Los Angeles, California*

Howard J. Edmonds - *1320 Lombard St., San Francisco, California*

George D. Edwards - *UKN*

John O. Edwards - *UKN*

Earl D. Eggers - *Post Falls, Idaho*

Herbert H. Eichlin Jr. - *1320 Spring Garden St., Easton, Pennsylvania*

Elliot J. Eilx - *UKN*

Burton C. Ellis - *2201 N.E. Hayes St., Minneapolis, Minnesota*

Jack L. Ellis - *2119 E. Gold Ave., Albuquerque, New Mexico*

John C. Ellis - *1277 S. Beverly Glen, Los Angeles, California*

William J. Ellis Jr. - *UKN*

Clyde E. Ely - *Silver City, New Mexico*

E. Carl Engelhart - *Box 854, R #1, Mill Valley, California*

Phillips B. England - *UKN*

Jimmie G. English - *Earle, Arkansas*

William R. English - *2900 Wilmott Ave., Columbia, South Carolina*

Albert W. Erickson - *Spearfish, South Dakota*

David G. Erickson - *2630 So. 15th St., Philadelphia, Pennsylvania*

Ervid E. Ericson - *2023 N. Calvert St., Baltimore, Maryland*

Norman L. Ernst - *122 Helena St., San Antonio, Texas*

Richard L. Errington - *UKN*

Alfred C. Espinoza - *318 E. La Patria St., Phoenix, Arizona*

Cecil J. Espy Jr. - *327 W. Maywood Dr., Portland, Oregon*

Franklins Evans - *UKN*

James W. Evans - *UKN*

Martin M. Evans - *61 E. 182 St., Apt. 4C, Bronx, New York*

Melvin W. Evans - *2315 S. Harvey St., Oklahoma City, Oklahoma*

Benjamin Evesson Jr. - *119 W. 46th Street, Bayonne, New Jersey*

Albert W. Everett - *213 "B" 6th Ave., San Francisco, California*

Austin Everett - *R #1, Mendenhall, Mississippi*

F

Norton R. Fairl - *59 Crowley Ave., Buffalo, New York*

Nickolas Fajnik - *UKN*

Anthony M. Falletta - *938 E. Abriende Ave., Pueblo, Colorado*

John S. Fantone - *1405 Claremont Ave., Norfolk, Virginia*

Carl G. Fansler - *1418 Davis Ave., Elkins, West Virginia*

William E. W. Farrell - *Warner Place, Bellemeade, Nashville, Tennessee*

Chester K. Fast - *UKN*

George C. Faulkner Jr. - *Woodside Way, Ross, California*

Ernial M. Feller - *2522 E. Preston St., Baltimore, Maryland*

Elbridge R. Fendall - *1214 Kincaid St., Eugene, Oregon*

Eahl W. Ferguson - *208 E. 51st St., New York, New York*

Harold M. Ferrell - *713 W. 133 St., Hawthorne, California*

John Filozof - *334 Prospect Ave., Brooklyn, New York*

Alva R. Fitsch - *UKN*

Hugh H. Fink - *1108 Upson St., El Paso, Texas*

Harold E. Finley - *18 N. 3rd St., Iola*

Douglas R. Fisher - *UKN*

Wayne A. Fisher - *2359 Van Buren, Ogden, Utah*

Orman L. Fitzhugh - *Tolar, Texas*

Morris A. Flagg - *UKN*

Peter M. Flame - *Union, Arizona*

Charles A. Fleming - *UKN*

John P. Flynn - *717 Bushwick Ave., Brooklyn, New York*

Jim G. Fong - *UKN*

Eugene A. Forbes - *UKN*

Jack A. Ford - *801 N. Vermont Ave., Los Angeles, California*

Ralph P. Ford - *321 W. 7th St., Charlotte, North Carolina*

Albert Fluck - *429 Quiricada, Manila, P.I.*

Herbert P. Fordham - *UKN*

Frank A. Forni - *UKN*

Eugene Forquer - *Carmichaels, Pennsylvania*

William J. Fossy - *UKN*

William N. Foster - *312 S. Zinc St., Deming, New Mexico*

Arthur E. Fouret - *Box 185, Trinchere, Colorado*

Paul W. Fouts - *3292 Flower St., Lynwood, California*

John M. Fowler - *3802 Olive St., Huntington Park, California*

Albert J. Foyt - *318 Mariposa, Apt. 402, Los Angeles, California*

Claud M. Fraleigh - *Veterans Hospital, Gulfport, Mississippi*

Earl C. Fradser - *409 S. 9th St., Norfolk, Nebraska*

Gus C. Francis - *UKN*

Charles B. Frank - *Mount Joy, Pennsylvania*

Stephen R. Franks - *Republic, Pennsylvania*

Ralph H. Free - *UKN*

Raymond A. Freel - *402 W. Walnut St., Hillsboro, Oregon*

Richard W. Freeman - *Cincinnati Post, Cincinnati, Ohio*

Samuel W. Freeney - *3 E. Lexington St., Baltimore, Maryland*

Edward P. Freiman - *UKN*

Paul W. French - *2423 Wellington Rd., Los Angeles, California*

Frank E. Fries - *124 W. 8th St., Madera, California*

Jack B. Frippts - *893 N. Prairie, Galesburg, Illinois*

Thomas W. Frutiger - *Red Lion, Pennsylvania*

John B. Fry - *Box 234, North Pleasanton, Texas*

Kenneth O. Fuelscher - *Perryten, Texas*

Robert B. Fugate - *1822 E. National Ave., Brazil, Indiana*

James W. Fulks - *R #2, Mena, Arkansas*

Albert L. Fullerton - *23 Union Place, Yonkers, New York*

Biagio O. Furnari - *342 21st St., Bellaire, Ohio*

G

Edgar S. Gable - *4400 Eagle Rock Blvd., Los Angeles, California*

Fritz O. Gaebler - *95 Ferry Street, Lawrence, Massachusetts*

Peter M. Gaffney - *1506 Jackne Ave., Covington, Louisiana*

Robert J. Gagen - *822 S. 11th St., Lafayette, Indiana*

Augustin R. Gagnon - *16 Birch St., Worcester, Massachusetts*

Howard J. Galbraith - *Bakersfield, California*

John D. Gamble - *Alvarado Hotel, Albuquerque, New Mexico*

Irwin W. Gamelguard - *117 S.E. 9th Ave., Portland, Oregon*

Warren A. Garnick - *158 S. Hoover St., Los Angeles, California*

Joseph S. Garcia - *UKN*

Robert L. Garcia - *519 S. Westmoreland St., Los Angeles, California*

Dwight E. Gard - *UKN*

Harold L. Gard - *R #1, Junction City, Kansas*

Louis K. Gardner Jr. - *UKN*

Burt C. Gay - *New London, New Hampshire*

William A. Gay - *Alexander City, Alabama*

Andrew A. Geiger - *407 W. Lake St., Horicon, Wisconsin*

Milton B. Geisman - *1651 E. Market St., Warren, Ohio*

Willis T. Geisman - *6 Ramona Ave., San Francisco, California*

Russell W. Genung - *1013 St. Charles Ave. N.E., Atlanta, Georgia*

Albert M. George - *1816 Richland Ave., Aiken, South Carolina*

Calvin S. George Jr. - *2013 E. 30th St., Baltimore, Maryland*

Paul T. George - *1645 Granada Ave., San Diego, California*

Edward A. Gerhard Jr. - *Winnetka, Illinois*

Herman F. Gerth - *409 E. Locust St., Bloomington, Illinois*

William C. Getchius - *317 Pearl St., Oshkosh, Wisconsin*

William Q. Gibbs - *UKN*

Marion J. Gibson - *UKN*

William A. Giddens - *General Delivery, Manchester, Texas*

Anthony L. Giebis - *1543 Packard Ave., Racine, Wisconsin*

Adolph H. Giesecke - *323 W. Granercy St., San Antonio, Texas*

Levis E. Giffin - *UKN*

Edward E. Gilbo - *735 W. Tuscarawas Ave., Barberton, Ohio*

Alfred D. Gilhan - *UKN*

Robert G. Gill Jr. - *109 W. 3rd St., Greensburg, Pennsylvania*

Mark E. Gimson - *UKN*

Edward E. Girsi - *1535 Larkin St., San Francisco, California*

William F. Glaab - *UKN*

Robert Glassburn - *UKN*

Robert L. Glatt - *518 20 Ave., Patterson, New Jersey*

Harry C. Glenn - *14206½ Sylvan St., Van Nuys, California*

Paul G. Glentzer - *1825 E. 2nd St., Pueblo, Colorado*

Wilson Glover - *36 Pickney St., Greenville, South Carolina*

John B. Glowacki - *709 Schuyler St., Syracuse, New York*

George W. Gobert - *Georgetown, Mississippi*

Grank Gossay - *UKN*

Albert K. Godwin - *UKN*

Roland E. Going - *Platte Center, Nebraska*

Harold H. Goldberg - *2900 Elmhurst St., Detroit, Michigan*

Francis X. Golden - *811 Roseneath Rd., Richmond Rd., Richmond, Virginia*

Leo B. Golden Jr. - *404 S. Ann St., Mobile, Alabama*

John C. Goldtrap - *c/o Galles Dairy, Box 1994, Casper, Wyoming*

Mark T. Goldstrire Jr. - *Chesterton, Indiana*

Abel O. Gomes - *1838 N. King St., Honolulu, Hawaii*

Walter Goodard - *El Rita, New Mexico*

Joseph Goodman - *6230 Old York Rd., Philadelphia, Pennsylvania*

Shields Goodman - *2425 Ransdell Ave., Louisville, Kentucky*

Benjamin D. Goodier - *Denver, Colorado*

Everett A. Goodiski - *New Kensington, Pennsylvania*

John A. Goodpasture - *818 Fairmont Ave., Bristol, Virginia*

Roy E. Goodpastor - *UKN*

Felix E. Goodson - *Kenton, Oklahoma*

Carl B. Gordon - *3500 64th Ave., Oakland, California*

Jack B. Gordon - *UKN*

Melvin E. Gordon - *UKN*

John J. Gorkiewicz - *UKN*

Andrew Gorman - *UKN*

Willis S. Gordon - *687 Jefferson Blvd., Memphis, Tennessee*

Alexander A. Gorski - *15 Arnold Ave., Newport, Rhode Island*

Charles H. Graff - *4551 Glenway, Seattle, Washington*

Hal C. Granberry - *c/o Pensacola Creasoting Co., Pensacola, Florida*

Robert W. Grandston - *18302 Ashworth Ave., Seattle, Washington*

Freelerick A. Grant - *UKN*

Marion D. Grant - *730 2nd St., Grand Rapids, Michigan*

Willard V. Grant - *UKN*

John E. Grantham - *El Paso, Texas*

Albert D. Gray - *20 W. Belmont St., Pensacola, Florida*

Harold W. Gaybeal - *11828 Wilshire Blvd., W. Los Angeles, California*

Billy B. Gray - *R #2, Shannon, Mississippi*

Sheldon F. Gray - *817 S. Hobart Ave., Los Angeles, California*

Warren Gray - *UKN*

Horace Greeley - *UKN*

Gerald B. Greeman - *709 S. Tin, Deming, New Mexico*

Carl Green - *R #2, Caddo, Oklahoma*

Franklin A. Green - *El Rey Theater, Tulare, California*

Leonard D. Green - *1042 Soniat St., New Orleans, Louisiana*

Ralph R. Green - *Inola, Oklahoma*

George H. Greenwood - *1224 Law-*

ton Street, San Francisco, California

Sydney R. Greer - *810 West Ave., Austin, Texas*

Mathew J. Gregorich - *RFD #1, Box 88, Naches, Washington*

Robert K. Gregory - *Genoa, Colorado*

Dwight M. Gribben - *181 Euclid Ave., San Leandro, California*

Edward R. J. Griffin - *2851 Kahawai St., Honolulu, Hawaii*

John C. Griffith - *222 East Popular St., San Antonio, Texas*

Andrew O. Grignon - *Winneconne, Wisconsin*

Edward M. Grimes - *516 So. 16th St., Fort Dodge, Iowa*

Joseph G. Groszek - *Rutland, North Dakota*

Gardner R. Gross - *Brookings, South Dakota*

Kenneth Grover - *Cumberland, Wisconsin*

Carroll M. Guin - *Rt. #3, Brainard, Minnesota*

John M. Gulick - *UKN*

George M. Gunter - *Gans, Oklahoma*

John Gure - *17 Rennell Court, Bridgeport, Connecticut*

Harry L. Gurner - *UKN*

Charles A. Guyon - *UKN*

Benjamin E. Gwynn - *48 Abbott St., Salinas, California*

Joseph Ganahl - *3280 Chadburne Road, Shaker Heights, Cleveland, Ohio*

H

Rueben G. Habockel - *243 So. Prospect Ave., San Bernardino, California*

Alvin C. Hadley - *1420 E. 8th St., Okmulgee, Oklahoma*

Olaf W. Hagomo - *UKN*

Robert F. Haggerty - *1660 N.E. Irving St., Portland, Oregon*

Alfred S. Hagstrom - *1720 Spring Garden St., Philadelphia, Pennsylvania*

Lucy E. Haines - *UKN*

John Gilbert Hair - *Enquirer Bldg., Cincinnati, Ohio*

Charles D. Hall - *Eagle Grove, Iowa*

Lee H. Hall - *1645 Francisca, Pasadena, California*

Stuart H. Hall - *1620 Monument Ave., Richmond, Virginia*

Winfield S. Halton - *UKN*

Alvah L. Hamilton Jr. - *Morehead City, North Carolina*

Donald W. Hamilton Jr. - *75 S. Broad St., Forwich, New York*

George D. Hamilton - *2730 Ivan Court, Los Angeles, California*

William A. Hamilton Jr. - *Board of Education, Dallas, Texas*

Homer H. Hammond - *UKN*

Clyder Handgham - *UKN*

Arda M. Hanenkrat - *Waynesfield, Ohio*

Donald Hanes - *672 Lindell Ave., Louisville, Kentucky*

Charles W. Hanson - *21 North Arapahoe St., Caldwell, Kansas*

Howard P. Hardegree - *Box 606, Ben Wheeler, Texas*

Harold L. Hardiwioke - *UKN*

Alvin R. Hatten - *UKN*

Jack Hargrove - *RFD #1, Olive Hill, Tennessee*

Harry J. Harper - *601 E. 3rd Ave., Mitchell, South Dakota*

Jay B. Harrelson - *Crossville, Alabama*

William B. Harrington - *Columbus, Mississippi*

Lawrence Harrington - *Box 42, Ged, Louisiana*

Hozie M. Harris - *Gould, Oklahoma*

Malvern P. Harris - *Norwood, North Carolina*

Mel L. Harrison - *Ajo, Arizona*

George B. Hart - *6738 Balkenton Place, Silverton, Ohio*

Allison L. Hartman - *317 Gray Ave., Winchester, Virginia*

John D. Hatch - *UKN*

Thomas E. Harvy - *UKN*

James O. Hase - *Dongola, Illinois*

Charles D. Harvy - *8616 A. Virginia Ave., South Gate, California*

Edward W. Hastings - *4225 Menlo St., San Diego, California*

Charles E. Hasse - *Pinconning, Michigan*

Graham M. Hatch Jr. - *City Health Dept., Dallas, Texas*

Basil M. Hatfield - *465 Cleveland, Fort Worth, Texas*

Carl William Hausmann - *730 Boulevard East, Weehawken, New Jersey*

Floyd A. Hawk - *1618 Cleveland Ave., Whiting, Indiana*

Thomas H. Hayes - *137 So. Fairfax St., Alexandria, Virginia*

Raymond C. Haynes - *Inman, South Carolina*

William Haynes - *UKN*

Hugh J. Haziett - *UKN*

John J. Heil - *1719 Otis Street NE, Washington, D.C.*

Clarence Heinrich - *Santo Tomas University, Manila, P.I.*

Samuel J. Hoisinger - *4207 Madison Street, Fresno, California*

Jack H. Heinzel - *4204 La Luz Street, El Paso, Texas*

Clifford D. Hendon - *UKN*

Lawrence E. Hendrickson - *5644 14th Ave., So. Minneapolis, Minnesota*

George R. Hennessey - *1554 "B" Ave., NE, Cedar Rapids, Iowa*

Patrick L. Hennessey - *4557 Pennsylvania St., Gary, Indiana*

Dale Henry - *Lesage, West Virginia*

Dudley A. Hensen - *140 Washington St., Dover, New Hampshire*

Louis H. Henson - *Spruce Pine, North Carolina*

Alfred J. Herbold - *UKN*

Harry P. Herr Jr. - *2036 No. Fifth St., Harrisburg, Pennsylvania*

Leroy W. Herrich - *UKN*

Robert W. Hey - *UKN*

Eugene S. Hicker - *Rt. #3, Burley, Idaho*

Gerban Hidmer - *UKN*

Raymond High - *15 Jessup St., San Rafael, California*

Earl W. Hill - *424 First Street, Stambaugh, Michigan*

Patrick G. Hilton - *705 Fayette Pike, Montgomery, West Virginia*

Richard F. Hill - *1418 Metropolitan Ave., Atlanta, Georgia*

John K. Hillemeier - *203 S. 6th St., Keokuk, Iowa*

Virgil L. Hinkel - *1012 Wm. H. Taft Road, Cincinnati, Ohio*

Jack M. Hinkson - *UKN*

James P. Hinton - *UKN*

Roy D. Hobbs - *Lovington, New Mexico*

Vernon D. Hobbs Jr. - *317 Southwest 5th St., Richmond, Indiana*

Welles G. Hodgson Jr. - *5057 Bel-*

mont Ave., Minneapolis, Minnesota

Harry C. Hoffmeyer - 3928 Palm Street, St. Louis, Missouri

William F. Hogaboom - 1625 Monroe St., Vicksburg, Mississippi

Emmet O. Hogan - Elmore, Alabama

Harry J. Hogue - 115 First St., Morgantown, West Virginia

Alvin R. Holden - 465 E. Second North, Payson, Utah

Willard B. Holdredge - 944 Westcotte St., Syracuse, New York

Arthur C. Holmes - 1012 Park Avenue, Hoboken, New Jersey

William T. Holloway - Cook-Lakeview, Washington

Dwight M. Holmes - UKN

George T. Holmes - 543 W. 123rd Street, New York, New York

Leslie H. Holmes - Nampa, Idaho

Stanley Holmes - 5 Church St., Stafford Springs, Connecticut

William E. Holton - Citizens State Bank, Hayfield, Minnesota

Albert H. Hook - 1327 Alma Street, Salinas, California

Thene H. Hooker - 209 Walnut Street, Rochester, Michigan

Pier J. Hoopmans - UKN

Armand Hopkins - 194 South Wilbur Ave., Syracuse, New York

John C. Hopper - UKN

Henry W. Horn - 1416 Birdie St., Burlington, Iowa

Jay M. Horowitz - Sweetwater, Tennessee

Edward L. Horton - 623 West Columbia, Farmington, Missouri

Karl H. Houghton - 2411 West Blvd., Los Angeles, California

John W. Hughes - UKN

Thomas W. House - 567 Capital View St., Atlanta, Georgia

James E. Houseknecht - UKN

Earl Houseal - Oswego, Montana

Houston P. Houser Jr.- Perry, Georgia

William T. Howell - UKN

Alfred R. Howland - UKN

Charles S. Hoyt - 882 Armada Point, Loma, California

Jaroslay F. Hrdina - UKN

Clyde R. Huddleson - Mandan, North Dakota

Jack D. Hudson - 3221 Hanes Ave., Richmond, Virginia

Arthur E. Huff - 8424 Roanoke Drive, St. Louis, Missouri

Joseph J. Hughes - 65 Rosewood St., Mattapan, Massachusetts

Orull L. Huling - 106 S. 29th St., Belleville, Illinois

Earl H. Hulsey Jr. - 4328 Overhill Drive, Dallas, Texas

Charles I. Humber - Adjutant General's Office, Washington, D.C.

Howard Humphreys - UKN

Dwight T. Hunkins - 657 Kennard St., St. Paul, Minnesota

J. B. Hunt - 441 S. 5th Ave., Tucson, Arizona

James E. Hunter - Silver City, New Mexico

Russell J. Hutchinson - 519 N. Hermosa St., Albuquerque, New Mexico

J

Peter S. Jackson - UKN

Robert Arnold Jackson - UKN

Eugene C. Jacobs - 827 Forest Ave., River Forest, Illinois

John R. Janson - *229 E. 79th St., New York, New York*

Leon H. Jay - *UKN*

Ralph Jewell - *2044 Mission St., San Francisco, California*

Lacy O. Jenkins - *Box 181, Mansfield, Missouri*

George M. Jenkins - *Box 35, Ruscola, Texas*

Sidney F. Jenkins - *Box 547, Walnut Creek, California*

Edmond E. Jennings - *UKN*

Owen E. Jensen - *2751 Blanche St., Pasadena, California*

Harold A. Jimerson - *2639 E. 7th St., Tucson, Arizona*

Paul L. Jeffrion - *62 S. First, West Salt Lake City, Utah*

Robert L. Johns - *110 E. Maine St., Grafton, West Virginia*

Byron L. Johnson - *Scotland Neck, North Carolina*

Bernard W. Johnson - *UKN*

Leo Johnson - *308 28th Ave., San Francisco, California*

Harold K. Johnson - *Grafton, North Dakota*

Lycurgus W. Johnson - *1379 Elm St., Denver, Colorado*

Lonnie M. Johnson - *R #2, Box 100, Dallas, Texas*

Chester L. Johnson - *704 Main St., So., Pendleton, Oregon*

Martin L. Johnson - *UKN*

Robert H. G. Johnson - *175 Prospect Place, Rutherford, New Jersey*

Wilburn D. Johnson - *Indio, California*

Howard D. Johnson - *UKN*

Donald E. Jones - *1157 N. Pacific Ave., Glendale, California*

Philip D. Johnson - *223 Spalding Drive, Beverly Hills, California*

Henry S. Jones - *Quezon City, San Francisco, Del Monte, P.I.*

Howard H. Jones - *UKN*

Sam C. Jones - *R #3, Box 100, Anaheim, California*

Daniel W. Jopling - *Ft. Summer, New Mexico*

Boder D. Jordon - *R #1, Box 220, Riverside, California*

Fred H. Jordan - *Box 956, Clovis, New Mexico*

James J. Jordan - *131 Trece Martiers, Cavite, P.I.*

Maurice Joses - *231 Alameda Blvd., Coronado, California*

Philip J. Joy - *UKN*

Henry C. Joyner - *UKN*

Mark C. Judy - *UKN*

Edward Junker Jr. - *109 E. Hill, Gallup, New Mexico*

K

James Kabakow - *715 F.B. Harrison, Pasay, Rizal, P.I.*

Darnell W. Kadlph - *2219 S. Hurley, Fort Worth, Texas*

Oliver R. Kamstra - *321 Bayview St., San Rafael, California*

Mac Kappelman - *Miltondale, Kansas*

Jack L. Kaster - *3003 Wheeling Street, El Paso, Texas*

Andrew Kastro - *UKN*

George M. Kaufman - *Machenzie Farms, Hampton, New Jersey*

William R. Kaye - *3040 45th Ave., S.W., Seattle, Washington*

Richard A. Keasey - *931 SE 32nd Ave., Portland, Oregon*

Dean R. Keating - *UKN*

Alexander E. Keegan - *Carrizo Springs, Texas*

Ralph Keeler - 3770 *Stuart St., Denver, Colorado*

James W. Keene - 1105 N. 9th Ave., *Pensacola, Florida*

James D. Koll - *R #1, Seneca, South Carolina*

George S. Kellogg - *UKN*

Mont C. Kellogg - 120 *Mountain View Ave., Vallejo, California*

Jack W. Kelly - *UKN*

Fred J. Kelsey - *Oden, Indiana*

John W. Kelsey - *North 3rd St., Burlington, Iowa*

Walter A. Kelso Jr. - 2215 Ave. C, *Galveston, Texas*

Lloyd H. Kelsey - Box 798, R #1, *San Jose, California*

Orich V. Kemph - 1610 *Live Oak St., Bell, California*

Marshall H. Kennedy Jr. - *UKN*

Thomas R. Kennedy - *Banking Oil Co., Maricopa, California*

William L. Kenney - 4537 SE 38th Ave., *Portland, Oregon*

Harry J. Kerbow - 256 *Broadway, San Diego, California*

Albert J. Kercher - *UKN*

Edwin V. Kerr - 26 *Springbrook Ave., Rhinebeck, New York*

Richard O. Kessler - *UKN*

Leland L. Keston - *UKN*

William N. Kindler - *Staples, Minnesota*

Andrew J. King - 133 *Pine Place, Stapleton, Staten Island, New York*

Edward E. King - *UKN*

John V. King - 1601 *Ursuline Ave., Bryan, Texas*

Leslie W. King - 1645 *Park Place, Wichita, Kansas*

Stuert W. King - 56 *Pitt St., Charleston, South Carolina*

William M. King - *UKN*

Berkley J. Kinrade - *R #1, Pawnee, Illinois*

Weldon H. Kirk - 8608 SW *Westlane, Portland, Oregon*

Ben E. Kirkpatrick - 2115 *Pierce Ave., Nashville, Tennessee*

Dale J. Kirnee - *UKN*

Jack R. Kirrland - *UKN*

James D. Kittredge - 122 *Prospect St., Cambridge, Massachusetts*

Louis C. Klein - 4424 *Rosedale Ave., Bethesda, Maryland*

Clarence A. Kline - *Upland, Indiana*

Aaron Klaitchke - *Plaridel, Bulacan, P.I.*

Leif R. Kloster - *Eagle Grove, Iowa*

Andrew G. Knizner - *UKN*

Charles H. V. Knowles - *UKN*

James C. Knowles - 612 *Narrow Lane Road, Montgomery, Alabama*

Raymond W. Koenig - 9718 34th *Ave., Corona, New York*

Richard B. Koenig - *UKN*

Hadson C. Kokjer - *Hotel Hyannis, Hyannis, Nebraska*

Louis G. Kolger - 300 N. 19th St., *Richmond, Illinois*

Edward P. Konik - 508 High St., *New Britain, Connecticut*

Morris H. Korrblum - 710 *Leland Ave., St. Louis, Missouri*

Oscar C. Kowalake - *Stewart, Minnesota*

Peter Koster - 2806 *Union St., San Francisco, California*

Joseph E. Krammer - *Coupeville, Washington*

Paul H. Krauss - *UKN*

Frank F. Krivanek - *UKN*

Edward H. Kuechler - *Coeur D'Alens, Idaho*

Lloyd W. Kuhn - *235 S. Walnut St.,* *Nousta, Oklahoma*

Clarence J. Kuncl - *1628 S. St., St.* *Louis Ave., Chicago, Illinois*

George J. Kusek - *R #1, Box 147,* *Oklahoma City, Oklahoma*

Zachary Kush - *Elbert, West* *Virginia*

Harold G. Kurvers - *UKN*

L

Marvin G. Lackey - *UKN*

Warren G. Lackey - *R #1, Box* *4598, Port Orchard, Washington*

Charles G. Lade - *1235 N. Ogden* *Drive, Hollywood, California*

Walter A. Laffoon - *RFD #1,* *Warner, Oklahoma*

Oriey A. Laird - *3022 Walton St.,* *Los Angeles, California*

Robert W. Lally - *40 W. York St.,* *Akron, Ohio*

Whitney A. Langlois - *UKN*

Harry R. Lane - *4511 Vine St.,* *St. Bernard, Ohio*

Benjamin B. Langdon - *350 Con-* *gress Ave., New Haven,* *Connecticut*

Leonard Langston - *UKN*

Edwin J. Laragay - *847 E. 27th St.,* *Paterson, New Jersey*

Peter F. Larson - *4033 Hanover St.,* *Dallas, Texas*

Lewis E. Lasth - *1106 N. Bowman* *Ave., Danville, Illinois*

Gordon K. Lambert - *646 West End* *Ave., New York, New York*

William J. Latimer Jr. - *132 Bethle-* *hem Pike, Philadelphia,* *Pennsylvania*

Philip G. Lauman Jr. - *3900 Cathe-* *dral Ave. NW, Washington, D.C.*

Stanley M. Lausen - *954 McLean* *Ave., St. Paul, Minnesota*

Ronald J. Latchford - *UKN*

Charles H. Langdon - *1419 E. Mar-* *ket St., York, Pennsylvania*

Leroy U. Lawler - *UKN*

Robert J. Lawler - *791 Neil Ave.,* *Columbus, Ohio*

Olive J. Lawter - *UKN*

Marion R. Lawton - *791 Neil Ave.,* *Columbus, Ohio*

Albert W. Leader - *UKN*

Stanley A. Leahigh - *804 SW Taylor,* *Portland, Oregon*

Cecil G. Lebrun - *New Hammond* *Hotel, Van Buren, Maine*

Charles F. LeCompte - *UKN*

Henry G. Lee - *1230 Milan Ave.,* *So. Pasadena, California*

Jesse E. Lee - *UKN*

Philip H. Leer - *5300 Lorain Ave.,* *Cleveland, Ohio*

Robert Lees - *Washburn, Illinois*

Robert A. Leger - *163 Stevens St.,* *St. Paul, Minnesota*

Harry R. Leighton - *20 Orange* *Drive, Salinas, California*

Charles B. Leinbach - *612 W. Main* *St., So. Pottstown, Pennsylvania*

Henry D. Leitner - *2510 Hayne* *Ave., Aiken, South Carolina*

Jack F. LeMire - *2791 Greenwich* *St., San Francisco, California*

Fred Lank - *UKN*

John T. Leonard - *555 Huger St.,* *Charleston, South Carolina*

Ben F. Leslie - *UKN*

Leon W. Lesner - *UKN*

Edward V. Lesnick - *837 E. Tazu-* *man, Manila, P.I.*

John E. Lester - *628 W. 7th St.,* *Dallas, Texas*

Tamlor A. Le Sueur - *Rt. #2, Okmulgee, Oklahoma*

Benjamin Levy - *UKN*

Theodore Lewin - *San Miguel, Manila, P.I.*

Donald D. Lewis - *UKN*

Eugene T. Lewis - *217 Burr Road, San Antonio, Texas*

Homer E. Lewis - *UKN*

John L. Lewis - *Box 709, Lake Village, Arkansas*

William L. Light - *Palo Pinto, Texas, Star Route*

Frank A. Lightfoot - *425 Fulton St., Alexandria, Louisiana*

Frederick R. Lincoln - *UKN*

Richard P. Lindemuth - *Maytown, Pennsylvania*

James R. Lindsay - *2325 Glenmary Ave., Louisville, Kentucky*

Arthur E. Lindstrom - *UKN*

Joseph R. Lippincott - *1256 W. Adams Blvd., Los Angeles, California*

Herman A. Little - *523 E. Locust St., San Antonio Texas*

Samuel W. Little - *Hotel Roosevelt, Washington, D.C.*

John O. Littig - *1945 Broadway, San Francisco, California*

Samuel W. Little - *UKN*

Alvin L. Lockridge - *UKN*

Hanford N. Lockwood Jr. - *9½ W. Walnut St., Westmont, New Jersey*

Jewel E. Loftin - *R #3, Cooper, Texas*

Carl E. Logan - *UKN*

Louis Loicano - *3723 18th Ave., Brooklyn, New York*

Andree W. Long Jr. - *UKN*

Paul L. Long - *Lincoln, Kansas*

Robert L. Long - *353 Woodfin St., Hot Springs, Arkansas*

Raymond Lopez - *R #3, Nampa, Idaho*

Gene Lotspech - *R #5, Floydada, Texas*

John M. Loupe - *2880 Vallejo St., San Francisco, California*

William F. Lovegreen - *Palmyra, Missouri*

John W. Lowery - *1512 7th Ave., Bessemer, Alabama*

Fred A. Ludwig - *Box 160, Salida, Colorado*

William P. Luetzel - *1591 Beverley Blvd., Berkley, Michigan*

John C. Lulkart - *600 Rencher St., Clovis, New Mexico*

Arthur C. Luis - *UKN*

Stanley F. Lukas - *2324 W. Armitage Ave., Chicago, Illinois*

John H. Luther - *Orleans, Nebraska*

Fred G. Lyda - *170 Jackson St., Greenwood, South Carolina*

James D. Lynch - *133 N. Pleasant St., Watertown, New York*

John J. Lynch - *96 Stearns St., Bristol, Connecticut*

Roy E. Lynch - *R #5, Waynesboro, Tennessee*

Thomas Lynch - *c/o Convent of Mercy, Victoria Square, Perth, W. Australia*

Leonard L. Lyons Jr. - *1820 Old Government St. Mobile, Alabama*

Julian V. Lyon - *R #2, Creedmoor, North Carolina*

M

Gordon E. Maccani - *923 E. Ayers St., Ironwood, Michigan*

Ronald G. MacDonald - *2395 Francisco St., San Francisco, California*

Daniel MacDugall - *381 E. 152 St., New York, New York*

Hubert MacGowan - *111 Boren Ave., Hudson Arms Apt., Seattle, Washington*

Edward C. Mack - *339 N. 17th St., Kansas City, Kansas*

Everett D. MacKay - *UKN*

Henry W. Macmer - *720 Noios St., Utica, New York*

Thomas K. MacNair - *San Jose, California*

John H. Macon - *738 W. Main St., Laurens, South Carolina*

Keith Madill - *Baker, Oregon*

Samuel A. Madison - *Williford, Arkansas*

Robert K. Magee - *UKN*

Lloyd H. Magill - *117 Oregon St., Bend, Oregon*

William H. Magill - *621 9th St., S., Fargo, North Dakota*

William H. Maguire - *416 W. Myrtle, San Antonio, Texas*

Harry C. Maguson - *602 Cottonwood Ave., Canon City, Colorado*

Steven Malevich - *230 Agnew Ave., Pittsburgh, Pennsylvania*

Irving R. Madelson - *540 Briar Place, Chicago, Illinois*

Warren H. Markham - *706 Roswell Ave., Long Beach, California*

Cyril Q. Marron - *109 Hillcrest Ave., Yonkers, New York*

Byrd F. Marshall - *Newville, Alabama*

James Martin - *Fulton, Kentucky*

Homer J. Martin - *UKN*

Howard A. Martin - *UKN*

John H. Martz - *6222 Flushing Ave., Maspeth, Long Island, New York*

William H. Marvel - *UKN*

Edward R. Mason - *535 Gadsden Court, Spartanburg, South Carolina*

Kenneth L. Mason - *UKN*

Claude E. Massie - *UKN*

Lester L. Mate - *610 W. 4th St., Quanah, Texas*

Andrew J. Mathiesen - *833 S. Sycamore Ave., Los Angeles, California*

John Matola - *401 3rd St., Monessen, Pennsylvania*

Clinton S. Maupin - *UKN*

Thompson B. Maury III - *10524 Wilkins Blvd., W. Los Angeles, California*

William H. Maverick - *Frost Bank Blvd., San Antonio, Texas*

Frank L. Maxwell - *4224 Jackson St., Birrington, Alabama*

Winsien R. Maxwell - *Columbus, Kansas*

Milton E. May - *Clarendon, Arkansas*

Richard H. Mayberry - *860 Orange Ave., Coronado, California*

Harold R. McBridge - *20 Stevens Ave., Westbrook, Maine*

Richard E. McCaffery - *R #1, Box 12A, Soledad, California*

John M. McAnerney - *UKN*

James H. McCahon - *310 S. Edith St., Albuquerque, New Mexico*

William H. McCann - *Rt. #2, Columbus, Ohio*

Joseph L. McCarthy - *445 N. 2nd West, Brigham, Utah*

Reed L. McCartney - *21 S. 53rd St., Philadelphia, Pennsylvania*

David McCeoch - *UKN*

Virgles W. McCollum - *511 N. Halageuno St., Carlsbad, New Mexico*

Henry M. McCullough - *134 Catalpa St., Clarksdale, Mississippi*

Deenah R. McCurry - *Erwin, Tennessee*

John J. McDonnell - *1017 Dahill Road, Brooklyn, New York*

Raymond E. McGee - *UKN*

William D. McGee - *UKN*

James M. McGrath - *1305 Euclid Ave., Santa Barbara, California*

John B. McGrew - *Rancho Santa Fe, California*

Vernald G. McIlhattan - *Spencer, Wisconsin*

Arch M. McKeever - *Spokane, Washington*

Clinton W. McKinley - *1315 Watt St., Reno, Nevada*

William J. McKenzie - *720 N. 2nd St., Albuquerque, New Mexico*

John A. Mclain - *5063 Lake Washington Blvd., Seattle, Washington*

James H. McLean - *UKN*

Lannie McLim - *UKN*

James T. McClellan - *8 Glenwood Ave., Portland, Maine*

John A. McCain - *5063 Lake Washington Blvd., Seattle, Washington*

Benjamin L. McMakin - *366 Virginia Ave., San Mateo, California*

Francis J. McManus - *6907 Hough Ave., Cleveland, Ohio*

William J. McMichael - *UKN*

Frank W. McMillan - *UKN*

James McMinn - *Carlsbad, New Mexico*

Dester L. McMullen - *UKN*

Joseph E. McNair - *Summit, Mississippi*

Roland C. McNaughton - *488 17th St., San Bernardino, California*

Samuel M. McReynolds - *113 29th St., Manhattan Beach, California*

Ernest C. McVittie - *UKN*

Everett V. Mead - *1508 Washington St., Hamburg, Iowa*

Joseph O. Meek - *UKN*

Poland C. Meeks - *1409 W. 13th St., Texarkana, Texas*

William G. Meese - *UKN*

Carl W. Meigs - *UKN*

Philip H. Meier - *1123 N. Orange Ave., Azuza, California*

Jack L. Melvin - *168 Pateros St., Caloocan, Rizal, P.I.*

Alfonso McIendez - *Box 57, Mora, New Mexico*

Cassa J. Mercer Jr. - *Baldwinsville, New York*

Jacques V. Merrifield - *1114 S. 5th Ave., Maywood, Illinois*

Grady M. Merritt - *General Delivery, Dardanelle, Arkansas*

Frederick Merton - *UKN*

John C. Metcalf - *101 Hawthorne Road, Duluth, Minnesota*

Vincent J. Mick - *Raquette Lake, New York*

Steve W. Mickey - *3447 France Ave., Robbinsdale, Minnesota*

Campbell N. Middleton - *2917 N.E. Alameda, Portland, Oregon*

Nicholas N. Mihailov - *5722 25th Ave. NW, Seattle, Washington*

John Miklo - *UKN*

Robert C. Milks - *UKN*

Julius J. Miller - *UKN*

Kenneth G. Miller - *Box 62, Port Arthur, Texas*

Leslie E. Miller - *Holton, Indiana*

Robert N. Miller - *UKN*

Wayne K. Miller - *4529 Beatty Drive, Riverside, California*

Lee G. Miles - *320 Fairfield St., Ligonier, Pennsylvania*

William F. Miles - *225 Ann St., Middletown, Pennsylvania*

Joseph C. Milligan - 22 E. St., Oxnard, California

Loyd E. Mills - UKN

John S. Miner - 1151 S. Broadway, Los Angeles, California

William D. Miner - Table Grove, Illinois

Harry C. Minsker - 308 Reynolds St., Charleston, West Virginia

Floyd A. Mitchell - US Military Academy, West Point, New York

Walter H. Mitchell - UKN

Winfred A. Mitchum - 2624 University Blvd., Houston, Texas

Harry H. Mittenthal - Pasig, Rizal, P.I.

Fred T. Miranda - Box 44, Plymouth, California

Chris D. Moeller - Box 64, Bostonia, California

Albert W. Moffett - 114 Desha Road, Lexington, Kentucky

Gerald L. Moffett - Ft. Knox, Kentucky

Lloyd C. Moffitt - 120 E. 8th Ave., Denver, Colorado

Alton L. Montgomery - UKN

Austin J. Montgomery - 14754 Greenleaf St., Sherman Oaks, California

Hampden E. Montgomery - UKN

John D. Mullaney - UKN

Jackson P. Montgomery - Plaunch, New Mexico

Charles Moore - 214 Columbia Ave., Albuquerque, New Mexico

Dennis M. Moore - 318 Arcadia Place, San Antonio, Texas

George B. Moore - 5807 Cornelia Ave., Chicago Illinois

Paul E. Moore - 212 E. Main St., Peru, Indiana

Robert B. Moore - 536 Knollwood Dr., Cedar Rapids, Iowa

Leslie E. Mocte - 11 First St., Quezon City, Manila, P.I.

Paul D. Morehouse - 2416 Gough St., San Francisco, California

Harold A. Morey - 417 S. Olympic, Tulsa, Oklahoma

Donald R. Morgan - 513 W. 23rd St., Vancouver, Washington

Jack P. Morgan - Ivyside Park, Altoona, Pennsylvania

Otis S. Morgan - Greenville Road, Laurens, South Carolina

John C. Morley - 10819 Magnolia Dr., Cleveland, Ohio

Garnet G. Morris Jr. - American Intern Camp, Mrs. Margert Morris, Baguio, P.I.

George E. Morris - UKN

Charles J. Morton - UKN

Roy Mosher - UKN

Edwin B. Moss - 2915 Bourland St., Greenville, Texas

Eugene Mott - UKN

Floyd J. Moyer - P.O. Box 295, Palmer, Nebraska

Victor A. Mueller - RR #2, Carroll, Iowa

James E. Mullen - 608 E. 8th St., Trinidad, Colorado

Jimmy Mullins - UKN

William L. Munro - 729 Shotwell St., San Francisco, California

William J. Murchison - 275 Ashland Ave., Pittsburgh, Pennsylvania

Lloyd G. Murphy - 213 Ave. NW, Bismarck, North Dakota

Louis F. Murphy - UKN

William W. Murphy - 3701 Divisadero St., San Francisco, California

Anthony Musso - 1625 Agriculture St., New Orleans, Louisiana

William Murphy - *UKN*
George A. Muzzey - *UKN*
Estel B. Myers - *525 Beacher St.,
Louisville, Kentucky*
Gordon R. Myers - *526 Monument
Square, Racine, Wisconsin*
Clayton H. Michelson - *947 S.W.
Broadway, Portland, Oregon*
Nateno Mirabel - *UKN*
John Mercurio - *1926 Chicago St.,
San Diego, California*
Howard I. Massey - *6 Caldwell
Ave., Apt. F, Fort Knox, Kentucky*
Walter P. Manning - *1926 Penn
Ave., S. Minneapolis, Minnesota*

N
David Nash - *Marett Hotel, India-
napolis, Indiana*
Peter Nathansen - *UKN*
Bernardo N. Navallo - *48th & Park
Ave., Des Moines, Iowa*
John C. Needham - *219 Lake Shore
Dr., Chicago, Illinois*
Edward J. Negel - *1409 United
Brethren Bldg., Dayton, Ohio*
Albert S. Negley - *310 Paseo Enci-
nal, San Antonio, Texas*
John Neiger - *7112 Wydown,
St. Louis, Missouri*
Robert R. Mangel - *UKN*
Edwin R. Nelson - *UKN*
Robert V. Nelson - *3952 12th Ave.
S., Minneapolis, Minnesota*
Russell J. Nelson - *UKN*
Theodore J. Neuwirth - *1652 36th
Ave., Oakland, California*
Fred R. Newell - *62 Western Ave.,
Brattleboro, Vermont*
Shelby F. Newman - *5714 Water-
bury Circle, Des Moines, Iowa*
John H. Newsom - *Palama Settle-
ment, Honolulu, Hawaii*

Ralph S. Ney - *UKN*
Alfred E. Nicholson - *Earlville,
Illinois*
Bruce Nicholson - *607 E. Ave., Na-
tional City, California*
Eugene H. Nirdlinger - *1327 S. Cen-
ter, Terre Haute, Indiana*
William F. Noble - *UKN*
Henderson B. Norris - *Jerkey City,
Arkansas*
William D. North - *139 Greenville
St., Newman, Georgia*
Walter L. Northby - *643 Van Buren
St. NE, Minneapolis, Minnesota*
Edward C. Northway - *UKN*
Amos H. Norton - *612 Maple St.,
Columbia, South Carolina*
Robert W. Nourse - *UKN*
Stanley E. Neyes - *1027 West 35th
St., Los Angeles, California*
Hugh R. Nutter - *5921 Bonsallo
Ave., Los Angeles, California*
Eugene J. Nyquist - *Soudan,
Minnesota*
James S. Neary - *Killian Ave.,
Bridgeport, Connecticut*
John B. Nixon - *UKN*

O
Edward J. O'Brien - *UKN*
John F. O'Brien - *154 S. Elliott
Place, Brooklyn, New York*
Kenneth J. O'Brien - *93 Scott St.,
San Francisco, California*
James N. Olmsted - *Watervliet,
Michigan*
Kenneth S. Olson - *#2 Park Drive,
Columbus, Georgia*
Herman Omansky - *355 St. Clair
St., St. Paul, Minnesota*
Norris O'Neal - *Hope, Arkansas*
Vincent T. O'Neill - *2340 Filbert St.,
San Francisco, California*

Maurice B. Ordun - *308 Ohio St.,*
La Porte, Indiana

James S. O'Rourke - *4215 Third St.*
NW, Washington, D.C.

George E. Orr - *259 28th Ave.,* *San*
Francisco, California

Oliver W. Orson - *Midland, Texas*

Gene Ortega - *505 E. 9th St.,* *Austin, Texas*

Alvan S. Ose - *UKN*

Thomas G. O'Shea - *2565 E. 24th*
St., Sheepshead Bay, Brooklyn,
New York

John H. O'Toole - *1516 NW 34th*
St., Oklahoma City, Oklahoma

Oscar Otere - *Rt. #1, Box 35, Los*
Lunas, New Mexico

Woody T. Owen - *UKN*

Andrew Lee Overton - *Rt. #4, Box*
67A, Norfolk, Virginia

P

Harry B. Packard - *Milo, Maine*

Richard Packer - *329 Parkdale,*
Great Falls, Montana

Leo C. Paquet - *1018½ S. Norton*
St., Los Angeles, California

Howard M. Rahl - *UKN*

Lawrence W. Parcher - *Peck, Kansas*

Rafe A. Parker - *Rt. #1, Lampasas,*
Texas

Ted E. Parker - *505 W. Slate Ave.,*
Albuquerque, New Mexico

William R. Parker - *UKN*

Robert F. Parks - *Glenn Ferry, Idaho*

William M. Parks - *601 Thorn St.,*
Marion, Illinois

Paul E. Parsons - *212 Howard St.,*
Bridgeport, Ohio

William A. Parson - *2313 W. 2nd*
St., Wichita, Kansas

Steve Pastyroryk - *UKN*

Thomas W. Patrick Jr. - *166 York*
St., Chester, South Carolina

Rufus A. Patterson - *UKN*

Thomas D. Patterson - *114 W. Lincoln, Harrisburg, Illinois*

Sidney F. Paul - *P.O. Box 62, Gresham, Oregon*

Claude W. Paulger - *UKN*

John R. Pearce - *Apt. 803, 67 So.*
Hunn Ave., E. Orange, New
Jersey

William W. Pearce - *UKN*

Lester J. Pearsall Jr. - *308 S. Main*
St., Caney, Kansas

Cecil J. Peart - *Cave Junction,*
Oregon

Allen L. Peck - *608 Michigan Ave.,*
Pullman, Washington

George H. Petts, Jr. - *UKN*

Thomas Pendlebury - *UKN*

Ralph R. Penick - *Heborn, Ohio*

Ulysses J. Peoples - *UKN*

George T. Perkins - *439 Eleanor, San*
Antonio, Texas

Paul E. Pearson - *721 Pierre St.,*
Manhattan, Kansas

Travis E. Perrenot - *313 E. Elmira*
St., San Antonio, Texas

Howard R. Perry Jr. - *816 Hill St.,*
Ann Arbor, Michigan

William G. Peryan - *UKN*

Michael E. Peshel - *1125 N. Brauer,*
Oklahoma City, Oklahoma

Arthur C. Peterson - *100 Lake St.,*
San Francisco, California

Neil B. Peterson - *UKN*

Malcolm O. Petrie - *East Side Savings Bank, Rochester, New York*

George K. Petritz - *Ottawa, Illinois*

Charles W. Pettis - *UKN*

Joseph P. Pevey - *UKN*

Robert C. Pettit Jr. - *63 Virginia*
Ave., Dayton, Ohio

Rudolfe Pfeifer - *UKN*

James A. Phillips - *223 26th St.,
Lewiston, Idaho*

Nelda L. Phillips - *213 4th St., Altoona, Pennsylvania*

Gaylord L. Philipps - *1437 4th Ave., Columbus, Georgia*

Bryan W. Pittman - *203 S. Fairfax St., Alexandria, Virginia*

William H. Plant - *853 Alamitos Ave., Long Beach, California*

Dominique Poirier - *119 Florence St., Providence, Rhode Island*

Curtis M. Polk - *627 E. Railroad St., Biloxi, Mississippi*

Hector J. Polia - *1848 Oneida St., Lexington, Missouri*

William D. Pope - *UKN*

William C. Porter - *3201 Piedmont St., El Paso, Texas*

Warner P. Portz - *3515 R. St. NW, Washington, D.C.*

Francis B. Powell - *Rt. #2, Box 156, Thayer, Missouri*

George R. Powell - *Hunnewell, Missouri*

Thomas N. Powell Sr. - *Massee Apts. College St., Macon, Georgia*

Nicholas Pramkgate - *UKN*

John F. Presnell Jr. - *253 Vaughan St., Portland, Maine*

Bernard E. Preston - *UKN*

Everett R. Preston - *Harrodsburg, Kentucky*

Finnie B. Price Jr. - *UKN*

James R. Price - *UKN*

Lawrence F. Prichard - *400 Alameda Circle, San Antonio, Texas*

William F. Prickett - *UKN*

William J. Priestley - *6026 32nd St., So. Seattle, Washington*

John H. Pringle - *UKN*

Dean O. Pronovost - *1605 S. 4th St., W. Missoula, Montana*

Vernon F. Puckett - *530 W. 27th St., Houston, Texas*

Henry H. Purvis - *UKN*

Frank P. Pysick - *Wells, Minnesota*

Chester A. Peyton - *2220 Santa Monica, San Antonio, Texas*

Robert C. Pettit Jr. - *UKN*

Gerald R. Pfaff - *6944 Fyler Ave., St. Louis, Missouri*

R

Elgin G. Radcliff - *Clearfield Ave., Rt. #2, Norristown, Pennsylvania*

Joseph R. Radosevich - *406 N. 2nd St., Gallup, New Mexico*

Patrick H. Rafferty - *3 High St., Brookline, Massachusetts*

John E. Rahe - *228 W. Main St., Dyersville, Iowa*

Jerome L. Raider - *1232 N. Edison St., Milwaukee, Wisconsin*

Jerman G. Ramsey - *UKN*

Kenneth W. Ramsey - *9014 Norma Place, W. Hollywood, California*

William P. Randolph - *UKN*

Cecil B. Rannale - *UKN*

Kenneth E. Ranson - *East Dubuque, Illinois*

Floyd C. Rapp - *El Dorado Springs, Missouri*

Richard E. Raschick - *5542 Shields Ave., Chicago, Illinois*

Cannon Rasmussen - *UKN*

Irving Rathblott - *UKN*

Fred L. Raymond - *Pond Hills, Amesbury, Massachusetts*

Nelson W. Raymond - *Washington, D.C.*

Martin E. Redfield - *Rt. #1, Box 139-B, Orlando, Florida*

George A. Reed - *Box 277, Rt. #3, Springfield, Missouri*

Leo Reider - *UKN*

Malcolm T. Reinhardt - *Margaret, Texas*

Warren A. Remnsnider - *512 NW 27th St., Oklahoma City, Oklahoma*

Joseph A. Revak - *1510 Madison Ave., Beaumont, Texas*

Gilbert H. Reynolds - *Devel, Oklahoma*

John B. Reynolds - *Martin, Kentucky*

Carl F. Rhodes - *49 White St., Clark Mills, New York*

Thomas H. Rhodes - *P.O. Box 581, Oak Hill, West Virginia*

John H. Rice - *251 Ashbury St., San Francisco, California*

Burton R. Richard - *30 Roessner Ave., Hagertown, Maryland*

Forest C. Richards - *5311 North 26th St., Omaha, Nebraska*

Grover C. Richards Jr. - *503 Donihan, Missouri*

James D. Richardson - *UKN*

Carlyle Ricks - *UKN*

Reginald H. Ridgfly - *3521 Voltaire St., San Diego, California*

Harvey H. Riedeman - *UKN*

Frank E. Riley - *2502 S. Second St., St. Joseph, Missouri*

Louis J. Rivet - *UKN*

James M. Robb - *Financial Center Bldg., Oakland, California*

Clifford E. Roberts - *506 E. 11th St., Long Beach, California*

Eustace O. Roberts - *Magazine, Arkansas*

Elton W. Roberts - *Clayton, Illinois*

Hugh H. Roberts - *UKN*

Robert K. Roberts - *Box 1736, Bisbee, Arizona*

Walter H. Roberts - *UKN*

Merville Robertson - *922 McAteer St., Houtzdale, Pennsylvania*

Joseph H. Robertson - *1009 Pilot Butte Ave., Rock Springs, Wyoming*

Ernest L. Robison - *R #2, Box 226, Kingman, Indiana*

Roy Robinton - *909 Kent Place N.E., Washington, D.C.*

Winfield N. Robinson - *R #2, New Bedford, Massachusetts*

William L. Robinson - *Adjutant General, Washington, D.C.*

Albert A. Roby Jr. - *Apopka, Florida*

Herbert Rochester - *1203 Drake St., Tallahassee, Florida*

Ellwood L. Roderick - *1029 Fedora St., Fresno, California*

Louis E. Roomer - *UKN*

Eugene F. Rogers - *Milroy, Indiana*

Harry W. Rogers - *RFD #1, Bluejacket, Oklahoma*

Ivan E. Rogers - *RT #1, Oakwood, Oklahoma*

Lloyd W. Rodgers Jr. - *229 Rosario Blvd., Sante Fe, New Mexico*

Paul D. Rodgers - *c/o American Red Cross, Manila, P.I.*

Jesse Rolfe - *Crosshore, North Carolina*

Walter A. Renowoki - *R #9, Box 222, Station F., Milwaukee, Wisconsin*

James O. Rooks - *UKN*

Arthur J. Root - *421 1st Ave. NE, Brainard, Minnesota*

Charles E. Roper - *1438 Kansas Ave., Atchison, Kansas*

Fred E. Rose - *861 G. Ave., Coronado, California*

Eric Z. Rosen - *3451 Sublette St., St. Louis, Missouri*

Melvin H. Rosen - *UKN*

Edgar S. Rosenstock - *1427 Magnolia St., Oakland, California*

Herbert J. Rosenthal - *Board of Education, Kansas City, Missouri*

Richard A. Roshe - *Tacoma, Washington*

Leslie G. Ross - *Langherns Place, Salem, Virginia*

Frederick J. Roth Jr. - *2122 Quimby Ave., Bronx, New York*

Frederick G. Roth - *UKN*

Arthur S. Rothrock - *Lawrenceville, Illinois*

Wilfred Rotherham - *335 Lytton Ave., Palo Alto, California*

Harlan F. Rousseau - *524 N. Broadway, East Depere, Wisconsin*

Robert E. Rouze - *UKN*

Ralph L. Rowland - *2914 Steiner St., San Francisco, California*

George D. Roy - *84 Pilgrim Ave., Worcester, Massachusetts*

Thomas A. Royal - *324 E. 4th St., Tulsa, Oklahoma*

James C. Ruby - *975 Westchester Place, Los Angeles, California*

John G. Rudgins - *UKN*

Arch B. Rue - *Harrodsburg, Kentucky*

Ralph E. Rumbold - *726 W. 30th St., Indianapolis, Indiana*

William E. Rushk - *UKN*

Robert E. Russell - *201 So. Grand Ave., Bozeman, Montana*

John D. Rutherford - *General Delivery, Magna, Utah*

Jay A. Ryan - *424 Garfield Ave., Del Rio, Texas*

Robert J. Ryan - *641 9th St., So. Wisconsin Rapids, Wisconsin*

S

Otis E. Saalman - *Tipton, Oklahoma*

James E. Sadler - *115 W. 2nd St., Junction City, Kansas*

Frederick G. Saint - *501 Franklin St., Alexandria, Virginia*

Joseph B. Sallee - *Bartle Court Apts., Eugene, Oregon*

Vern R. Sallee Jr. - *UKN*

Eddy Samethini - *UKN*

John F. Samord - *UKN*

Aster N. Saniers - *UKN*

Cecil M. Sanders - *Kensett, Arkansas*

Chester Sanders - *UKN*

Fred R. Sanders - *5825 SE 44th Ave., Portland, Oregon*

Kenneth F. Sarer - *324 S. Terrace Dr., Wichita, Kansas*

Wilburn R. Saunders - *Mathiston, Mississippi*

Columbus Savage - *Kennedy, Alabama*

Carl J. Savoie - *UKN*

Robert L. Saxton - *UKN*

Howard J. Say - *413 Elk St., Franklin, Pennsylvania*

Francis H. Scarborough - *Bishopville, South Carolina*

Lester A. Schade - *Abbotsford, Wisconsin*

Max W. Schaeffer - *UKN*

Harry W. Schenck - *UKN*

Harold E. Schenk - *Oregon, Missouri*

Alexander B. Schlaten - *UKN*

George Schnicks - *UKN*

Charles W. Schnabel - *702 E. 23rd St., Oakland, California*

John L. Schock - *Balls City, Nebraska*

Lawrence S. Schoenck - *1239 E. Valley Blvd., Rosemead, California*

Robert D. Scholes - *2955 Twentieth Ave., San Francisco, California*

George Scholtis - *UKN*

Linus L. Schramski - *326 E. Rock St., Mankato, Minnesota*

Murl R. Schroeder - *1283 Elm St., El Paso, Texas*

Paul W. Schurtz - *Deming, New Mexico*

Abe Scwartz - *88 Inverness St., Saint Anna, Manila, P.I.*

Jack W. Schwartz - *301 Washington Ave., Kennett, Missouri*

Jerome J. Schwbich - *UKN*

Daley H. Scott - *Yuba City, California*

Robert V. Scott - *UKN*

Walter E. Scott - *Coopersville, Michigan*

Warwick P. Scott - *1035 Land Title Bldg., Philadelphia, Pennsylvania*

Willis A. Scrivener - *UKN*

Beresford O. Seale - *UKN*

Byron T. Search - *Pampa, Texas*

Charles K. Seawright - *UKN*

Michael A. Sedlak - *12 Lawrence St., Yonkers, New York*

Fred Sehmann Jr. - *1205 Polk St., Wichita Falls, Texas*

Kenneth J. Scitler - *128 S. 13th St., Olean, New York*

Ignac D. Senkyrik Jr. - *UKN*

John W. Sewall - *5920 Manola Way, Hollywood, California*

John N. Shanks - *UKN*

Otho L. Shamblin - *412 Madison St., Amarillo, Texas*

Carl E. Shaw - *UKN*

John C. Shaw - *Kerr, North Carolina*

Henry C. Shawver - *3728 Jackson St., El Paso, Texas*

James W. Sheares - *R #1, Ridgeway, Ohio*

Charles P. Shearn - *UKN*

Charles B. Sheed - *UKN*

Charles A. Sheeley - *1133 Beaulah Ave., Pueblo, Colorado*

Ford Shelton - *Cane River, North Carolina*

John H. Sherk - *Beaumont, California*

Robert H. Sherk - *Beaumont, California*

Dennis P. Sheridan - *145 Elizabeth Rd., San Antonio, Texas*

Frederick S. Sherman - *704 S. Zinc Ave., Deming, New Mexico*

Herman V. Sherman - *4501 S. Gramercy Place, Los Angeles, California*

Raymond G. Sherman - *UKN*

Lloyd E. Sherwood - *219 Waverly St., Palo Alto, California*

Clifford Shiflett - *R #1, Cedartown, Georgia*

Earle M. Shiley - *West Annapolis, Maryland*

Andrew D. Shoemake - *Box 417, La Grade, Oregon*

Thomas B. Shone - *Boca, California*

Edward L. Short - *Cebu, P.I.*

Arthur L. Shreve - *502 Wingate Road, Baltimore, Maryland*

Sanford Shrout - *Carlisle, Kentucky*

Paul Shultz - *UKN*

Clayton O. Shupp - *UKN*

Arthur N. Sidebottom - *UKN*

Benjamin F. Siegel - *UKN*

Henry E. Sigrist - *55 Grand Ave., Long Branch, New Jersey*

Oswald Sika - *R #2, Silverton, Oregon*

Fred L. Siler - *237 Taft Ave., Pocatello, Idaho*

Jeff S. Sills - *UKN*

Frank Sima Jr. - *UKN*

Norman R. Simmonds - *56 Wellesley St., Weston, Massachusetts*

Carter B. Simpson - *9 Elliewood Ave., Charlottesville, Virginia*

Earl R. Simpson - *UKN*

Cash T. Skarda - *Citizens Bank, Clovis, New Mexico*

Beverly N. Skardon - *#1 Fishburne St., Walterboro, South Carolina*

Charles F. Skill - *UKN*

Russell E. Skiver - *UKN*

Glen P. Slipsager - *UKN*

Fred M. Small - *317 Walnut St., Boulder, Colorado*

Lawrence K. Smarr - *UKN*

Charles L. Smelour - *912 W. 23rd St., Tulsa, Oklahoma*

Carey M. Smith - *4709 Edgeward Road, San Diego, California*

Edgar B. Smith - *211 North 7th St., Mayfield, Kentucky*

Edward I. Smith - *RFD #1, Dexter, New Mexico*

Elmer N. Smith - *177 W. 2nd St., Port Clinton, Ohio*

Elza R. Smith - *R #1, Box #52, Summer, Illinois*

Frank Smith - *UKN*

Harvey L. Smith - *UKN*

John S. Smith - *UKN*

Joseph F. Smith - *UKN*

Milo O. Smith - *Rt. #2, Chanute, Kansas*

Richard A. Smith - *1090 W. 5th St., Dubuque, Iowa*

Walter C. Smith - *3351 30th St., San Diego, California*

Due Smithwick - *Windsor, North Carolina*

Thomas B. Smothers Jr. - *UKN*

Thaddeus E. Smyth - *2522 Tulare Ave., Richmond, California*

David M. Snell - *3921 Shenandoah St., Dallas, Texas*

Maynard G. Snell - *UKN*

Donald R. Snoke - *185 E. Katherine Ave., Washington, Pennsylvania*

Sidney G. Snow - *222 So. Broadway, Corpus Christi, Texas*

Campbell H. Snyder - *1301 Ten-eighth Way, Sacramento, California*

Robert O. Snyder - *1583 W. Macon, Decatur, Illinois*

Paul E. Solmon - *UKN*

Erven C. Somerville - *21 Third Ave., Bellaire, Ohio*

Julius J. Spanovich - *UKN*

Theodore I. Spaulding - *Sherwood, North Dakota*

Eugene Specht - *727 E. Saint John St., San Jose, California*

Jefferson W. Speck - *Frenchman's Bayou, Arkansas*

Clinton W. Sperry - *5174 Christy Blvd., St. Louis, Missouri*

Thomas W. Spickard - *406 Eagle St., Princeton, Kentucky*

Benjamin F. Stakes - *UKN*

Darrel S. Staley - *2114 Jersey Ave., Norfolk, Virginia*

Loren E. Stamp - *Navy Department, Washington, D.C.*

Henton H. Stearns - *Duluth, Minnesota*

Arthur Steele - *Rt. #1, Plan City, Ohio*

Leslie Steele - *UKN*

Lewis Q. Steele - *Rt. #4, Lancaster, South Carolina*

Harry J. Stempin - *2024 S. 20th St., Milwaukee, Wisconsin*

Will K. Stenis - *Koloa, Kauai, Hawaii*

Joseph O. Stensland - *Madison, South Dakota*

William H. Stephens - *400 Cortex, Prescott, Arizona*

Lee E. Stevens - *722 Cornelia Ave., Chicago, Illinois*

Karl M. Stewart - *UKN*

Sidney J. Stewart - *Watonga, Oklahoma*

Roland E. Stickney - *8 Williams St., Lancaster, New Hampshire*

Lemoyne B. Stiles - *315 W. 9th St., Los Angeles, California*

Lloyd H. Stinson - *Greenwood, Mississippi*

Joseph W. Stirri - *1231 Langley Field Rd., Hampton, Virginia*

Henry B. Stober - *3092 Celeron Place, Cincinnati, Ohio*

Wesley D. Stookey - *Thorp, Wisconsin*

Dick D. Strauss - *UKN*

Lowell H. Strand - *UKN*

William W. Streso - *617 1st Ave., Durand, Wisconsin*

James E. Strickland - *2117 E. Cypress, Altus, Oklahoma*

Walter S. Strong Jr. - *131 East Fall Creek Blvd., Indianapolis, Indiana*

Arthur W. Sullivan - *UKN*

Leon Sullivan - *c/o Bureau of Navigation, Washington, D.C.*

James M. Sullivan - *UKN*

Michael C. Sult - *740 E. 15th St., Eugene, Oregon*

William E. Surber - *UKN*

Roger W. Swain - *1111 Urban Ave., Durham, North Carolina*

Roy Swain - *UKN*

Robin C. H. Swan - *2 Sandrock Rd., Tunbridge Wells, Kent, England*

Thomas E. Swann - *UKN*

Wendell F. Swanson - *2926 Grove St, Denver, Colorado*

Clifford E. Sweet - *UKN*

Melvin R. Swensen - *3455 Elliot Ave., S., Minneapolis, Minnesota*

Fred H. Swope - *c/o U.S. Penitentiary, Terre Haute, Indiana*

John H. Shales - *167 Chester St., Blackburn, Lancashire, England*

Dorris P. Simmons - *1010 N. Willows St., Sherman, Texas*

Harold Stevenson - *UKN*

Edmund Starke Jr. - *UKN*

Erhard Sgoblom - *UKN*

T

Lester J. Tacy - *Raleigh Dr., Virginia Beach, Virginia*

Fred O. Tally - *UKN*

Marvin A. Tarnehill - *Box 495, Woods Cross, Utah*

Lester R. Tappy - *UKN*

Donald E. Tapscott - *331½ Winnipeg Place, Long Beach, California*

Howard F. Taquin - *UKN*

Thomas M. Tarpley Jr. - *110 Park Rd., Portsmouth, Virginia*

Clarence M. Taylor - *1357 Rerbaugh St., Philadelphia, Pennsylvania*

George S. Taylor - *UKN*

Herbert H. Taylor - *4907 Colorado St., Long Beach, California*

Marion W. Taylor - *1821 So. Preston St., Louisville, Kentucky*

Robert P. Taylor - *Fort Worth, Texas*

Linzia C. Teem - *UKN*

Elmer C. Tenney - *Rt. #1, Box 50, Merrill, Maine*

James H. Terry - *UKN*

Samuel C. Terry - *UKN*

Allen Thayer - *19 King St., Putnam, Connecticut*

Frank C. Thomas - *803 Black St., Silver City, New Mexico*

William R. Thomas - *216 Chesnut St., Evansville, Indiana*

Arnold W. Thompson - *UKN*

Frank Thompson - *UKN*

Robert E. Thompson - *908 E. 76th St. Terrace, Kansas City, Missouri*

Walter H. Thompson - *UKN*

Russell C. Thorman - *565 S. Fremount St., Janesville, Wisconsin*

Charles S. Thornton - *Weweka, Oklahoma*

Joseph D. Thorpe - *412 S. 7th St., Artesia, New Mexico*

Fred G. Threatt - *Manila, P.I.*

Clarence F. Thurman - *Higley, Arizona*

Robert N. Thwing - *Murdo, North Dakota*

Hugh A. Tistadt Jr. - *Garuthersville, Missouri*

Wendelin F. Tixier - *Stead, New Mexico*

Cyril H. Toensend - *UKN*

Robert F. Tokoly - *1760 Oakwood Ave., Youngstown, Ohio*

William J. Tooley - *UKN*

Charles P. Towne - *1334 Marion St., Salem, Oregon*

William H. Traeger - *c/o H. W. Meekin Rienzi, Fond Du Lac, Wisconsin*

Edwin Trapp - *Hopewell, Swindon Road, Cheltenham, Gloucester, England*

Thomas J. Trapnell - *UKN*

George H. Treacy - *1383 Osceola Ave., St. Paul, Minnesota*

Herbert R. Trump - *1392 East Mound St., Columbus, Ohio*

Chester H. Tucker - *4014 Xenia Ave., Robinsdale, Minnesota*

Lee C. Tucker - *301 S.W. 2nd St., Perryton, Texas*

James R. Tuggle - *Bow, Kentucky*

Harry L. Turner - *503 5th Ave., Twin Falls, Idaho*

John W. Turner Jr. - *1200 6th St., Silver City, New Mexico*

Jess Turnipseed - *4247 35th St., San Diego, California*

Albert J. Tybur - *UKN*

W

Ernest M. Wade - *226 Granada Ave., Long Beach, California*

William H. Waggener Jr. - *5708 Branch Ave., Tampa, Florida*

Lloyd E. Wagner - *5631 Woolworth Ave., Omaha, Nebraska*

George M. Wagnon - *5117 N. Delaware Ave., Portland, Oregon*

William L. Wagner - *UKN*

Custer E. Wake - *2219 Broadway Inn, Seattle, Washington*

Allan B. Walker - *646 E. 5th St., Tucson, Arizona*

Edward L. Walker - *25 Garfield St., Santa Cruz, California*

Jack K. Walker - *924 College Ave., Ft. Worth, Texas*

Robert R. Walker - *UKN*

Joseph E. Wilks - *UKN*

Guy L. Waldron - *UKN*

Harold A. Wallace - *Box 88, RFD #4, Battle Creek, Michigan*

Wilbur W. Walton - *UKN*

Emmett A. Warfel - *Clyde Park, Montana*

Everett L. Warner - *9 Waldron Ave., Pikesville, Maryland*

Miller P. Warren - *Midlothian, Texas*

Bennett H. Waters - *Rt. #1, Black-shear, Georgia*

Donald J. Watson - *4160 23rd St., San Francisco, California*

Roy B. Watson - *UKN*

Ivan J. Weaber - *2759 N.W. 19th, Oklahoma City, Oklahoma*

John T. Webb - *R.R. #2, Ironton, Ohio*

Joseph R. Webb - *501 6th Ave., Salt Lake City, Utah*

William E. Webb - *2200 N.E. 21st St., Oklahoma City, Oklahoma*

Cecil E. Welch - *Pierre, South Dakota*

George R. Weeks - *1227 E. Ocean Blvd., Long Beach, California*

John L. Welch - *831 Olive Ave., Coronado, California*

Lawrence Weffer - *UKN*

Cecil R. Welchke - *Bonner's Ferry, Idaho*

Vernon E. Weldon - *Rt. #1, Nevada City, California*

Max Well - *UKN*

Clyde L. Welsh - *5006 36th Ave. NE, Seattle, Washington*

Daniel N. Weitzner - *1539 Fairfield Ave., Bridgeport, Connecticut*

Earl H. Wheeler - *UKN*

Melden V. Werner - *UKN*

Edward R. Wernitznig - *UKN*

Arthur W. Wermuth - *Traverse City, Michigan*

Charles J. Weschler - *709 Riverview Ave., Portsmouth, Virginia*

Floyd E. Weittenburg - *UKN*

Milton Whaley - *Petros, Tennessee*

Robert I. Wheat - *Lonoke, Arkansas*

John Z. Wheeler - *759 Fairmont Ave., St. Paul, Minnesota*

Kenneth R. Wheeler - *211 W. Maple Ave., Fullerton, California*

Harold J. Whitcomb - *UKN*

Alfred F. White - *18 Mellen St., Ashmont-Boston, Massachusetts*

Clarence H. White - *3808 S. St. Andrews Place, Los Angeles, California*

Mondell White - *Wharton, West Virginia*

John T. White - *UKN*

Fred S. Whiteneck - *1824 Myrtle Ave., Long Beach, California*

Doug G. Whiteman - *710 E. 21st St., Sioux Falls, South Dakota*

Harry Gill Witman Jr. - *235 Union Ave. SE, Grand Rapids, Michigan*

Laurel W. Whitworth - *Boerne, Texas*

Timothy J. Wholey - *20 Irring St., Ridgewood, New Jersey*

George S. Wiggins - *Lyons, Kansas*

Chester J. Widman - *UKN*

Albert P. Wilcox - *UKN*

Emil Wilk - *UKN*

Alfred J. Wilkins - *103 W. Boston, Seattle, Washington*

Lee V. Willeford - *UKN*

Cliff C. Williams - *17 Percy St., Charleston, South Carolina*

Francis H. Williams - *205 S. Jackson St., Wilmington, Delaware*

John W. Williams - *Wewahitchka, Florida*

Raymond H. Williams - *Yolo, California*

Robert M. Williams - *Box 2003, Shawnee, Oklahoma*

William R. Williams - *309 S. Main St., Culpepper, Virginia*

Richard R. Williams - *310 No. Duluth St., Sioux Falls, South Dakota*

Albert M. Willis - *Grandview, Washington*

Alvin T. Wilson - *1546 16th Ave.,*
Columbus, Georgia

Charles H. Wilson - *35 Charlton St.,*
New York, New York

James M. Wilson - *Caneville,*
Kentucky

Ovid O. Wilson - *233 Howard St.,*
San Antonio, Texas

Peronneau B. Wingo - *1304 Park*
Ave., Richmond, Virginia

James H. Winiker - *1257 Buena Vis-*
tas, Ventura, California

Rollo D. Winne - *UKN*

John H. Winschuh - *Ravine Drive,*
Matawan, New Jersey

Henry H. Weira - Almond,
Wisconsin

John T. Wislocki - *RFD 2, Box 50,*
Greensburg, Pennsylvania

James E. Wilstead - *Provo, Utah*

Oliver B. Witten - *Deming, New*
Mexico

Edward G. Woof - *UKN*

Leonard L. Wolfenbarger - *R #3,*
Clovis, New Mexico

Joseph W. Wolf - *Saint Marys,*
Missouri

Michael F. Wolf - *UKN*

Siles C. Wolf - *224 W. Seminole,*
McAlester, Oklahoma

Allen O. Wood - *157 Ivy St., Spar-*
tanburg, South Carolina

John A. Wood - *UKN*

Nathan Wood - *UKN*

John P. Woodbridge - *231 Brondon,*
San Antonio, Texas

John S. Woodside - *425 B. S. Shirley*
Place, Beverly Hills, California

Gerald C. Worthington - *2302 Vil-*
lage Dr., Louisville, Kentucky

Robert S. Worthington - *R #2,*
(Houston Lake) Parkville,
Missouri

Paul Werezdiniac - *UKN*

Elmer R. Wright - *623 W. 6th, Still-*
water, Oklahoma

Edgar B. Wright - *Cottonwood,*
Idaho

Harold B. Wright - *Barnsdale,*
Oklahoma

John M. Wright Jr. - *4833 Elmwood*
Ave., Los Angeles, California

Robert R. Wuest - *6 W. Marshall*
Road, Lansdowne, Pennsylvania

Hueston R. Wynkoop - *Headquar-*
ters 6th Corps Area, Chicago,
Illinois

John E. Wchlmacher - *UKN*

Frank H. Wilson - *UKN*

Charles M. Wilkins - *UKN*

Joseph V. Iacobucol - *1545 Race St.,*
Cincinnati, Ohio

Frank Ignaszewski - *111 S. Broom*
St., Madison, Wisconsin

Herbert V. Ingersoll - *61 Marl-*
borough Road, Waltham,
Massachusetts

Arthur L. Irons - *UKN*

John T. Istock - *UKN*

Lawrence L. Qualls - *Baxter*
Springs, Kansas

Clinton D. Quinlan - *590 Douglas*
St., Pasadena, California

John L. Quinland - *UKN*

Calvin D. Quimn - *UKN*

David L. Quinn - *Crisfield,*
Maryland

Frank J. Quesnell - *UKN*

U

Homer H. Uglow - *723 Grayson St.,*
San Antonio, Texas

Emil M. Ulanowicz - *2229 Bank St.,*
Baltimore, Maryland

John C. Ulmer - *5722 Meade Ave.,*
San Diego, California

Melvin E. Underwood - 409 Dodds
Ave., Chattanooga, Tennessee
George Urabick - UKN
Gordon A. Utke - UKN

V

George A. Van Arsdall - UKN
Guy Vance - UKN
Joseph G. Vanderheiden - 409 E. 1st
Ave., Nebraska City, Nebraska
Zacharias Van Diggeie - UKN
Jan Van Doorne - UKN
Walter E. Van Horn - 3A North
Spring Ave., St. Louis, Missouri
William Van Nostrand - 529
Madison St., New Orleans,
Louisiana
Adrinmus J. Van Oesten - 13 E.
Lake St., Addison, Illinois
Clarence E. Van Ray - Valley City,
North Dakota
George D. Vanture - Summerville,
Georgia
Jacob Van Tiwel - UKN
Josef Varak - UKN
Alfred Vepsala - 1987 29th Ave.,
San Francisco, California
Robert J. Verde - 502 Spruce St.,
Dowagiac, Michigan
Robert J. Verde - UKN

John F. Vernon - UKN
Kenneth Vick - 724 N. Grand Ave.,
Sherman, Texas
Ben Vidal - Box #B70, RR #5,
Floresville, Texas
Simon D. Vilar - UKN
Anthony G. Volney - 4700 Market
St., Oakland, California

Y

Robin W. Yearsley - Manila, P.I.
Deck Yee - UKN
Joseph M. Youmans - 485 Mayhew
Court, So. Orange, New Jersey
Winbon D. Youngblood - RFD #3,
Gordon, Georgia

Z

Peter A. Zanirato - 1021 S. Com-
merce St., Stockton, California
Mathias E. Zerfes - Twin Lakes,
Wisconsin
Paul Zimmerman - UKN
George R. Zimmerman - Sturgis,
South Dakota
Fred W. Zimpher - UKN
Lerian G. B. Zonneveld - UKN
Andrew B. Zwaska - 1825 E. La-
Fayette Place, Milwaukee,
Wisconsin

Index

American Prisoners of War Mentioned in *Some Survived*

C30941

940.   Lawton, Manny, 1918-
54
Law   Some survived
                        16.95

C30941

940.   Lawton, Manny, 1918-
54
Law   Some survived
                        16.95

DATE	BORROWER'S NAME	

Ⓡ THE BAKER & TAYLOR CO.

RECEIVED JUN 5 1985